The Travels of
Ibn Battuta

The Travels of
Ibn Battuta

A GUIDED ARABIC READER

David DiMeo and Inas Hassan

The American University in Cairo Press
Cairo New York

First published in 2016 by
The American University in Cairo Press
113 Sharia Kasr el Aini, Cairo, Egypt
420 Fifth Avenue, New York, NY 10018
www.aucpress.com

Exclusive distribution outside Egypt and North America by I.B. Tauris & Co Ltd., 6 Salem Road,
London, W4 2BU

Dar el Kutub No. 25539/14
ISBN 978 977 416 715 7

Dar el Kutub Cataloging-in-Publication Data

DiMeo, David
        The Travels of Ibn Battuta: A Guided Arabic Reader / David DiMeo,
    Inas Hassan—Cairo: The American University in Cairo Press, 2015.
        p.   cm.
        ISBN 978 977 416 715 7
        1. Arabic literature
        2. Ibn Battuta, Mohamed

        1387—1304
        I Hassan, Inas (Jt. auth.)
        II Title

        892.7

1 2 3 4 5   19 18 17 16 15

Designed by Shehab Abdullah
Printed in Egypt

Contents

Introduction

The Travels of Ibn Battuta: A Guided Reader is designed for Arabic students striving to reach, or already at, the Advanced level of proficiency. It introduces students to classical Arabic literature through a detailed, but guided, study of one the greatest works of classical literature—*The Travels of Ibn Battuta*. In this book, students will read the actual text of the great travel writer, but with sufficient supporting explanatory notes to make the text accessible to students at the third or fourth year of Arabic study. From there, students are offered an extensive series of exercises to test their comprehension, develop interpreting and critical-reading skills, and apply the linguistic structures to their own speaking and writing. To suit students of varying proficiency levels, the exercises cover a spectrum of tasks from the Intermediate to the Advanced level.

Beyond language proficiency, this book is designed to offer a window into an important period in Arab culture and world history. Without question, Ibn Battuta is one of the most fascinating writers of the medieval period. His voyages offer unparalleled portraits of Middle Eastern, African, and Asian societies during the height of Muslim power and influence. There is no better lens to view the glories of Islamic civilization at the time, and its place in the world than through the writings of Ibn Battuta. His was also a time of great transition. The united Islamic empire of the caliphates had fallen, and the Arab Muslim states were under attack from many sides. At the same time, however, Muslim religion and culture were spreading throughout Asia and Africa. For the first time, the most powerful Muslim states were non-Arab and a large portion of the Muslim population lived as minorities. It was into this milieu that Ibn Battuta traveled as an Islamic judge to help establish Islamic law in recently converted states. This book will offer students an opportunity to learn the histories of many cultures, such as the Chinese empire, the Golden Horde, Timbuktu, Mecca, and Constantinople through the eyes of a fourteenth-century traveler.

The lessons in this book do not have to be completed in order; students and teachers are free to use the chapters they choose in the order they desire.

The Source Text

The Arabic selections in this book come directly from the original text penned over six centuries ago, rather than modern paraphrases or revisions. As such, the history of the text is of great importance in itself. Shortly after his return to Morocco in 1354, Ibn Battuta was directed by his sultan to dictate the memoirs of his travels to a gifted scribe of the royal court, Muhammad Ibn Juzayy, whom Ibn Battuta had met earlier in Spain.[1] Thus, the authoritative version of the travels is a collaboration between Ibn Battuta the traveler, and Ibn Juzayy the writer. Much is based on Ibn Battuta's recollections, so in some places dates are uncertain and facts may be questionable. As Ibn Battuta was a public official—a Muslim judge—and an unofficial anthropologist, he often does not distinguish between what he saw firsthand and stories he heard during his travels. Ibn Juzayy further embellished the accounts. The text contains, for instance, liberal quotation from an earlier traveler Ibn Jubayr, often without identification. Later scholars have questioned some parts of his travels—for example his trip to Beijing during his stay in China—but overall, the record is believed to be a generally honest account of the world as he knew it.

This text, although today viewed as one of the most important medieval historical narratives, was unknown in the West before the 1800s. The German explorer Ulrich Jasper Seetzen acquired and translated a selection of excerpts from Ibn Juzayy's text in 1818. The first English translation of the partial texts came in 1829 by Professor Samuel Lee. The most important discovery was the French acquisition of five copies of the original text in Algeria in 1830, one of which carries the signature of Ibn Juzayy himself. In 1858, French scholars Charles Defrémery and Beniamino Sanguinetti published the first full translation of *The Travels* and an annotated

---

1 See Lessons 18 and 19 for more information about Ibn Juzayy and the Marinid sultan.

version of the Arabic text. The most authoritative English translation and historical study of Ibn Battuta's narrative was written by the reknowned Scottish historian Sir H.A.R. Gibb between 1929 and 1958 (the final volume being completed by Charles Beckingham in 1994). In short, the excerpts that students will read in this book come straight from one of the most important historical and cultural texts ever written in Arabic.

Lesson Format

Each lesson is divided into several parts, as described below:

Historical Background

This introductory section sets the stage for the reading and helps students frame what they will encounter in Ibn Battuta's text. It begins with a general overview of the historical context and the significance of the location visited (For example: Why was Cairo so important at the time? What was the relationship between China and the Muslim world? How was the Muslim influence in Spain changing?). Next, key terms, such as locations, dynasties, people, groups, sects, and factions are identified and placed in their proper context. The emphasis is on the lasting legacy of these groups. For instance, how is the Mamluk influence felt in Egypt today? What great landmarks have these people left behind? What terms and names in our present day came from them?

From the Writings of Ibn Battuta

Key excerpts, in the actual words of Ibn Battuta, are presented with sufficient explanatory notes to situate them contextually. Here, students will not rely on paraphrases, but the actual words of the writer, and thus gain an appreciation for his style and skill. Each sentence is numbered, and key or difficult terms and phrases linked to explanatory definitions.

Vocabulary Terms

Presented in the order they appear in the text, students will find both unfamiliar vocabulary and key names and titles. The consolidated glossary at the end of the book lists all terms from all lessons in alphabetical order.

Comprehension Exercises
This section begins with questions to test students' general understanding of the text, then moves on to questions that prompt students to identify idioms and phrases based on their existing knowledge of Arabic. Hints are given in parentheses as to from which lines of the text the questions come.

Interpreting the Text
These questions, in Arabic, prompt students to read between the lines, applying their knowledge of history and the background notes given for the texts. They are often "why" questions, such as "Why would Ibn Battuta visit Cairo before going to Mecca?" These questions can form the springboard for class discussions or serve as useful short answer questions for tests that emphasize critical reading and reasoning.

Using Grammar and Context Clues
These are hints on reading strategies and stylistic devices that will better enable students to read this text and other classical texts. They are also designed to give students practice in applying their knowledge of the language and culture to effective reading. This section offers guided practice on strategic reading of Arabic texts, providing students with techniques for effectively breaking down difficult texts and using their knowledge of Arabic structure to determine meaning. After describing a technique, the book will direct students to apply it to specific lines of the text to sharpen their skills and become more effective readers.

Writing Exercises
This section offers several different types of exercises to cement student comprehension of the text as well as build student writing skills. The exercises prompt students to apply the idioms and stylistic techniques discussed in order to enhance their own writing, with hints given as to where to look in the text for clues.

Discussion Questions
These are general, open-ended questions about Ibn Battuta, his travels, his world, and the countries he visited. These encourage students to go beyond the material in the text and apply the information to their own interpretations

of Arab culture. In this way, students do not merely comprehend the text, but are encouraged to make it their own, and develop their own viewpoints.

Research and Presentation
This section offers a general question for further research by students as a capstone to their study of the lesson. These can serve for both written projects and oral presentations that can be integrated into a classroom framework.

Classical Arabic literature need not be daunting for students nor involve an excessively difficult 'jump' from intermediate texts. The sequence of exercises presented here will guide students to become increasingly more confident and independent readers of Arabic Literature.

Happy travels with Ibn Battuta!

1
Setting off on the Greatest Journey

(Tangier, Morocco, 1325)

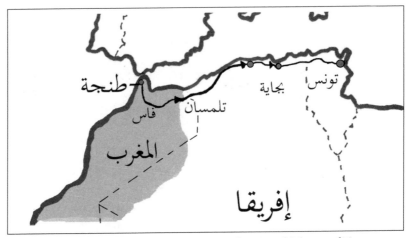

Ibn Battuta's departure from his home country, the Marinid Sultanate of Morocco

Although he is remembered today as the greatest traveler of his day, Ibn Battuta did not start out with that intent. The journey of some 75,000 miles over nearly 30 years began as the most familiar of travels for a pious Muslim—the Hajj to Mecca. Ibn Battuta grew up in a respected family of Muslim legal scholars in the coastal Moroccan city of Tangier (طنجـة), and his primary vocation and reputation throughout his life was as a Muslim jurist or qadi (قـاضٍ). In fact, it seems that this young scholar of exceptional talent had exhausted the limited educational opportunities in his hometown, so that when he began his Hajj journey in 1325 at age twenty-one, he also intended to visit some of the larger and more respected centers of Islamic learning. Throughout his travels, Ibn Battuta details the great attention he paid to the jurists and Islamic scholars of all the cities he visited. This extension of his pilgrimage into a lifetime journey throughout the known world of his day was the result of several factors: the demand for his service and expertise as a *qadi*, particularly in the more remote regions of the Muslim world; his pursuit of learning in great centers of Islamic knowledge; the need to move due to shifting political conditions; and lastly, his own love of travel. In his early journeys, we see the authenticity that made Ibn Battuta's memoir so valuable. He openly confesses his loneliness, longing for home, seasickness, fear, illness, and blunders.

The Kingdom of Morocco

Ibn Battuta's home country, though clearly in decline from the unified kingdom which had ruled over Spain and much of the Maghreb, was enjoying something of a renaissance in his lifetime. The Marinid sultans (1244–1465) had built Fez into a major political and intellectual capital, and restored the official status of the Maliki school of Islamic jurisprudence, of which Ibn Battuta was a scholar. The sultan of the day, Abu Sa'id Uthman II (1310–31), had established relative calm with the neighboring kingdoms, which made travel to the East possible. With the decline of Muslim Spain, the great centers of Islamic learning and power lay to the East, and it was to these that Ibn Battuta headed. Nonetheless, wherever Ibn Battuta traveled, he never ceased to consider Morocco his home, nor doubt that he would one day return.

Tunis

When Ibn Battuta arrived there in 1325, Tunis was the most prosperous and respected center of commerce and learning in the Maghreb. Many eminent scholars from Muslim Spain had fled to Tunis over the previous century, greatly enhancing its status. Its position on the North African coastal route also made it a major departure point for the yearly pilgrimage convoy. As could be expected, the twenty-one-year-old Ibn Battuta spent his time in one of the leading Islamic schools of Tunis. His talents were quickly recognized, however, and this young man found himself appointed as the *qadi* for the annual Hajj caravan from this great city. Here, the pattern was set for the rest of his travels, as his skills as a jurist, diplomat, and leader would call him to travel to the farthest corners of the Muslim world.

From the Writings of Ibn Battuta

The greatest journey begins with a very simple purpose. Here, Ibn Battuta describes his humble intent upon setting out from his home on a journey that would turn out to be much longer than he ever envisioned:

(١) كان خروجي من طنجة مسقط رأسي في يوم الخميس الثاني من شهر الله رجب الفرد عام خمسة وعشرين وسبعمائة[1] (٢) معتمداً حجّ بيت الله الحرام وزيارة قبر الرسول، عليه أفضل الصلاة والسلام، (٣) منفرداً عن رفيق آنَسُ بصحبته، (٤) وركب أكون في جملته، لباعث على النفس شديد العزائم، وشوق إلى تلك المعاهد الشريفة كامن في الحيازم. (٥) فجزمت أمري على هجر الأحباب من الإناث والذكور. (٦) ففارقت وطني مفارقة الطيور للوكور. (٧) وكان والدي بقيد الحياة فتحمّلت لبعدهما وصباً، ولقيت كما لقيا من الفراق نصباً، وسني يومئذ ثنتان وعشرون سنة.[2]

Early on, Ibn Battuta is struck by the physical hardships of a fourteenth-century land journey, yet demonstrates his determination to continue until death:

(٨) ولما وصلنا إلى بجاية ...أصابتني الحمى (٩) فأشار عليّ أبو عبد الله الزّبيدي بالإقامة فيها حتى يتمكّن البرء مني (١٠) فأبيت وقلت: «إن قضى الله، عزّ وجل، بالموت فتكون وفاتي بالطريق، وأنا قاصد أرض الحجاز.» (١١) فقال لي: «أما إن عزمت فبع دابّتك وثقّل المتاع وأنا أُعيرك دابّةً وخباء، وتصحبنا خفيفاً، (١٢) فإنّا نجدّ السير خوف غارة العرب في الطريق.» (١٣) فكنت أشدّ نفسي بعمامة فوق السرج خوفَ السقوط بسبب الضعف، ولا يمكنني النّزولُ من الخوف.

Upon arriving in Tunis, Ibn Battuta is struck by emotional hardship, as loneliness and homesickness affect him. Yet he also experiences the kindness of those he meets along the way, which will sustain him in much of his journey:

(١٤) وصلنا مدينة تُونُس، فبرز أهلها للقاء الشيخ أبي عبد الله الزّبيدي (١٥) فأقبل بعضهم على بعض بالسلام والسؤال (١٦) ولم يسلّم عليّ أحدٌ لعدم معرفي بهم (١٧) فوجدت من ذلك في النفس ما لم أملك معه سوابقَ العبرة، وأشتدّ بكائي (١٨) فشعر بحالي بعض الحجّاج، فأقبل عليّ بالسلام والإيناس.

---

1 1325 CE
2 lunar (Islamic calendar) years

Ibn Battuta is chosen to be the *qadi* of the pilgrims leaving Tunis. He will serve as a *qadi* throughout his life in locations all over the Muslim world:

(١٩) وبعـد مـدّة تعـيّن لركب الحجـاز الشريـف شيخُه يعـرف بـأبي يعقـوب السـوسي مـن أهـل أقـل مـن بـلاد إفريقيـة، وأكثـره المصادمـة، (٢٠) فقدمـوني قاضيـاً بينهـم (٢١) وخرجنـا مـن تونـس في أواخـر شـهر ذي القعـدة.

Vocabulary

مَسقط رأس (١)	birthplace
رَجب (١)	Rajab, the seventh month of the Islamic calendar
مُعتمداً (٢)	intending, targeting
مُنفرداً (٣)	alone, solitary
العزائم (٤)	intentions, resolutions
حيزوم (الحيازم - .sing) (٤)	the front of the chest
جَزَم (٥)	to assert, resolve
إناث (٥)	females
ذُكور (٥)	males
وكور (وكر - .sing) (٦)	nests
بقيد الحياة (٧)	alive, still living
يو مئذ (٧)	at this time
وَصَباً، نصباً (٧)	pain (in classical usage)
الحُمّى (٨)	fever
البَرء (٩)	healing, cure
أبيْتُ (١٠)	I refused
قَضى (١٠)	to predestine
الحِجاز (١٠)	The Hijaz (region in Saudi Arabia where Mecca & Medina are located)
دابّة (١١)	ride
خِباء (١١)	tent
نجدّ السيرَ (١٢)	speed up
شدّ (١٣)	to tighten
العَبرة (١٧)	crying, weeping
الإيناس (١٨)	sociability
ذي القعدة (٢١)	the eleventh month of the Islamic calendar

Comprehension Exercises

A. Answer the following questions in complete Arabic sentences (numbers refer to the lines in which the information can be found):

١.   متى بدأ ابن بطوطة رحلته ؟ وماذا كان السبب الرئيسي لرحلته؟ (١-٢)

_____

_____

_____

٢.   ما الصعوبات التي واجهها[3] ابن بطوطة عندما بدأ رحلته ؟ (٥-٨)

_____

_____

_____

٣.   بماذا نَصح[4] أبو عبد الله الزبيدي ابن بطوطه عندما أصابته الحمى في أول الرحلة؟ (٨-١٠)

_____

_____

_____

٤.   هل اتّبع[5] ابن بطوطة نصيحة صديقه؟ ماذا قال له؟ (٩-١٢)

_____

_____

_____

---

3 faced
4 advised
5 followed

٥. ماذا فعل أهل مدينة تونس مع ابن بطوطه عند وصوله؟ (١٤–١٩)

_____

_____

_____

B. Find Arabic phrases in the text that approximate the following meanings in English:

1. without a companion : _____

2. I had resolved : _____

3. if God has destined : _____

4. for fear of : _____

5. each other : _____

C. Find Arabic synonyms or equivalents in the text for the following words and phrases:

_____ : صديـق .١

_____ : تـرك .٢

_____ : عُمـري .٣

_____ : الشـفاء .٤

_____ : رفـض .٥

D. Find Arabic antonyms or opposites for each of the following words in the text and use each in a complete sentence:

١. غـــادر: _____

_____

٢. المـرض : _____

_____

٣. اشـترى : _____

_____

٤. ثقيــل : _____

_____

Interpreting the Text

١. أين وُلد ابن بطوطة ؟ كيف عرفتم ذلك؟ (١)

_____

_____

_____

٢. كيف وصف ابن بطوطة حالته عندما فارق وطنه و أهله؟ و هل بالَغَ⁶ في هذا الوصف؟ (٣-٦)

_____

_____

_____

٣. لماذا كان المسافرون يسيرون بسرعة أثناء رحلتهم؟ (١٢)

_____

_____

_____

6 exaggerated

٤. ما رأيكم في استقبال أهل مدينة تونس لابن بطوطة، وردّ فعله⁷ على ذلك؟ (١٤-١٨)

_____

_____

_____

٥. كم كان عُمر ابن بطوطة عندما أصبح قاضياً؟ (١٩-٢١)

_____

_____

_____

Grammar, Structure, and Context Clues

1. In line 2, Ibn Battuta describes himself as "مُعتمداً حجّ بيت الله".
    This sentence is a good example of the importance of reading for con-
    text. The word معتمد is an active participle derived from the verb اعتمد.
    In this text, the word means intending, planning, or targeting.
    In other contexts, the verb may carry many different meanings, such
    as: 'to approve,' as in اعتمد الرئيس القرارات الجديدة or ' to accredit,' as in
    اعتمد الرئيس الدبلوماسيين الجدد. When followed by the preposition على, the
    verb means 'to rely on or to depend on,' as in the sentence:
    اعتمد الطالب على الكتاب في المذاكرة. The verb in this configuration can also
    mean 'to base (something) on.' The context of Ibn Battuta describing
    his departure on a trip, however, indicates that the word refers to his
    intended destination.

2. In line 10, Ibn Battuta begins his oath "إن قضى الله، عزّ وجلّ." The verb
    قضى, like many Arabic verbs, has multiple meanings and is used in
    many idioms. In this case, قضى means 'to predestine,' or 'to decree.' The
    context of being collocated with 'if…God' indicates that this is the
    proper meaning. The same verb can also mean 'to judge' (قضى بالعدل)

---

7 reaction

and relates to Ibn Battuta's career title as a قاض . Yet it can also mean 'to accomplish' (قضى الغرض), 'to carry out' (قضى العهد), or even 'to urinate' (قضى حاجته). The objects which collocate with the verb are important clues to the meaning. The most familiar modern day to you usage may be 'to spend (a unit of time),' as in قضى العطلة مع أسرته.

3. In line 6, Ibn Battuta claims "ففارقت وطني مفارقةَ الطيور للوكور". The word مفارقة in this sentence is used as an absolute object (مفعول مطلق), a distinctive form of object that serves to highlight the main verb. The absolute object uses the *masdar* (المصدر) form of the primary verb placed in the accusative case. The absolute object is very often modified by adding an adjective or *idaafa* that further qualifies the meaning.

    For example:

    ضربه ضرباً قوياً.

    Literally, "He hit him a strong hitting." The underlined word is the absolute object. It repeats the meaning of the basic verb, but when qualified here with the adjective, makes it clear what type of hitting was involved. While a literal translation sounds very awkward in English, the root and pattern system gives this a rather poetic quality in Arabic, as in the example above.

    Another example:

    ركض ركضاً سريعاً.

    He ran fast (literally, "He ran a fast running").

4. The absolute object can also be modified by making it part of an *idaafa*, to clarify the type of action.

    مات الرجل موتَ الشهداء.

    "The man died the death of martyrs."

In line 6, Ibn Battuta has used this form, saying that he has left his homeland "فارقت وطني", describing this as the departure of the birds from the nest "مفارقة الطيور للوكور." This meaning could be approximated in English by using a simile "like the departure of a bird from its nest," but the Arabic construction conveys more power, as it does not rely on a 'like' or 'as.'

5. In line 16, "لَم... أَحَدٌ" is a general negation meaning "no one" (in this case, "no one greeted me"). A negative particle (لا، لم، لن) followed by an accusative noun has the meaning of a general, category negation, and can be translated as "no_____", "_____less", "non-_____", or any general negative in English. For example, لا سلكي from the word سلك, meaning 'wire,' thus means 'wireless.'

    What do you think the following compounds mean?

    لا جنسية: _____

    لا ديني: _____

    لا مكان: _____

6. The particle فَ has many uses and can be a useful signal of changes in the flow of the text. Since it attaches directly to the beginning of the word, it is important to be on the lookout for it. The excerpt from lines 8–13 includes several examples. When used in conjunction with a conditional 'if' (إذا، لو، إن، فـ) it signals the follow-on 'then' statement. Although the 'if' clause must always be in the perfect (past) tense, the فَ also allows the 'then' clause to be in a tense other than the perfect. This is instrumental in line 10, where the فَ allows the author to put the resulting clause in the imperfect, thus strengthening the dramatic impact of the first clause, which indicates that God's will on future events is sealed:

    إنْ قضى الله، عزّ وجل، بالموت فتكون وفاتي بالطريق.

"If God has ordained [my] death, then my death will be on the road."

The other uses of فَ in the paragraph (at the beginning of lines 9, 10, 11, and 12) all introduce new statements. In these cases, the particle فَ functions like وَ and need not be translated into English, but has the effect of indicating a closely related series of immediately following events. This increases the dramatic effect of the peril and urgency in the narrative, and supports the repeated use of خوفَ (fearing), by indicating that Ibn Battuta and his companions are moving rapidly from one action to another without delay.

7. In line 1, Ibn Battuta refers to the month of Rajab as رجب الفرد, with فرد meaning 'solitary,' or 'alone.' This refers to the fact that Rajab is the only one of the four sacred months (الأشهر الحُرُم) of the Islamic calendar that does not come in sequence with the rest. The four sacred months in which fighting was not allowed, as identified in the Quran (Quran 9:36), are:

the eleventh month of the year —(ذو القعدة) Dhu al-Qaʿda

the twelfth month of the year — (ذو الحجة) Dhu al-Hijja

the first month of the year — (محرم) Muharram

Rajab, as the seventh month, is non-consecutive with these.

Writing Exercises

A. Translate the following sentences into Arabic, using vocabulary from this reading. Hints in parentheses indicate which lines to look at for similar structures:

1. I left my birthplace, intending to travel to the Middle East (1–2):

_____

_____

_____

2. He lived alone in the desert (3):

_____

_____

_____

3. My grandfather was still alive when I left home (7):

_____

_____

_____

4. I was struck by a fever, and was unable to talk, due to weakness (9):

_____

_____

_____

5. The people of the city greeted one another (16):

_____

_____

_____

B. Rearrange the words below into coherent sentences:

١. والدي كان ذلك الحياة في على قيد الوقت

_____

_____

_____

٢. رأسي مِن مسقط خرجتُ الأوسط زيارة الشرق معتمداً

_____

_____

_____

٣. أهل بعضهم سلّم على المدينة بعضا

_____

_____

_____

٤. البيت النزول من يمكنني البرد لا بسبب

_____

_____

_____

٥. في لم يزرني المستشفى أحد

_____

_____

_____

Discussion Questions

١. ما أول رحلة قمت بها في حياتك ، و كم كان عُمرك حينئذٍ⁸؟

٢. ما أوجه <u>الشبه و الاختلاف</u>⁹ بين السفر الآن و السفر في زمن ابن بطوطة؟

٣. هل يمكن وصف¹⁰ ابن بطوطة بالمصطلح¹¹ العربي القديم : "شديد البأس"¹²؟ لماذا؟

٤. هل تشعرون بالوحدة أو بالغربة في بعض الأحيان؟ متى و أين؟

٥. تحتاج وظيفة القاضي لمؤهلات¹³ علمية و شخصية معينة ، ما أهم هذه المؤهلات من وجهة نظركم؟

Research and Presentation

ابحثوا في الانترنت عن واحدة من أهم المدن في بلاد المغرب العربي، و اكتبوا تقديها مصورا عنها وبيّنوا سبب اختياركم لهذه المدينة تقريراً.

---

8   at this time
9   similarities and differences
10   describe
11   idiom
12   stout-hearted
13   qualifications

2

The Lighthouse at Alexandria, One of the Wonders of the World

ذكر منار الإسكندرية (Alexandria, Egypt, 1326)

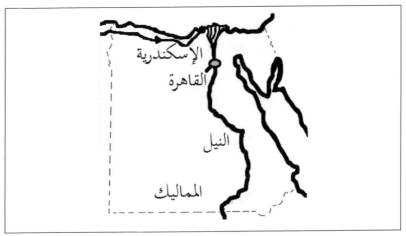

الإسكندرية

القاهرة

النيل

المماليك

Ibn Battuta followed the coastal route to reach Alexandria

Ibn Battuta was an astute observer of world political events and history. The fall of the eastern reaches of the once-great caliphate to the Mongols and the decline of Islamic Spain during the Spanish Reconquista contributed to the elevation of Mamluk Egypt as the most powerful state in the Islamic world. Successfully checking the Mongol advance and establishing firm control over the trade connections between the Mediterranean and the Red Sea, the Mamluks led Egypt into a new era of power that was quite evident to Ibn Battuta as he entered the Mediterranean port city of Alexandria. Although Cairo to the south was the largest city in the world and the greatest center of Islamic teaching, Ibn Battuta stayed in Alexandria for a few weeks to study its history and architecture. He later ranked it as one of the five greatest port cities of the world.

Alexandria
Named after Alexander the Great (356–23 BC), who founded the city in 331
BC, Alexandria (الإسكندرية in Arabic) was a cosmopolitan port from the very
start. Although the Suez Canal was more than 500 years in the future, Egypt
in Ibn Battuta's time had already become the vital connection between
Asian and Mediterranean maritime trade. Goods from Asia were unloaded
at the Red Sea port of Aydhab (عَيـذاب) and carried overland by camel to
Aswan on the Nile, eventually traveling to the Mediterranean port of Alexandria. Then, as now, it was a city full of European shippers and merchants.

The Lighthouse of Alexandria
One of the 'Seven Wonders of the World,' as described by Philo of Byzan-
tium, the lighthouse was for several hundred years the second-tallest structure in the world, after the Pyramids of Giza. Constructed by the Ptolemaic
(Greek) rulers of Egypt in approximately 280 BC, it was situated on Pharos
Island in Alexandria's harbor, connected to the mainland by a causeway, and
stood around 120 meters tall. It was the model for lighthouses around the
world, but by Ibn Battuta's time had fallen into disrepair. Although it was re-
portedly in use as late as the twelfth century CE, well over a millennium after
its construction, three major earthquakes, the last occurring shortly before
Ibn Battuta's visit, had damaged the structure. Despite being unable to enter
the lighthouse, Ibn Battuta was a keen student of history and architecture,
and nonetheless marveled at the significance of the building. A century
later, the remnants of the lighthouse would be removed by Mamluk sultan
Qaytbay to build the fort bearing his name, which still stands in Alexandria's
port.

An Amazing Prediction
While in Alexandria, Ibn Battuta visited its scholars, jurists, and Sufis. One
of the last, al-Zahid Burhan al-Din, predicted that Ibn Battuta would journey to China and India, although the young man had given no thought to
going farther than Mecca. The prediction would remain in Ibn Battuta's
mind throughout the following decades as these outlandish fortunes came
to pass. Of course, the only record of the incident is Ibn Battuta's own recollection after his long journey, so we will never know what may have actually
occurred. Nonetheless, the story does capture the improbability of a minor
scholar in his early twenties traveling from Morocco to China.

From the Writings of Ibn Battuta

Ibn Battuta describes the glory of the city of Alexandria:

(١) وصلنا في أوّل جمادى الأولى إلى مدينة الإسكندرية، حرسها الله (٢) وهـي الثغـرُ المحـرُوس والقطـرُ المأنـوس، العجيبـة الشـأن الأصيلـة البنيـان، (٣) بهـا مـا شـئتَ مـن تحسـين وتحصـين، ومآثـر دنيـا وديـن (٤) فهـي الفريـدة في تجـلّي سـناها، والخريـدة تجـلى في حلاهـا.

The port and gates of Alexandria are among the greatest in the known world:

(٥) لمدينـة الإسكندرية أربعـة أبـواب، (٦) بـاب السّـدرة، وإليـه يـشرَعُ طريق المغـرب. (٧) وبـاب رشيد، وبـاب البحـر، والبـاب الأخضر، وليـس يُفتـحُ إلا يـوم الجمعـة، (٨) فيخرج النـاس منـه إلى زيـارة القبـور (٩) ولهـا المَرسَـى العظيـم الشـأن، (١٠) ولم أرَ في مَـراسي الدنيـا مثلَـه، إلا مـا كان مـن مَرسَـى كـولم وقاليقـوط ببـلاد الهنـد، و مَرسَـى الكفـار بـسُرَادق ببـلاد الأتـراك، ومَرسَـى الزيتـون ببـلاد الصّـين وسـيقع ذكرها.

Description of the lighthouse of Alexandria, one of the Wonders of the World:

(١١) قصدتُ المنـار في هـذه الوجهـة فرأيـتُ أحـد جوانبـه متهدّمـاً. (١٢) وصفتـه أنّـه بنـاء مربّـع ذاهـبٌ في الهـواء، وبابـه مرتفـعٌ عـلى الأرض (١٣) وداخـل المنار بيـوتٌ كثـيرة (١٤) وهـو عـلى تـل مرتفـع. (١٥) ومسـافة مـا بينـه وبـين المدينـة فرسـخ واحـد في بـرّ مستطيل يحيـط بـه البحـر مـن ثـلاث جهـات إلى أن يتّصـل البحـر بسـور البلـد (١٦) فـلا يمكـن التوصّـل إلى المنـار في البـرّ إلا مـن المدينـة. (١٧) وفي هـذا البـرّ المتصـل بالمنـار مقبرة الإسـكندرية.

Thirteen years later, upon Ibn Battuta's return trip, the lighthouse had fallen into disrepair:

(١٨) قصـدتُ المنـار عنـدَ عـودي إلى بـلاد المغـرب عـام خمسـين وسبعمائة[14] فوجدتـه قـد استـولى عليـه الخـراب بحيـث لا يمكـن دخولـه ولا الصعـود إلى بابـه. (١٩) وكان الملـك النّـاصر[15]، رحمـه الله، قـد شرع في بنـاء منـار مثلـه بإزائـه فعاقـه المـوت عـن إتمامـه.

---

14 1349 CE
15 See Lesson 3 for more on Sultan al-Nasir Muhammad.

While in Alexandria, Ibn Battuta receives auspicious predictions from the Imam al-Zahid Burhan al-Din about future travels which he had not yet even considered:

(٢٠) دخلتُ عليه يوماً فقال لي: "أراك تحبّ السياحة والجولان في البلاد." (٢١) فقلتُ له: "نعم إني أحبّ ذلك." (٢٢) ولم يكن حينئذٍ بخاطري التوغّل في البلاد القاصية من الهند والصين. (٢٣) فقال: "لا بدّ لك إن شاء الله من زيارة أخي فريد الدين بالهند، وأخي ركن الدين زكريّاء بالسند، وأخي برهان الدين بالصين." (٢٤) فعجبتُ من قوله وألقىَ في رُوعي التوجّه إلى تلك البلاد، ولم أزل أجول حتى لقيتُ الثلاثة الذين ذكرهم وأبلغتهم سلامه.

Vocabulary

جُمادى الأولى (١)	Jumada al-Ula, the fifth month of the Islamic calendar
الثَّغْر (٢)	a coastal city or town, a fortified border city
المأنوس (٢)	popular, familiar
مآثر (٣)	finest works
الخريدة (٤)	virgin girl or pearl
تجلِّي(b)/ تجلَّى(a) (٤)	(a) to flaunt/(b) to appear, transfigure
سنا (٤)	glow
يشرَع (٦)	to begin, pave
كولم وقاليقوط (١٠)	Kollam and Calicut, India
الكفّار (١٠)	infidels
سُرَادق (١٠)	Sudak, in the Crimea
ذاهبٌ (١٢)	going
الهواء (١٢)	air
فرسخ (١٥)	old measure of distance (approx. five kilometers)
البرّ (١٦)	mainland
المتصل (١٧)	linked, connected
استولى عليه (١٨)	to seize

إزاء (١٩)	in the face of
عاق (١٩)	to prevent, hinder
الجَوَلان (٢٠)	wandering
توغّل (٢٢)	to go deep into
السِند (٢٣)	the Sindh, a region of southern Pakistan
رُوعي (٢٤)	my mind
أَبلغ (٢٤)	to convey

Comprehension Exercises

A. Answer the following questions in complete Arabic sentences (numbers refer to the lines in which the information can be found):

١.   متى وصل ابن بطوطة إلى مدينة الإسكندرية؟ (١)

_____

_____

_____

٢.   كيف وصف ابن بطوطة هذه المدينة؟ (٢-٤)

_____

_____

_____

٣.   كم عدد أبواب الإسكندرية وما أسماؤها؟ (٥-٨)

_____

_____

_____

٤ . ما الهيئة¹⁶ التي كان عليها المنار عند زيارة ابن بطوطة الأولى له؟ (١١–١٦)

_____

_____

_____

٥ . ماذا طلب الإمام برهان الدين من ابن بطوطة؟ وكيف كان وَقْعُ¹⁷ هذا الطلب عليه؟ (٢٣–٢٤)

_____

_____

_____

B. Find Arabic phrases in the text that approximate the following meanings
in English:

1. well built; of solid construction :_____

2. very tall; reaching into the sky :_____

3. fallen into ruin :_____

4. such that; to the extent that :_____

5. had not occurred to me :_____

C. Find Arabic synonyms or equivalents in the text for the following words
and phrases:

_____ البلـــد : ١ .

_____ ما تريـــد : ٢ .

16 shape
17 impact

٣. جمالها : ـــــــــــــــــــــــ

٤. الميناء : ـــــــــــــــــــــــ

٥. بـدأ في : ـــــــــــــــــــــــ

D. Find Arabic antonyms or opposites for each of the following words in the text and use each in a complete sentence:

١. الآخرة : ـــــــــــــــــــــــ
ـــ

٢. منخفض : ـــــــــــــــــــــــ
ـــ

٣. ينفصل : ـــــــــــــــــــــــ
ـــ

٤. الهبـوط : ـــــــــــــــــــــــ
ـــ

Interpreting the Text

١. لماذا كان يُفتَح الباب الأخضر يوم الجمعة فقط من كل أسبوع؟ (٧-٨)
ـــ
ـــ
ـــ

٢. متى كانت زيارة ابن بطوطة الثانية للمنار؟ وما التغييرات التي وجدها عليه؟ (١٨-١٩)
ـــ
ـــ
ـــ

٣. ما الفكرة التي أراد الملك الناصر تنفيذها[18] ؟ هل نجح فيها؟ لماذا؟ (١٩)

_____

_____

_____

٤. في رأيكم، كيف لاحظ[19] الإمام برهان الدين شغف[20] ابن بطوطة بالسفر والترحال؟ (٢٠)

_____

_____

_____

٥. لماذا تعجّب ابن بطوطة من طلب الإمام برهان الدين؟ (٢٤)

_____

_____

_____

---

18 implement
19 recognize
20 passion

Grammar, Structure, and Context Clues

1. Although not written in poetry, Ibn Battuta's style makes use of parallelism and rhyme to enhance its sense of eloquence, or بلاغة. In the first excerpt (lines 1–4), his description of Alexandria uses many pairs of rhymes or near-rhymes that have complementary meanings. Note the following pairs:

الثغرُ المحرُوس والقطرُ المأنوس؛ تحسين وتحصِين؛ الفريدة في تجلّي ... والخريدة تجلى

Understanding this structure can help you deduce what his overall theme is as well as predict the meaning of unfamiliar words. تحسين, for example, means 'embellishing' or 'beautifying,' while its pair, تحصِين means 'strengthening' or 'fortifying.' Ibn Battuta is pairing, in a memorable way, the qualities of Alexandria's fortifications and beauty, which are two central characteristics of the architecture of a great medieval city. This stresses both the strategic importance of Alexandria and its elevated culture. As you read the rest of Ibn Battuta's text, look out for these rhetorical devices. It follows logically that the other pairings will have similar themes, which can help you deduce unfamiliar words. These techniques tend to appear often in his descriptive passages of cities and locales, and less so in his narrative sections.

2. In line 5, Ibn Battuta uses a fronted predicate in the sentence "للمدينة الإسكندرية أربعةُ أبواب". The subject of this sentence is أربعةُ أبواب and أربعةُ is the word that carries the case-ending mark of the subject. Although Ibn Battuta wants to communicate that the city of Alexandria has four gates, an Arabic sentence cannot start with an indefinite noun, so he has delayed the subject by starting with the prepositional phrase للمدينة الإسكندرية.

What are some other ways to express this basic idea? Remembering that Ibn Battuta's goal in this excerpt is to stress the greatness of Alexandria, how does placing this predicate first strengthen or weaken the description?

By contrast, would the sentence هناك أربعة أبواب في مدينة الإسكندرية carry the same power of emphasis on the glory of Alexandria as a whole?

3. In line 7, Ibn Battuta notes of the gate: "وليس يفتح إلا يوم الجمعة." *Laysa* (ليس), as you have learned, is one of the 'sisters of kaana' (فعل ناقص من), أخوات كان), and is used to negate nominal (non-verbal) sentences. You may have been taught in Modern Standard Arabic never to use ليس to negate a verb. This construct, however, is used in classical texts. When used this way, you can assume there is an implied pronoun that acts as the noun of *laysa* (اسم ليس) and the entire verbal sentence is being negated, thus being essentially the predicate of *laysa* (خبر ليس). In this sentence, the implied pronoun is هو: ليس هو يفتح.

4. In line 10, the words "لَمْ أَرَ" are used when describing the port at Alexandria. The verb negated in this instance is رأى (to see). This is one of the trickiest verbs in the language to recognize and thus it is worth learning its different forms. This is a 'doubly weak' verb, in the sense that it has a *hamza* for a middle radical and an *alif maqsura* for the final radical. As you may know, the particle لم (did not) requires that the verb be in the jussive, which is a mood based on the present tense. This creates some problems with this verb, as the middle radical normally drops out entirely in the present tense. The jussive mood, as you may remember, causes the final long vowel to drop as well. Thus, our three-letter verb is reduced to one letter: رأى ← رَ. The initial *alif* is a conjugation prefix for 'I.' It is important to recognize this verb when you see it, because trying to look it up under its three-letter root when only one letter remains can be quite difficult.

Writing Exercises

A. Translate the following sentences into Arabic, using vocabulary from this reading. Hints in parentheses indicate which lines to look at for similar structures:

1. I had never seen a city like Cairo (10):

_____

_____

_____

2. The new commerce building stretches into the sky (12):

_____

_____

_____

3. He weakened to the extent that he couldn't walk (18):

_____

_____

_____

4. The city had fallen into ruin after the war (18):

_____

_____

_____

5. When I first went to college, it had not occurred to me to study Arabic (22):

_____

_____

_____

B. Rearrange the words below into coherent sentences:

١. أرَ الدنيا مثلها لم مدن في

_____

_____

_____

٢. يمكن من لا إلى المنار الوصول المدينة إلا

_____

_____

_____

٣. في نيسان مدينة شهر إلى القاهرة وصلنا أوّل

_____

_____

_____

٤. تُفتح المدينة إلا الجمعة يوم أبواب لا هذه

_____

_____

_____

٥. خاطري يكن حينئذٍ بـ لم السفر إلى الصين

_____

_____

_____

Discussion Questions

١.   ما المدينة أو المدن التي يمكن أن نصِفها كما وصف ابن بطوطة مدينة الإسكندرية ؟ لماذا؟

٢.   ما أغرب[21] وصف ذكره ابن بطوطة عن مدينة الإسكندرية و معالمها[22]؟

٣.   بماذا تفسرون[23] زيارة ابن بطوطة لمنار الإسكندرية مرةً أخرى في طريق عودته؟

٤.   ما أهم الكوارث[24] الطبيعية التي تحدث في المناطق الساحلية ؟ اذكروا أمثلة لها.

٥.   هل تستطيعون رسم صورة لمنار الإسكندرية وفقا[25] لوصف ابن بطوطة؟

Research and Presentation

ابحثوا في الإنترنت عن أهم معالم مدينة الإسكندرية القديمة والحديثة واكتبوا مقالا تفصيليا عن أحد هذه المعالم وأسباب اختياركم له.

---

21   strangest
22   landmarks
23   explain
24   disasters
25   based on

3
The Mamluk Sultan of Egypt

ذكر سلطان مصر (Cairo, Egypt, 1326)

The borders of the Mamluk state in Ibn Battuta's time

The Islamic world was going through a great transition during Ibn Battuta's lifetime. The unified caliphate of the Golden Age was in ruins, its great
capital of Baghdad sacked by the Mongols. Salah al-Din's (صــلاح الديــن)
Ayyubid dynasty, which had battled Crusader armies in Palestine, had fallen.
In its place, the Mamluk state in Egypt emerged as the most powerful force
in the Middle East. As the Mamluk warriors defeated both the Mongols and
Crusaders, Cairo became the center of economic, political, and military
power in the Middle East, a position it arguably retains to the present. By all
estimates, Cairo was the largest city outside of China at the time, as well as a
refuge for scholars and artists from besieged territories. For better or worse,
both the location and nature of power in the Islamic world had shifted. An

astute political observer and diplomat, Ibn Battuta recognized that he was entering the most important city of his day, and that the support and favor of the Mamluk sultan—whom he may have never actually met—would be crucial for the success of his further travels.

Mamluks

The Mamluks were originally slaves trained to be warriors during the Ayyubid dynasty (the term مملوك, from the root م-ل-ك 'to own,' means 'owned' or 'possession'). Selected for their physical strength and usually from Turkic families, they were taken away from their homes for specialized training and became fiercely loyal fighters. Rising to key positions in the Ayyubid army, Mamluk leaders would eventually seize power and found their own dynasty. Shortly before Ibn Battuta's birth, the great Mamluk ruler Baybars had defeated the Seventh Crusade, captured King Louis IX of France, and ended the westward expansion of the Mongols. Mamluk control ranged from Syria down into present-day Saudi Arabia, and the Mamluk sultan became the protector of the Two Holy Sites of Mecca and Medina.

The Mamluk period was marked by great turbulence as well as achievement. Rather than establishing a monarchy, Mamluks ruled as 'sultans' (the Arabic term سلطان, related to سلطة or 'power,' means exactly that—the 'holder of power'). The three centuries of Mamluk rule were marked by very short reigns, frequent coups, assassinations, and domestic struggles. The sultan that Ibn Battuta describes—al-Nasir Muhammad—seized power three times, and was one of few to die of natural causes while in office. Despite the violence of the times, however, Mamluk rulers were often prolific builders and generous supporters of arts and of religion. Much of the classical architecture of Islamic Cairo, in fact, is the result of Mamluk building projects, and the names of Mamluk sultans can be found on hundreds of historic buildings in the city.

Interestingly, the most famous of Egypt's monuments was of only minor interest to Ibn Battuta. Indeed, from his brief description of the Pyramids of Giza, it is clear that he didn't actually visit them. Yet this does not seriously undermine the value of his narrative. More than just a witness, Ibn Battuta was a collector of stories and reports that he heard along the way. In some cases, these are identified as secondhand accounts (حكاية) but often not, as in the case of the Pyramids. Ibn Battuta was extremely accurate about those things that concerned him and his readers. The pharaonic monuments, which would only receive great attention after the arrival of the Europeans, were of so little interest in Ibn Battuta's time that they were being used as spare bricks in Cairo walls. Mamluk Cairo was the political, military, and cultural capital of the Islamic world, and its glories lay very much in the present. Accordingly, Ibn Battuta's narrative focuses on the Mamluks.

From the Writings of Ibn Battuta

Before arriving in Cairo, Ibn Battuta first describes the Nile River:

(١) نيــل مــصر يفضــل أنهــار الأرض عذوبــة مــذاق، واتّســاع قطــر، وعظــم منفعــة، (٢) والمـدن والقـرى بضفتيـه منتظمـة ليـس في المعمـور مثلهـا. (٣) ولا يُعلـم نهـر يُـزرع عليـه مـا يُزرعُ عـلى النيـل (٤) وليـس في الأرض نهـرٌ يُسـمّى بحـراً غـيره.

Ibn Battuta then relates his impression of Cairo at the time of his arrival:

(٥) وصلـت إلى مدينـة مــصر (٦) هـي أم البــلاد. (٧) ذات الأقاليـم العريضـة والبـلاد الأريضـة المتناهيـة في كثرة العـمارة المتباهيـة بالحسـن والنضارة. (٨) مجمـع الـوارد والصادر، ومحـط رحـل الضعيـف والقادر، وبهـا مـا شـئت مـن عـالم وجاهـل وجـادّ وهـازل وحليـم وسـفيه ووضيـع ونبيـه وشريـف ومشـروف ومنكـر ومعـروف. قهـرت قاهرتهـا الأمـم. (٩) وتمكنـت ملوكهـا نـواصي العـرب والعجـم. (١٠) وأرضهـا مسـيرة شـهر لمجـدّ السـير، كريمـة التربـة مؤنسـة لـذوي الغربـة. (١١) وأمـا المـدارس بمـصر، فـلا يحيـط أحـد بحـصر هـا لكثرتهـا، (١٢) وأمـا المارسـتان الـذي بيـن القصريـن عنـد تربـة الملـك المنصـور قـلاوون، (١٣) فيعجـز الواصـف عـن محاسـنه.

Ibn Battuta's description of the sultan of Egypt:

(١٤) وكان سـلطان مـصر عـلى عهـد دخـولي إليهـا الملـك النـاصر أبـو الفتـح محمـد بـن الملـك المنصـور سـيف الديـن قـلاوون الصالحـي. (١٥) وكان قـلاوون يعـرف بالألفـي لأن الملـك الصالـح اشـتراه بألـف دينـار ذهبـاً، وأصلـه مـن قفجـق. (١٦) وللملـك النـاصر — رحمـه الله — السـيرة الكريمـة والفضائـل العظيمـة. (١٧) وكفاه شرفـاً انتـاؤه لخدمـة الحرميـن الشريفيـن، (١٨) ومـا يفعلـه في كل سـنة مـن أفعـال الـبرّ التـي تُعيـن الحجـاج مـن الجـمال

التـي تحمـل الـزاد والمـاء للمنقطعـين والضعفـاء، (١٩) وتحمـل مـن تأخـر أو ضعـف عـن المشـي في الدربـين المـصري والشـامي.

(٢٠) كان الملـك النـاصر – رحمـه الله – يقعـد للنظـر في المظالـم ورفـع قصـص المتشـكين كل يـوم اثنـين وخميـس. (٢١) ويقعـد القضـاة الأربعـة عـن يسـاره.

Vocabulary

مذاق (١)	taste
منفعة (١)	usefulness, benefit
المعمور (٢)	civilization, the civilized world
متناهية في (٧)	of the greatest ...
متباهية بـ (٧)	flaunting, showing off
نضارة (٧)	grace, beauty
نواصي (٩)	front of the head (the finest)
العجم (٩)	Persians, or more generally, non-Arabs
مجدّ السير (١٠)	diligent traveler
مؤنسة (١٠)	welcoming, friendly
مارستان (١٢)	medieval hospital, usually part of a mosque complex
الملك الناصر...الصالحي (١٤)	Mamluk sultan, known as al-Nasir Muhammad (reigned 1293–94, 1309–1341)
الملك المنصور سيف الدين قلاوون الصالحي (١٤)	Qalawun al-Salahi, father of al-Nasir Muhammad, Mamluk sultan 1279—90
قفجق (١٥)	Kipchak, a Turkic state in Central Asia
برّ (١٨)	charity, reverent deeds
زاد (١٨)	(as used here) food and provisions
منقطعين (١٨)	cut-off, i.e. those without support
الدربين (١٩)	the two paths

شامي (١٩)	Syrian or Levantine
يقعد (٢٠)	to sit (to hold audience)
متشكين (٢٠)	those with complaints

Comprehension Exercises

A. Answer the following questions in complete Arabic sentences (numbers refer to the lines in which the information can be found):

١.   بماذا يتميز نهر النيل عن بقية أنهار العالم؟ (١-٤)

_____

_____

٢.   لماذا عُرف السلطان قلاوون باسم ''الألفي''؟ (١٥)

_____

_____

٣.   كيف يصف ابن بطوطة مدينة القاهرة ومدارسها؟ (٥-١٣)

_____

_____

٤.   اذكروا بعض المساعدات التي قام بها الملك الناصر مع الحجاج. ما رأيكم فيها؟ (١٧-١٩)

_____

_____

١ . أحسن من :

٥ . ما المهمة التي كانت تشغل الملك الناصر يومي الاثنين و الخميس؟ (٢٠)

_____

_____

_____

B. Find Arabic phrases in the text that approximate the following meanings in English:

1. There is none like them in the civilized world : _____

2. No one could count them : _____

3. Their goodness cannot be described: _____

4. The works which he does every year : _____

5. Those who delayed or became weak : _____

C. Find Arabic synonyms or equivalents in the text for the following words and phrases:

١ . أحسن من :

_____

_____

_____

٢ . سيطروا على العرب والأجانب :

_____

_____

_____

٣. في وقت : _____

_____

_____

٤. لا يستطيعون أن يمشوا : _____

_____

_____

٥. يجلس ويستمع : _____

_____

_____

D. Find Arabic antonyms or opposites for each of the following words in the text and use each in a complete sentence:

١. ضيـق :_____

_____

٢. قــوي :_____

_____

٣. متبعثرة :_____

_____

٤. موحِشـة : ــ

٥. شـاكرين : ــ

Interpreting the Text

١. لماذا يُسمّي المصريون نهر النيل بحراً؟ (١-٤)

_____

_____

٢. كان المماليك مقاتلين بارعين. في رأيكم، لماذا ذكر ابن بطوطة شهرتهم وتفوقهم في فن العمارة؟ (١١-١٢)

_____

_____

٣. هل كان السلطان الناصر على قيد الحياة[26] عندما كتب ابن بطوطة هذا التقرير؟ كيف نعرف ذلك؟ (٢٠)

_____

_____

٤. ما علاقة السلطان قلاوون بالملك الصالح؟ (١٥)

_____

---

26 the idiom here means 'alive'

_____

_____

٥. هل تظنون أن ابن بطوطة التقى السلطان خلال زيارته للقاهرة؟ ما الدليل؟

_____

_____

_____

Grammar, Structure, and Context Clues

1. Names: Identifying names can be one of the trickiest parts of reading a classical text, as most names are also common adjectives or nouns. This is much more of an art than a science, and the most useful technique is to be aware of terms that are used frequently in the text and seem to be in the position of subjects of sentences. An Arabic name is usually a sequential enumeration of the person's lineage, and may contain titles and accomplishments. In common address, most of these are dropped, but for important persons, the full sequence may be used to emphasize the person's significance, typically the first time they are mentioned. Look at the full name of Sultan al-Nasir Muhammad from line 14.

الملك الناصر أبو الفتح محمد بن المنصور سيف الدين قلاوون الصالحي

This name consists of three main parts. Using the signal words بن (son) and أب (father), can you identify the components of the sultan's name?

His title: _____

His name: _____

His nickname or _kuniya_: _____

Father's name: _____

See the analysis below for further explanation:

الناصر أبو الفتح محمد بن المنصور سيف الدين قلاوون الصالحي

The sultan's name is الناصر محمد, but Ibn Battuta will refer to him in the
text simply as الناصر. Notice the title الملك 'king' is used out of respect,
although al-Nasir is a sultan.

His father's name is that following بن, in this case: المنصور سيف الدين
قلاوون الصالحي, and he is commonly referred to as قلاوون, as Ibn Battuta
does in line 15.

Lastly, Ibn Battuta includes أبو الفتح in his title. This could indicate
that he is the father of a son named 'al-Fath,' or, as is the case here, the
name is an honorific, meaning the 'Father of Conquest.' Such titles
were often given to powerful people. In any case, it is a part of the
name and need not be translated.

2. Invoking blessings: Ibn Battuta uses several formulaic religious
    blessings as the situation requires. For example, رحمه الله or رحمه الله يرحمه 'God
    have mercy on him' is used to refer to the dead, and indicates here that
    Sultan al-Nasir Muhammad was dead by the time this memoir was
    written.

3. غير: The term غير, meaning 'other than …', is often used in compounds. In
    line 4, for example, غيره means 'other than it' or 'besides it.' This is frequent-
    ly used with a negative statement, to say 'there is no____ besides it.' With
    this structure in mind, what is line 4 saying about the Nile River?

4. Active and passive verbs: Note the verb structure يعرف...بـ in line 15:
    وكان قلاوون يعرف بالألفي. What would be the voweling (and thus the
    correct pronunciation) of the verb? Hint: Is the verb here passive or
    active? Is Qalawun knowing or being known?

5. لـ: The preposition لـ ('for' or 'belonging to') can change the meaning of an entire sentence. It is very easy to overlook, particularly when attached to the definite article. Note how للملك الناصر at the beginning of line 16 could easily be mistaken for الملك الناصر.

With attention to this function of لـ, how should those opening words of line 16 be read? How should the entire sentence be translated?

6. Using case endings to identify subject and object: In line 17, which reads وكفاه شرفاً انتماؤه لخدمة الحرمين الشريفين, identifying the subject of the sentence will assist in understanding the meaning. Here, as is common, the first word is a verb—كفى (to suffice). Context tells us that the pronoun suffix ـه (him, his) refers to the sultan.

Which of the next two words, however, tells us what sufficed the sultan? The clue is in the case endings for each word. Notice شرفاً (honor) is in the accusative case, meaning it cannot be the subject of the verb 'to suffice him.' The word انتماؤه (his association), however, is in the nominal case, indicated by the و, meaning it could be the subject. Given these limitations, how would you translate line 17?

Writing Exercises

A. Translate the following sentences into Arabic, using vocabulary from this reading. Hints in parentheses indicate which lines to look at for similar structures:

1. The king was known as 'The Father of the Sword' (15):

_____

_____

_____

2. There was no other person besides him in the room (4):

_____

_____

_____

3. Her association with the university was sufficient (17):

_____

_____

_____

4. There is no one who knows what he knows (3):

_____

_____

_____

5. The pilgrims carried the weak and old with them (18–19):

_____

_____

_____

B. Rearrange the words below into coherent sentences:

١. دولة أسست سقوط الأيوبيين بعد المماليك

٢. هزم المغول المماليك والصليبيين جيوش محاربون

_____

_____

_____

٣. بغداد القاهرة مركز العرب سقوط أصبحت بعد سلطة

_____

_____

_____

٤. كبيرة السلطان خدمة للحجاج وفّر المملوك

_____

_____

_____

٥. الملوك المباني الدينية في العديد من القاهرة بنى المملوك

_____

_____

_____

Discussion Questions

١. كتب ابن بطوطة عن أهمية ومكانة نهر النيل بالنسبة لمصر وللمصريين. وضّحوا ذلك مع بيان مدى توافق كلامه مع الوضع الحالي لنهر النيل.

٢. مازالت مصر تحتفظ بدورها الريادي والمحوري في الشرق الأوسط منذ عهد ابن بطوطة وحتى الآن. هل تتفقون أم تختلفون مع هذه المقولة ولماذا؟

٣. كيف تحلّى الملك الناصر بصفات وأخلاق القائد الوَرِع[27]؟

٤. لماذا كانت خدمة الحرمين الشريفين وحجاج البيت مسؤولية سلطان مصر في هذا العهد؟ ومن يضطلع بهذه المسؤولية اليوم؟

٥. هل زرتم أو قرأتم عن مدينة في العالم تضاهي[28] مدينة القاهرة وأبنيتها كما وصفها ابن بطوطة؟

Research and Presentation

ابحثوا عن مقالة أو خبر مقروء أو مسموع على الإنترنت يتناول موضوعا ثقافيا أو سياسيا أو اجتماعيا حول'' مصر و المصريين في القرن الحادي والعشرين'' واكتبوا ملخصا ونقدا له.

---

27 godly
28 emulate

4
Jerusalem and
the Dome of the Rock

(Jerusalem, 1326) ذكر قبة الصخرة

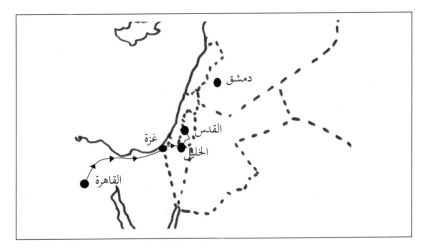

Ibn Battuta's route from Cairo to Jerusalem

Ibn Battuta had planned to travel to Mecca across the Red Sea. The Egyptian
port of Aydhab as a key link in the spice trade, had a ferry link to Jeddah in
Saudi Arabia and was a major Hajj transit point for pilgrims. A local rebellion
of the Beja bedouins against the Mamluks had closed the port and forced Ibn
Battuta to return to Cairo. Even then, it was clear that he had more than a Hajj
journey on his mind. Rather than join the official Mamluk Hajj caravan out of
Cairo, he traveled northward through Palestine toward the city of Damascus,
the second great city of the Mamluk Sultanate, before heading back on the
route to Mecca. Ibn Battuta stopped at many important religious sites in Palestine, including the city of Jerusalem, and recorded his impressions.

Jerusalem

While Jerusalem today is a huge city of tremendous political importance, in Ibn Battuta's time it was a neglected town administered by Damascus. In part this was due to the stability and security that Mamluk rule had brought to the region. The Crusaders had been driven out of Palestine at the end of the previous century and the town was no longer the site of major religious conflict. Meanwhile, Mamluk trade routes bypassed Jerusalem, such that only religious pilgrims had an interest in visiting. Ibn Battuta was certainly one of these, being fascinated not only by its mosques, but by its Christian churches as well. A budding historian, Ibn Battuta looks beyond the evident destruction in the town to the way the city's walls reflect the heroic campaign of liberation waged by the eminent Salah al-Din.

The Dome of the Rock

Constructed in CE 691 by the Umayyad Caliph 'Abd al-Malik, the Dome of the Rock was at the time, and remains today, one of the most visually striking buildings in the world. It was constructed at the center of the Temple Mount, believed to have been the site of Solomon's Temple. The mosque takes its name from the stone at its center, believed to have been the site of the Prophet Muhammad's Night Journey to Heaven (المعراج). Although Muslims now pray facing Mecca, the original direction of prayer was toward Jerusalem. The octagonal structure, with its eighteen-meter dome, was patterned after Byzantine churches. For much of its early history, the site was open to Christian pilgrims, and attacks on the pilgrims became the ostensible justification for the Crusades. After the Crusader occupation in 1099, the mosque was turned into a church and the Knights Templar set up their headquarters on the site. Salah al-Din, who recaptured Jerusalem in AD 1187CE, reconsecrated the site as a mosque.

Despite Ibn Battuta's fascination with Palestine, he had to leave after about a week as the annual Hajj caravan from Syria was departing. Knowing the desert portion of the journey (through present-day Saudi Arabia) to be the most difficult, he recognized the importance of joining the well-provisioned caravan.

From the Writings of Ibn Battuta

Ibn Battuta's route through Palestine takes him to several holy sites:

(١) ثمّ سافرتُ من غـزّة إلى مدينـة الخليـل، صلّى الله عـلى نبينـا وعليه وسلّم تسليماً، (٢) وهـي مدينة صغيرة السـاحة، كبيرة المقـدار، مشرقـة الأنـوار، (٣) ومسجدها أنيق الصنعة (٤) وفي داخـل المسـجد الغـارُ المكـرمُ المقـدّسُ، فيـه قـبرُ إبراهيـم وإسـحاق ويعقـوب، صلوات الله عـلى نبينا وعليهـم (٥) ثمّ سافرتُ مـن هـذه المدينـة إلى القـدس (٦) فـزرتُ في طريقـي إليـه تربـةَ يونـسَ، عليـه السـلام، وعليهـا بنيّـةٌ كبيرة، ومسـجد (٧) وزرتُ أيضاً بيـتَ لحـم موضـعَ ميـلاد عيسـى، عليـه السـلام، وبـه أثـر جـذع النخلـة، وعليـه عـمارة كثـيرة (٨) والنصـارى يعظّمونـه أشـد التعظيـم، ويُضيّفـونَ مـن نـزّل بـه.

Upon arriving in Jerusalem, the traveler reflects on the city's significance in Islam and its recent history:

(٩) وصلنـا إلى بيـت المقـدس شرّفـه الله ثالـثِ المسـجدين الشريفـين في رتبـة الفضـل (١٠) ومصعد رسـول الله، صلّى الله عليـه وسلّم تسـليماً، ومَعرَجِـه إلى السـماء (١١) وكان الملك الصـالـح الفاضـل صـلاحُ الديـن بـن أيّـوب، جزاه الله عـن الإسـلام خـيراً، لمـا فتـحَ هـذه المدينـة هـدم بعـض سـورها.

Among the marvels of Jerusalem, Ibn Battuta is amazed by the Dome of the Rock:

(١٢) وهـي مـن أعجـب المبـاني وأتقنهـا وأغربهـا شـكلاً، (١٣) قـد توفّـر حظّهـا مـن المحاسـن، وأخـذتْ مـن كلّ بديعـة بطـرفٍ، (١٤) وهـي قائمـة على نشـز في وسـط المسـجد، يُصعدُ إليهـا في درج رُخـام، (١٥) وفي ظاهرهـا وباطنهـا مـن أنـواع الزواقـة ورائـق الصّنعـة مـا يُعجـزُ الواصـف، وأكثر ذلـك مغشّى بالذهـب، (١٦) ويقصرُ لسـان رائيهـا عـن تمثيلها (١٧) وفي وسـط القبّـة الصخـرة الكريمـة التي جـاء ذكرهـا في الآثـار، (١٨) فإنّ النبيّ، صلّى الله عليـه وسلّم، عَـرَجَ منهـا إلى السـماء.

During his week-long visit, he also noted some historic churches in Jerusalem:

(١٩) بَعَدوةِ الـوادي المعـروف بـوادي جهنّـم في شرقـي البلـد عـلى تـلّ مرتفـع هنالـك بنيّـة يُقال إنهـا مصعـد عيسـى، عليـه السـلام، إلى السـماء (٢٠) وفي بطـن الـوادي المذكور كنيسـة يعظّمهـا النصـارى، ويقولـون: "إنّ قـبرَ مريـمَ، عليهـا السـلام بهـا" (٢١) وهنالـك أيضاً

كنيسـة أخـرى معظمـة يحجّهـا النصـارى، وهـي التـي يكذبـون عليهـا، ويعتقـدون أنّ قـبر
عيسـى، عليـه السـلام، بهـا (٢٢) وعـلى كلّ مـن يحجّهـا ضريبـةٌ معلومـةٌ للمسـلمين.

Vocabulary

الخليل (١)	Hebron, a city in the West Bank
مِقدار (٢)	size, extent, expanse
غار (٤)	cave
تُربة (٦)	land, soil, burial ground
جِذع النخلة (٧)	trunk of the palm tree
النَصارى (٨)	Christians
تعظيم (٨)	glorification, magnification
يُضيّفونَ (٨)	they host
مِصْعَد (١٠)	elevator (in this case, place of ascent)
مَعرَج (١٠)	route of ascent (refers to the Prophet Muhammad's ascent into Heaven)
فاضل (١١)	excellent, kind
صلاحُ الدين بن أيّوب (١١)	Salah al-Din (Saladin 1137–93), founder of the Ayyubid dynasty in Syria and Egypt
جزاه الله عن الإسلام خيراً (١١)	Islamic expression meaning may God reward him
محاسن (١٣)	good qualities, advantages
بديعة (١٣)	terrific, impressive
نشز (١٤)	elevated place
دَرَج رُخام (١٤)	marble stairs
مُغَشّى (١٥)	coated, plated
عَرَجَ (١٨)	to ascend, rise
جهنّم (١٩)	the Valley of Gehenna (which gave its name to 'Hell)
ضريبة (٢٢)	tax

Comprehension Exercises

A. Answer the following questions in complete Arabic sentences (numbers refer to the lines in which the information can be found):

١. كيف وصف ابن بطوطة مدينة الخليل؟ (١-٣)

_____

_____

_____

٢. ما المعالم التي زارها ابن بطوطة في الطريق إلى مدينة القدس؟ (٦-٨)

_____

_____

_____

٣. ماذا فعل صلاح الدين عندما فتح مدينة القدس؟ (١١)

_____

_____

_____

٤. كيف صوّر ابن بطوطة بناية مسجد قبة الصخرة؟ وما أهم ما يميزه[29]؟ (١٣-١٨)

_____

_____

_____

---

29   distinguish it

_____

_____

_____

B. find Arabic phrases in the text that approximate the following meanings in English:

1. of elegant construction :_____

2. third in rank (or importance) :_____

3. most unusual in shape :_____

4. to defy description :_____

5. said to be, alleged to be :_____

C. Find Arabic synonyms or equivalents in the text for the following words and phrases:

١. الأضـواء : _____

٢. الكهـف : _____

٣. احـترام : _____

٤. الزينة : _____

٥. مكان مرتفع : _____

D. Find Arabic antonyms or opposites for each of the following words in the
text and use each in a complete sentence:

١. الأرض : ــــــــــــــــــــــــــــــ

٢. بنى : ــــــــــــــــــــــــــــــ

٣. هبــط : ــــــــــــــــــــــــــــــ

٤. منخفــض : ــــــــــــــــــــــــــــــ

Interpreting the Text

١. مَن الأنبياء والرُّسل[30] الذين زار ابن بطوطة قبورَهم في مدينتي الخليل والقدس؟ (١-٦)

٢. بيت المقدس أو المسجد الأقصى[31] هو ثالث المسجدين الشريفين. فما هما المسجدان الأول
والثاني؟ (٩)

٣. لماذا تُعد قبة الصخرة مكاناً مقدساً عند المسلمين؟ (١٢-١٨)

---

30 messengers and prophets
31 the 'furthest mosque' as mentioned in the Prophet Muhammad's miraculous night
journey.

4. هل تشبه بناية قبة الصخرة —كما وصفها ابن بطوطة— أحد الأماكن التي زرتموها[32] من قبل؟ (١٢-١٨)

٥. ما أوجه الشبه والاختلاف بين الكنيستين اللتيْن زارهما ابن بطوطة في وادي جهنم؟ (١٩-٢٢)

Grammar, Structure, and Context Clues

1. It is a common sign of reverence to follow the names of important Muslim figures with a standard blessing. These are derived from the Quran or hadith. You are likely familiar with the blessing that normally follows the name of the Prophet Muhammad—صلّ الله عليه وسلّم, often rendered in English as 'peace and blessings upon him' or abbreviated as 'PBUH.' Abbreviating these phrases is controversial, however, as it can be seen as a sign of laziness. The name of God is also followed by a statement of exaltation. As you can see from the text, however, there are a great many more standard blessings, and they are very important to a devout Muslim like Ibn Battuta. Note some of the following, along with their meanings and to whom they are normally applied:

---

32 you (plural) visited

Arabic	English	Applied to	Abbreviation
صلّى الله عليه وسلّم	God's peace and blessings upon him	the Prophet Muhammad	PBUH
عليه السلام	peace upon him (her)	any prophet or archangel	
عليه الصلاة والسلام	prayers and peace upon him (her)	the Prophet Muhammad	
رضي الله عنه	may God be pleased with him	companions of the prophet	
سبحانه وتعالى	exalted and glorified is He	God	SWT

2. Many of the common names found in Islamic texts are the same as in Christian or Jewish writing, although spellings and pronunciations may vary. A large number of the names mentioned in this section of the text are Biblical as well as Quranic figures, and recognizing the names will help to understand Ibn Battuta's account. Becoming familiar with the most common pronunciation changes between names derived from Arabic and Hebrew will also help you recognize Quranic people and place names. Note the following important names:

إبراهيم (٤)	Abraham
إسحاق (٤)	Isaac
يعقوب (٤)	Jacob
يونسَ (٦)	Jonah
بيتَ لحم (٧)	Bethlehem (Beth equates to بيت in Arabic and appears in a number of place names.)
عيسى (٧)	Jesus
أيّوب (١١)	Job
جهنّم (١٩)	Gehenna (the valley gave its name to the name for 'Hell' in both Arabic and Hebrew)
مريم (٢٠)	Mary

3. In line 14, the word نشز is a noun. The verb form of this word means 'to be elevated' or 'to protrude.' The unvoweled spelling gives no clue to the usage, but the context makes it clear. The word is preceded immediately by the preposition على in the phrase "قائمة على" (situated upon), and followed by "في وسط المسجد" (in the middle of the mosque). This arrangement clearly calls for the noun 'a rise, an elevated place,' rather than the verb. Using context is very important, as a great number of verbs have verbal nouns that look the same as the verb. The same word نشز can also be used in other contexts, giving a very different meaning. When one says نشز في الغناء, it means 'he sang out of tune,' that is, his voice protruded, or stood out from, the others. The related active participle (اسم الفاعل ناشز) thus means 'discordant, inharmonious' or 'elevated, protruding.' The context here is very important, since Ibn Battuta is praising the beauty and glory of the Dome of the Rock and the entire Aqsa complex, not criticizing the site as disharmonious.

4. The verb عَرَج with the vowel pattern used in line 18 means to ascend and is related to the معراج, the Prophet Muhammad's famous ascension into Heaven. The same verb, however, with a *kasra* on the middle consonant ر means 'to be lame' or 'to walk lamely,' as in the sentence عَرِج الرجل في مشيه. Since most texts are not voweled, the context is of great importance in extracting the correct meaning, as these two meanings have vastly different implications.

5. Similarly, the participle معلومة in line 22 has several possible meanings. It is most commonly used to mean 'known' as in مخاطر معلومة (a known risk). This usage lends itself to the word معلومات (information). As it is used in this sentence, however, the word means 'fixed, specified.' Since it is associated here with the word ضريبة (tax), this usage makes the most sense. In other contexts, the word can function as a noun, meaning 'a notion, a fact.' The structure, however, of ضريبةٌ معلومةٌ shows that it is not being used as a noun in this sentence.

Writing Exercises

A. Translate the following sentences into Arabic, using vocabulary from this reading. Hints in parentheses indicate which lines to look at for similar structures:

1. This prince[33] was third in rank among the princes of the kingdom (9):

   _____

   _____

   _____

2. The size of the city of Cairo defies description (15):

   _____

   _____

   _____

3. Her dress was of the most unusual color (12):

   _____

   _____

   _____

4. Damascus is said to be the oldest city in the world (19):

   _____

   _____

   _____

أمير، أمراء 33

5. The people of the city host all pilgrims who visit (8):

_____

_____

_____

B. Rearrange the words below into coherent sentences:

١. الله خيرا الإسلام جزاه عن

_____

_____

_____

٢. أعجب المباني أهرامات و شكلا من أتقنها الجيزة

_____

_____

_____

٣. يضيّفون سكان و المدينة كل يكرمون الزّوار هذه

_____

_____

_____

٤. أجمل إن الزيتون من يُقالُ في كنائس دمشق العالم كنيسة

_____

_____

_____

_____

_____

_____

Discussion Questions

١. لماذا تعد القدس مَهْد[34] الأديان السماوية الثلاثة؟

٢. ما المعلومات التي عرفتموها عن مدينة القدس قبل وبعد دراستكم لهذا الفصل؟

٣. ناقشوا ما أعجبكم وما لم يعجبكم من آراء[35] ابن بطوطة في هذا الفصل؟

٤. ما أثر الصراع العربي– الإسرائيلي على مدينة القدس في العصر الحديث؟

٥. إذا قمتم برحلة إلى مدينة القدس، فما الأماكن المفضلة التي ستزورونها ولماذا؟

Research and Presentation

ابحثوا في الإنترنت عن أغنية زهرة المدائن[36] (يا قدس) للمطربة اللبنانية فيروز.

استمعوا للأغنية وترجموا بعض كلماتها للإنجليزية ثم قوموا بتسجيل مقطع منها بصوتكم للتقديم في الصف.

---

34 cradle
35 views
36 the old name of Jerusalem means 'the flower of cities'

5
Damascus, Paradise of the East

(Damascus, Syria, 1326) ذكر مدينة دمشق

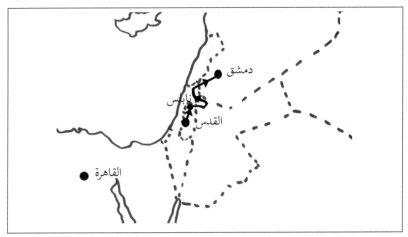

On to Damascus, the second city of the Mamluk Sultanate

Ibn Battuta's journey through Palestine was more rushed than he would have liked. He had a Hajj caravan to catch from Damascus, and no doubt had much interest in seeing the great city itself. After a brief stay in Jerusalem, he was off for one of the most celebrated cities in Islamic history.

Damascus is believed to be the oldest continuously inhabited city in the world. An important center of ancient Christianity, it became the capital of the Umayyad Caliphate (661–750), the second Islamic caliphate, and, at the time the largest empire the world had ever seen. Damascus' status fell with the shift of the caliphate to Baghdad in 762 and several Crusader and Mongol invasions. As was the case in so many places Ibn Battuta visited, Damascus was enjoying something of a renaissance at the time. It had been spared from the Mongol conquest by the brilliant Mamluk victory over the

Mongols at 'Ayn Jalut in 1260, and effectively became the second capital of the Mamluk Sultanate. Mamluk rule had brought stability and solidified Damascus' position as a major center of inland trade. As a terminus of the 'Silk Road,' it was so renowned, in fact, that it gave its name to a particular silk fabric, 'damask.' While the wars had greatly diminished this trade, the power of Mamluk rule had not only driven off the Mongol threat, but turned Mongol states into valuable trading partners. Nonetheless, the Mamluks maintained a sizable military presence in the city.

The centerpiece of Damascus was the famous Umayyad mosque, built on the site of an important church and named after the Umayyad Caliphs. While Ibn Battuta gives due praise to the glory of the mosque, he is careful also to detail the history of its founding and construction as an example of the governing practices of the Muslim caliphs. In an elegant image—likely more metaphoric than precise—he describes how half the cathedral on the site was seized by force, while the other half was entered peacefully. When the two Umayyad generals met in the center of the cathedral, they decided to keep the half willingly opened by the Christians as a church; the other half became a mosque. The caliph Walid I (705–15) offered the Christians compensation to sell their half, but when they refused, he seized it by force. The remaining church was destroyed and the Grand Mosque was built on the site. Those same Christians predicted a curse would fall upon the Muslims, but none did. Ibn Battuta's account implies clear lessons for those who came under Islamic rule.

The most striking aspect of Ibn Battuta's account of Damacus, however, is its contrast with his later visit. When he returned through the city in 1348[37], Damascus had been devastated by the Black Plague and countless people—including his own son—had died from the disease. As in all the places he visited during that period, the plague paralyzed economic, cu tural, and religious growth.

Little aware of any of these future calamities, Ibn Battuta quickly acquired a new wife and sired a son (whom he would never meet) and headed off with

---

37   See Lesson 20

the caravan for his long-anticipated Hajj to Mecca after less than a month in Damascus.

In his description of Damascus, Ibn Battuta quotes the twelfth-century geographer and traveler Ibn Jubayr, who visited many of the locations on Ibn Battuta's route a century earlier. In this account, he clearly attributes Ibn Jubayr's words to him, but that is not always the case in the text. Ibn Battuta, in fact, makes frequent use of Ibn Jubayr's descriptions and those of other travelers—some sections of Ibn Battuta's text are copied directly from Ibn Jubayr. This has caused some modern historians to doubt the veracity of some of Ibn Battuta's accounts. Here, however, Ibn Battuta's text clearly distinguishes first-person narrative (where he describes what "I" or "we" saw) from passages that are simply descriptions of people and locations written in the third person. More importantly, Ibn Jubayr's narrative is evidence that Islamic exploration and travel writing was an established genre before Ibn Battuta's grand journey.

From the Writings of Ibn Battuta

The surpassing beauty of Damascus:

(١) ودمشـق هـي التـي تَفضُـل جميـع البـلاد حسـناً وتتقدّمهـا جمـالاً، (٢) وكلّ وصـف، وإن طـال، فهـو قـاصر عـن محاسـنها (٣) ولا أبـدع ممّـا قالـه أبـو الحسـين بـن جُبـير، رحمه الله تعـالى، في ذكرهـا قـال: "وأمّـا دمشـقُ، فهـي جنّـةُ المـشرقُ ومطلـعُ نورها المـشرق (٤) وخاتمـة بـلاد الإسـلام التـي استقرَيْناهـا، وعـروسُ المـدن التـي اجتَلَيناهـا" (٥) تَزَيَّنـت في منصّتهـا أجمـل تزيـين. (٦) وتشرَّفـت بـأن أوى المسـيح، عليـه السـلام، وأمّـه منهـا إلى ربـوة ذات قـرار معـين. (٧) ولله صـدقُ القائلـينَ عنهـا: "إن كانـت الجنّـة في الأرض فدمشـقُ لا شـكَّ فيهـا."

The unmatched glory of the Umayyad Mosque of Damascus:

(٨) وهـو أعظـم مسـاجد الدنيـا احتفـالاً، وأتقنهـا صناعـة، وأبدعهـا حسـناً وبهجـة وكمالاً، (٩) ولا يُعلـم لـه نظـير ولا يوجـد لـه شـبيه. (١٠) وكان الـذي تـولّى بنـاءه وإتقانـه أمـير المؤمنـين الوليـد بـن عبـد الملـك بـن مـروان، (١١) ووجّـه إلى ملـك الـروم بقسـطنطينية يأمـره أن يبعـث إليـه الصُّنـاع فبعـث إليـه اثنـي عـشر ألـف صانـع.

The story of the founding of the Umayyad Mosque:

(١٢) وكان موضـع المسـجد كنيسـة فلمّا افتتـح المسـلمون دمشـق دخـل خالـد بـن الوليـد، رضي الله عنـه، مـن إحـدى جهاتهـا بالسـيف، فانتهـى إلى نصـف الكنيسـة، (١٣) ودخـل أبـو عبيـدة بـن الجـرّاح، رضي الله عنـه، مـن الجهـة الغربيـة صلحـاً، فانتهـى إلى نصـف الكنيسـة. (١٤) فصنـع المسـلمون مـن نصـف الكنيسـة الـذي دخلـوه عَنوةً مسـجداً، وبقـي النصـف الـذي صالحـوا عليـه كنيسـة. (١٥) فلمّا عـزم الوليـد عـلى زيـادة الكنيسـة في المسـجد طلب مـن الـروم أن يبيعـوا منـه كنيسـتهم تلـك بـما شـاؤوا مـن عـوض، (١٦) فأبـوا عليـه، فانتزعهـا مـن أيديهـم، (١٧) وكانـوا يزعمـون أن الـذي يهدمهـا يُجَـنّ، (١٨) فذكـروا ذلـك للوليـد فقـال: "أنـا أوّل مـن يُجَـنّ في سـبيل الله". وأخـذ الفـأس وجعل يهـدم بنفسـه، (١٩) فلمّا رأى المسـلمون ذلـك تتابعـوا عـلى الهـدم، (٢٠) وأكـذب الله زعمَ الـروم.

Vocabulary

أبو الحسين بن جُبير (٣)	Abu al-Husayn Ibn Jubayr (1145–1217), geographer and traveler who preceded Ibn Battuta by over a century
استقرَيْنا (٤)	we followed, tracked
اجتَلَينا (٤)	we explored
منصّة (٥)	podium, dais, stage
أوى/ أوى إلى (٦)	to be sheltered, moved to
رَبوة (٦)	hummock, knoll
ذات قرار مَعين (٦)	fertile and flowing with water, promised land (refers to Damascus)
صدقُ (٧)	honesty
أتقن (٨)	the most perfect
بهجة (٨)	joy, delight
شبيه (٩)	one like it
أمير المؤمنين (١٠)	'Commander of the Faithful,' a title given to the caliph (also used by Ibn Battuta to refer to the sultan of Morocco, his patron)

الوليد بن عبد الملك بن مروان (١٠)	Al-Walid Ibn 'Abd al-Malik Ibn Marwan (668–715); Umayyad caliph
الروم (١١)	'Rome' here meaning Christendom in general
قسطنطينية (١١)	Constantinople
خالد بن الوليد (١٢)	Khalid Ibn al-Walid (592-642); general who captured Damascus along with Ibn al-Jarrah
أبو عبيدة بن الجرّاح (١٣)	Abu 'Ubaydah Ibn al-Jarrah (583–638), a Muslim commander
عَنوةً (١٤)	forcibly
صالحوا (١٤)	they made peace with
عَزَم على (١٥)	he was determined to
شاؤوا (١٥)	they wanted
عوض (١٥)	indemnity, compensation
أبوا (١٦)	they refused
فأس (١٨)	axe
أكذب (٢٠)	to prove a liar

Comprehension Exercises

A. Answer the following questions in complete Arabic sentences (numbers refer to the lines in which the information can be found):

١. عن أية³⁸ مدينة يتحدث ابن بطوطة وكيف وصفها؟ (١–٨)

_____

_____

_____

---

38 which

٢. بِمَ³⁹ يتميز الجامع الأموي عن بقية الجوامع؟ (٨-١٠)

_____

_____

_____

٣. مَن صاحب الفضل في بناء الجامع الأموي؟ وضّحوا ذلك. (١٠-١٢)

_____

_____

_____

٤. ما قصة الجامع الأموي التي ذكرها ابن بطوطة في كتابه؟ (١٢-١٨)

_____

_____

_____

٥. ما الخرافة⁴⁰ التي زَعَمَها الروم حول هدم الكنيسة؟ وماذا كان ردّ فعل⁴¹ خالد بن الوليد
    عليها؟ (١٧-٢٠)

_____

_____

_____

---

39 بماذا
40 myth
41 reaction

B. Find Arabic phrases in the text that approximate the following meanings in English:

1. he didn't exaggerate (lit. he didn't invent) : _____

2. it knows no equal : _____

3. for (in exchange for) whatever they desired : _____

4. they claimed, alleged :_____

5. disproved, exposed as a lie :_____

C. Find Arabic synonyms or equivalents in the text for the following words and phrases:

١. آخــر : _____

٢. احتمى : _____

٣. مثيـل : _____

٤. يرسـل إلى : _____

٥. مكان : _____

D. Find Arabic antonyms or opposites for each of the following words in the text and use each in a complete sentence:

١. الجنّـة: _____

_____

٢. الأرض : ــ

٣. يأمـر : ــ

٤. إنتهي : ــ

Interpreting the Text

١ . ما الصورة الفنية التي رسمها ابن بطوطة لمدينة دمشق؟ (١-٧)

ــ

ــ

ــ

٢ . ما الأهمية الدينية لمدينة دمشق؟ (١-٧)

ــ

ــ

ــ

٣ . لماذا يُعد المسجد الأموي تُحفة معمارية[42] نادرة؟ (٨-١١)

ــ

ــ

ــ

---

42 architectural masterpiece

٤ . كيف صوّر لنا ابن بطوطة قصة الفتح الإسلامي لدمشق؟ وما دلالتها[43]؟ (١٢-١٤)

_____

_____

_____

٥ . هل تؤمنون أحيانا بالخرافات؟ وهل تؤيِّدون موقف[44] الوليد من خرافة هدم كنيسة
الروم؟ (١٥-١٩)

_____

_____

_____

Grammar, Structure, and Context Clues

1. In line 1, Ibn Battuta describes the city of Damascus using the verb
تَفضُل. The vowel pattern indicates that this is measure (I) of the verb,
which means 'it exceeds, it is better than.' This is in distinction from
the more commonly used measure (II) verb تفضّل, meaning 'she prefers,' which lends itself to derived forms, like 'favorite,' and 'preferred'
(مُفضّل). This is a fairly common pattern, in which the first measure of a
root means to have a quality or characteristic, and the second measure means to cause or consider something to have that quality. For
example:

صَدَقَ: to tell the truth, to be honest (I)

صَدَّقَ: to believe, to consider truthful (II)

عَظُمَ: to be great (I)

---

43 its significance
44 attitude

عَظَّمَ: to glorify, to treat as great (II)

In this case, the vowel pattern on the verb indicates the writer's intent, but in unvoweled texts, the context will be the best clue. Even if the phrase in line 1 were stripped of its diacritics, the context makes clear that Ibn Battuta is talking about Damascus being better than other cities, not preferring other cities:

دمشق هي التي تَفْضُل جميع البلاد حسنا

2. In line 6, the familiar word قرار appears. In modern media texts, this word almost always means 'decision.' From the context, however, it is clear that this meaning does not work:

أوى المسيح، عليه السلام، وأمّه منها إلى ربوة ذات قرار معين

In classical usage, this word has several meanings, all related to the basic meaning of the root, which is 'to be stable, settled, at rest' (as indeed, the usage of 'decision' also takes its meaning, being something that is 'settled'). Here, the text refers to Jesus and his mother seeking refuge, so the meaning of 'a place of rest' makes the most sense.

3. As you know, Arabic prefers to attach prefixes and suffixes to a base word where English would use separate modifying words. Thus, Arabic typically takes fewer words to express the same idea. In this text, we find several examples of an entire sentence contained in a single word:

Line 4: استقريناها

استقرى: verb (to follow, track)

نا: subject (we)

ها: object (her, it)

اجتليناها: Similarly in line 4, Ibn Battuta notes

Can you find the following:

verb: _____ meaning _____

subject: _____ meaning _____

object: _____ meaning _____

4. In line 1, Ibn Battuta uses a *tamyiz* (تمييز) construction following a superlative adjective (تفضيل). The *tamyiz*, or noun of specification, is an indefinite noun in the accusative case (recognizable here by the ً ending), which clarifies an element in the preceding statement. Its use includes an implied preposition بـ or مِن, implying 'in terms of.' In English, the construction is typically translated using 'in terms of' or a similar phrase. Note Ibn Battuta's description of Damascus:

دمشق هي التي تَفضُل جميع البلاد <u>حسناً</u> وتتقدّمها <u>جمالاً</u>

Without the two underlined words, we would know that Damascus is the place that exceeds all other countries and precedes them. While Ibn Battuta is not averse to such sweeping praise in his description of cities, he wants to clarify in which aspects Damascus exceeds its rivals. The underlined nouns (perfection, beauty) tell us in what categories Damascus tops the list. To express the same idea in English, we would need to say 'in beauty,' 'in terms of its beauty,' or something similar.[45]

In the sentence below describing the Umayyad Mosque, from line 8, note the underlined nouns of specification. As you can see, multiple nouns can be used to clarify a single object. What does each mean, and what is the overall meaning of the sentence?

وهو أعظم مساجد الدنيا <u>احتفالاً</u>، وأتقنها <u>صناعة</u>، وأبدعها <u>حسناً</u> <u>وبهجةً</u> <u>وكمالاً</u>

5. In line 14, note how the object of the sentence is separated from the verb:

---

45 for more on the uses of the *tamyiz*, see Lesson 12

فصنع المسلمون من نصف الكنيسة الذي دخلوه عَنوةً مسجداً

The case endings (ون on the subject and ا on the object) tell us what the function of each word is. However, even without these, context dictates that 'mosque' is the only logical object for the verb 'made' in this sentence. It is quite common in Arabic to have a large separation between the subject and verb. The subject of the sentence often comes between and may be quite elaborate. Here, however, not only the subject (المسلمون) appears, but a clarification of the verb, specifically, out of what the Muslims made a mosque. Typically, this information would go after the object, but the writer's intent here is to highlight this piece of information. In the narrative, the different way the Muslim conquerors handled the two halves of the church is the key message in the story, and Ibn Battuta foregrounds this theme by placing this clarification before the object.

6.   Note the construction in line 2:

وكلّ وصف، وإنْ طال، فهو قاصر عن محاسنها

In this sentence, the phrase وإن is the key to the rhetorical device. In his praise of Damascus, Ibn Battuta tells us that 'all description' (كلّ وصف) falls short of its beauties or charms (literally, 'is short of its beauties or charms', قاصر عن محاسنها). The compound وإن here means 'even if.' Here Ibn Battuta is not challenging whether other descriptions are accurate, but is using the phrase in the sense of 'no matter how much.' In other words, all description, no matter how complete, falls short of the true charm of Damascus. This is an elegant phrase emphasizing the magnitude of something.

Writing Exercises

A. Translate the following sentences into Arabic, using vocabulary from this reading. Hints in parentheses indicate which lines to look at for similar structures:

1. This city is the finest in the world, in terms of its construction (1):

    _____

    _____

    _____

2. Our university surpasses all universities in the country in terms of its research (1):

    _____

    _____

    _____

3. He was determined to build a mosque in the capital city (15):

    _____

    _____

    _____

4. They claim that their city is the oldest in the world (17):

    _____

    _____

    _____

5. The eye witnesses[46] exposed his claim as a lie (20):

_____

_____

_____

B. Rearrange the words below into coherent sentences:

١.   القاهرة و جمالاً المدن لا جميع حسناً تَفضُل

_____

_____

٢.   شبيه لا يُعلَم له نظير يوجد ولا له

_____

_____

٣.   المبنى الأمير من صنع جميلاً مسجداً

_____

_____

٤. أَجَلَ العَروس يوم تَزيين زفافها تَزَيَّنَت

_____

_____

_____

٥. أوّل من الوطن في سبيل أنا يحارب

_____

_____

_____

Discussion Questions

١. كتب ابن بطوطة عن جمال وسِحر مدينة دمشق. قارنوا بين دمشق الماضي والحاضر.

٢. علاَمَ[47] يُبرهِن[48] قول ابن بطوطة: "إن كانت الجنة في الأرض فدمشق بلا شك فيها"؟

٣. لماذا تُعد رواية[49] هدم الوليد لكنيسة دمشق- من وجهة نظركم — من الروايات المثيرة للجدل[50] في كتب التاريخ الإسلامي؟

٤. ناقشوا رأي ابن بطوطة في قصة هدم الكنيسة ومزاعم الروم. هل تتفقون أم تختلفون معه؟

٥. يشتهر الجامع الأموي باسم 'دُرّة[51] دمشق،' فما سبب هذه التسمية في رأيكم؟

Research and Presentation

اكتبوا مقالا قصيرا عن بلاد الشام وأهميتها التاريخية والجغرافية.

---

47 على ماذا
48 prove
49 narration
50 controversial
51 pearl

6
The Hajj Journey and Medina

(Medina, Saudi Arabia, 1326) ذكر مسجد رسول الله صلى الله
عليه وسلم

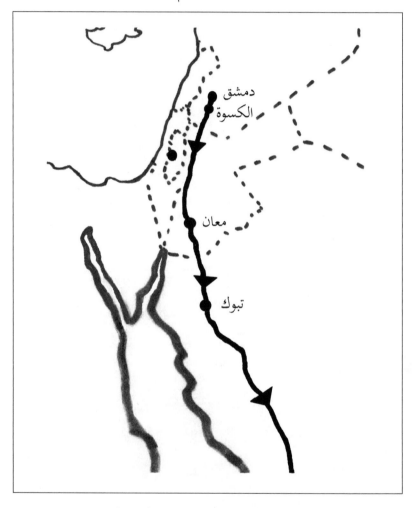

The perilous journey into the Arabian desert

The Hajj today is a marvel of modern technology, remarkable for the speed and efficiency with which the Saudi Arabian government manages the rapid flow of some two million pilgrims through specialized airline terminals and into air conditioned, fireproof tent cities. Modern technology has changed the journey so much, in fact, that the annual number of pilgrims today is over 200 times what it was just a century ago. In Ibn Battuta's time, it was a slow and very arduous journey on which many lost their lives. The journey from Ibn Battuta's starting point in Damascus to Medina was just over 1,300 kilometers, but required some fifty days of land travel through unforgiving desert. Ibn Battuta mentions a point on a recent Hajj caravan where water sold for a thousand dinars a drink, but "both the drinker and seller died."

Then, as now, protection and oversight of the Hajj travelers and the holy sites was a key responsibility of the Muslim sovereigns of the area. Today, the king of Saudi Arabia is normally referred to in Arabic by his title 'Custodian of the Two Holy Mosques' (خــادم الحرمـين الشريفـين) to emphasize this central responsibility, while a government agency, the Ministry of the Hajj, overseas the logistics of the massive pilgrimage. In Ibn Battuta's time, the Mamluk sultan in Cairo had emerged as the preeminent defender of the Islamic community, and in addition to ruling over Egypt and the Levant, had effective control over the holy cities of Mecca and Medina. Organizing, equipping and protecting the large Hajj caravans from Cairo and Damascus was a duty of high honor for the Mamluk sultan. Today, the Saudi king's role as guardian of the Hajj sites is symbolized by an annual ceremonial washing of the Ka'ba, the black cube in the center of the Great Mosque. In the 1300s, the equivalent ceremony was the Egyptian sultan's presentation of the *kiswa*, the huge embroidered black cloth covering for the Ka'ba, which traveled with his official caravan from Cairo. Aside from the ceremonial value of the Mamluk caravans making the annual journey, Ibn Battuta notes the very practical dangers that necessitated traveling in a convoy of several thousand people under Mamluk military escort.

Although the city of Medina (referred to as مدينــة رســول الله by Ibn Battuta and المدينــة المنـوّرة today) was not a required part of the Hajj, most pilgrims also made the journey there. Ibn Battuta's great joy upon entering the city came not only from the spiritual experience of seeing this holy site, but also relief on surviving a very perilous desert crossing. For those coming from the north like Ibn Battuta, it was a welcome rest before the remaining 320-kilometer trip across the desert to Mecca.

Medina was the site of the first Islamic community, founded by the Prophet Muhammad after he was invited to live there by some of the people of that town. So significant was the date, CE 622 , that it marks the beginning of the Islamic (*hijri*) calendar. Among the most important sites in Medina was the Mosque of the Prophet (المسجد النبوي or المسجد الكريم), which held the tombs of the Prophet Muhammad (الروضةُ المقدسةُ), his daughter Fatima and the Rashidun caliphs Abu Bakr and 'Umar. As Ibn Battuta describes, the arrangement of the tombs was of great significance. Yet even upon reaching one of the two holy sites, he still faced another very difficult 320-kilometer journey on to Mecca.

From the Writings of Ibn Battuta

Ibn Battuta joins the annual Hajj caravan as it leaves Damascus for Medina and Mecca:

(١) لما استهلّ شَـوّالُ ... خـرج الركبُ الحجـازي إلى خـارج دمشـق ونزلـوا القريـة المعروفة بالكسوة، (٢) فأخـذتُ في الحركـة معهـم، (٣) وكان أمـير الركـب سـيفُ الديـن الجوبـان مـن كبـار الأمـراء، (٤) وقاضيـه شرف الديـن الأذرُعـي الحـوراني.

As the Hajj caravan travels through the desert to Medina, Ibn Battuta describes the hardships of the journey:

(٥) ارتحلنـا إلى مَعـان، وهـو آخـرُ بـلاد الشـام، (٦) ونزلنـا مـن عقبـة الصّـوان إلى الصحـراء التـي يقـال فيهـا: "داخلُهـا مفقـودٌ وخارجهـا مولـودٌ" (٧) وبعـد مسـيرة يومـين نزلنـا ذاتَ حـجّ ولا عـمارة بهـا. (٨) ثـم إلى وادي بلـدحَ ولا مـاءبـه. (٩) ثُـم يرحـل الركـبُ مـن تبـوك ويجـدّون السـيرَ ليـلاً ونهـاراً خوفـاً مـن هـذه البريـة، وفي وسـطها الـوادي الأخيـضر كأنّـه وادي جهنّـم، أعاذنـا الله منهـا، (١٠) وأصابَ الحُجّـاجَ بـه في بعـض السـنين مشـقّةٌ بسـبب ريـح السَّـموم التـي تهـبّ، فانتشـفتِ الميـاه، (١١) وانتهـت شربـةُ المـاء إلى ألـف دينـار، ومـات مشربهـا وبائعهـا.

After an arduous journey, the caravan enters the city of Medina:

(١٢) دخلنـا الحـرَم الشريـف، وانتهينـا إلى المسـجد الكريـم، (١٣) فوقفنـا بـاب السـلام مُسَـلّمينَ، وصَلّينـا بالرّوضـة الكريمـة بـين القـبر والمنـبر الكريـم. (١٤) وانصرفنـا إلى رَحلنا مسرورين بهـذه النعمـة العظمـى مستبشرين بنيـل هـذه المنّة الكـبرى (١٥) حامديـن الله تعـالى عـلى البلـوغ إلى معاهـد رسـوله الشريفـة ومشـاهده العظيمـة المنيفـة داعـين أن لا يُجعَل ذلـك آخـرَ عهدِنـا بهـا، (١٦) وأن يجعلنـا ممّـن قُبلـت زيارتُـه وكُتبـت في سـبيل الله سـفرتُه.

Ibn Battuta describes the customs of Muslims upon entering the mosque:

(١٧) المسـجد المعظّـم مسـتطيل (١٨) والروضـةُ المقدسـةُ، صلـواتُ الله وسـلامه عـلى سـاكنها، في الجهـة القِبلية ممّـا يـلي الشـرق مـن المسـجد الكريـم. (١٩) وشـكلها عجيـب لا يتأتّـى تمثيلـه (٢٠) وهنالـك يقـفُ النـاسُ للسـلام مستقبلين الوجهَ الكريـمَ مُسـتدبرين القِبلـة، (٢١) فيسـلّمون وينصرفـون يميناً إلى وجـه أبي بكـر الصديـق، (٢٢) ورأسُ أبي بكرَ، رضي الله عنـه، عنـد قدمـي رسـول الله، صلّـى الله عليـه وسـلّم، (٢٣) ثـمّ ينصرفـون إلى عمـرَ ابـن الخطّـاب، (٢٤) ورأسُ عمـرَ عنـد كتفـي أبي بكـر، رضي الله عنهما.

Vocabulary

استهلّ (١)	it began	
شَوّال (١)	Shawwal, the tenth month of the Islamic calendar	
رَكْب (١)	caravan	
أمير الركب (٣)	amir (leader) of the caravan	
ارتَحَلْنا (٥)	we departed	
بلاد الشام (٥)	Greater Syria	
البريّة (٩)	wilderness	
كأنّه (٩)	it is as if it were	
جهنّم (٩)	Hell	
ريح السَّموم (١٠)	a severe hot and dry wind	
انتشَفَت (١٠)	it ran dry	
مشقّة (١٠)	difficulty	
انتهت إلى (١١)	to reach	
الحرَم الشريف (١٢)	the Noble Sanctuary	

المسجد الكريم (١٢)	the Prophet's Mosque in Medina
الرّوضة الكريمة (١٣)	a section within the Prophet's Mosque which holds the tomb of the Prophet Muhammad and the first two caliphs
مُستبشرين (١٤)	optimistic
المنّة (١٤)	merit
عهْد (١٥)	time, era
مَنيف (١٥)	lofty
الجهة القِبلية (١٨)	the direction of the Qibla
لا يتأتّى (١٩)	it is not easy
مُستدبرين (٢٠)	unwelcoming, opposite of مستقبلين
أبي بكر الصديق (٢٢)	Abu Bakr, the first caliph
عمرَ ابن الخطّاب (٢٣)	'Umar ibn al-Khattab, the second caliph

Comprehension Exercises

A. Answer the following questions in complete Arabic sentences (numbers refer to the lines in which the information can be found):

١. إلى أين ذهب ابن بطوطة وأصحابه في بداية شهر شوّال؟ (١-٣)

_____

_____

_____

٢. لماذا تحاول القافلة[52] أن تسير سريعا لتخرج من مدينة تبوك؟ (٩)

_____

_____

_____

52 caravan

٣.   ما الصعوبات التي واجهت[53] الحجّاج في رحلتهم؟ (١٠-١١)

_____

_____

_____

٤.   ماذا فعل ابن بطوطة وأصحابه عندما وصلوا إلى الحرم الشريف وماذا كانت أُمْنِيَتهم[54]؟
     (١٣-١٦)

_____

_____

_____

٥.   كيف وصف ابن بطوطة المسجد المعظم والرّوضة المقدسة؟ (١٧-٢٤)

_____

_____

_____

B. Find Arabic phrases in the text that approximate the following meanings
in English:

1.   known as :_____

2.   waterless :_____

3.   rejoicing :_____

4.   unique, distinct :_____

5.   at the feet of :_____

---

53 faced, confronted
54 their wish

C. Find Arabic synonyms or equivalents in the text for the following words and phrases:

١.   بـدأ: _____

٢.   ذهبنـا إلى : _____

٣.   تركنا المـكان : _____

٤.   في منتصفها : _____

٥.   صعوبة : _____

D. find Arabic antonyms or opposites for each of the following words in the text and use each in a complete sentence:

١.   أول: _____
_____

٢.   جنّـة : _____
_____

٣.   رُفِضَـت : _____
_____

٤.   الغـرب : _____
_____

Interpreting the Text

١.   يقول ابن بطوطة عن الصحراء: ''داخلها مفقود وخارجها مولود. ''كيف تفسرون[55] هذه الجملة وهل هناك مكان تعرفونه ينطبق[56] عليه نفس الوصف؟ (٦)
_____

---

55   to explain
56   the same description applies to

٢. لماذا عُرف[57] الوادي الأخضر باسم 'وادي جهنم'؟ (٩)

٣. ما سِرُّ[58] الفرحة والسعادة التي شعر بها ابن بطوطة وأصحابه عند زيارتهم للحرم الشريف؟ (١٤-١٦)

٤. ما الشكل الهندسي[59] الذي بُني عليه المسجد النبوي؟ (١٧)

٥. ما الخطوات التي يجب أن يتبعها زائرو الروضة الشريفة؟ (٢٠-٢٣)

---

57 was known
58 what is the secret of
59 geometric shape

Grammar, Structure, and Context Clues

1. Line 6 is an excellent example of the poetic qualities of the Arabic language: "داخلُها مفقودٌ وخارجها مولودٌ". The Arabic here is far more concise than the English, which would require the addition of several words implied in the Arabic phrase before producing the translation "whoever enters it is lost, and whoever leaves it is born." This sentence takes advantage of the distinct word shapes and case endings of Arabic to make a much more compact, poetic statement than its English equivalent. The words داخِل and خارج are both active participles, referring to the 'doer' of an action, or the state of 'doing' that action, in this case, entering and leaving. The ٗ ending indicates we are talking about the subject—the one who enters and leaves. The 'to be' verb is implied by the equational sentence. The words مفقودٌ and مولودٌ are passive participles, referring to one who has received an action, or the state of that action being completed. Here again, the case endings on the two words tell us they are the second halves of equational sentences—that is, the resulting information about 'one who enters' and 'one who leaves.' The predictable pattern of vowels and consonants for each of these types of words, as well as the predictable case ending gives us a compact sentence, the two parts of which share a common rhythm and rhyme.

2. This text includes several examples of the *hal* (الحال) construction, also known as the circumstantial accusative. This construction defines the conditions under which an action occurs, such as 'he entered the home laughing' or 'we made haste, fearing the desert wind.' The *hal* is frequently preceded by و which is not itself translated. The circumstantial part of the phrase that tells *how* the action occurs will be in the accusative case (*mansub,* منصوب). There are many types of *hal* clauses, but the one used often in this text is an active participle—'praising,' 'fearing,' and so on. In line 13, for example, Ibn Battuta notes that he and his companions stopped at the gate مُسَلِّمِينَ. While in an unvoweled form this could look like the word 'Muslims,' the vowel pattern and the *shadda* indicate that this is an active participle meaning 'salut-

ing,' and describes what they were doing as they stopped at the gate of Medina after an arduous journey. This excerpt includes several *hal* constructions of the same pattern.

Can you identify at least four more examples of this form and what the sentences mean?

_____

_____

_____

_____

_____

_____

_____

_____

3. The word يُجِدّون in line 9 means 'to strive' or 'to hurry.' Measure (II) of this root can mean 'to renew'. The *shadda* tells us that this is not the verb وَجَد meaning 'to find,' although the two would look the same in a completely unvoweled text. The context here is the best clue to the meaning, as Ibn Battuta describes traveling day and night (something not typically done in a desert) due to the dangerous conditions. We can assume that his party is making haste and striving to get across this dangerous stretch of desert.

4. The word نَيْل in line 14 is the *masdar* of the hollow verb نال meaning 'to gain' or 'to receive.' Here it refers to the blessing and favor that Ibn Battuta has received from his visit to the Mosque of the Prophet. This form is similar to other hollow *masdar* forms, like قَوْل from قالَ, but since the root letter in the middle of نالَ is ي, the ي appears in the *masdar*. It is important to remember that a hollow verb could have either a و or ي in its *masdar*, depending on its root.

Writing Exercises

A. Translate the following sentences into Arabic, using vocabulary from this reading. Hints in parentheses indicate which lines to look at for similar structures:

1. When the caravan left, I went with it (1–2):

_____

_____

_____

2. The Empty Quarter in Saudi Arabia is a desert with no water and no buildings (7–8):

_____

_____

_____

3. We made haste in our travel across the desert (9):

_____

_____

_____

4. The price of oil[60] reached $100 a barrel[61] (11):

_____

_____

_____

---

60 النفط

61 برميل

5. We entered the city, rejoicing in our safe arrival (15):

_____

_____

_____

B. Rearrange the words below into coherent sentences:

١.   أمـير من الركب الأمراء كان كبار

_____

_____

٢.   المدينة يومين نزلنا بـ بعد مسـيرة

_____

_____

٣.   وادياً لا ماء عبرنا به

_____

_____

٤.   و مثيله عجيب لا يوجد البناية شـكل

_____

_____

٥. السيرَ ليلاً الشـديد خوفاً من الريح و نهاراً نَجِدُّ

_____

_____

_____

Discussion Questions

١. قارنوا بين أطول رحلة قمتم بها ورحلة ابن بطوطة إلى الحج من حيث[62] الهدف والتحدّيات والنتائج.

٢. لماذا قال ابن بطوطة إن الروضة المقدسة يصعُب أن نجد لها مثيلاً[63] ؟

٣. تبدأ مناسك[64] الحجّ في أوائل شهر ذي الحجة، فكم يوماً—تقريباً—استغرقت رحلة ابن بطوطة للحجّ؟

٤. أركان[65] الإسلام خمسة، والحجّ هو الركن الخامس منها، فما هي الأركان الأربعة الأخرى؟

٥. هل كان ابن بطوطة دقيقاً[66] في وصف رحلته إلى الحج؟ لماذا؟

Research and Presentation

اكتبوا تقريرا مختصرا عن واحد من أشهر الأماكن الدينية المقدسة في العالم.

---

62 in terms of
63 one like it
64 rituals
65 pillars
66 precise

7
The Hajj to Mecca

ذكر مدينة مكة المعظمة (Mecca, Saudi Arabia, 1326)

المدينة المنورة

مكة المكرمة

The two Holy Cities of Mecca and Medina

Ibn Battuta originally set out for Mecca and, more than a year later, finally reached his destination. Although Ibn Battuta's journey to Mecca was quite different than that experienced by a modern-day pilgrim, his experience once inside the holy city sounds very similar. Despite the dramatic increase in the number of pilgrims and the expansion of the Great Mosque (المسجد الحرام), the Hajj rituals have remained the same as in Ibn Battuta's time. Ibn Battuta changed into the plain, white, unsewn *ihram* garment outside Mecca, performed the seven circuits around the Ka'ba (*tawwaf*, طواف), kissed the foundation stone, drank from the well of Zamzam, and recited prayers on the Mount of Arafat. At the same time, he details the layout of the mosque down to precise measurements for his readers, as if to emphasize the central importance of Mecca among his world travels.

In truth, this emphasis was more than just symbolic. Ibn Battuta's freedom to travel the extent of his known world owed much to the stabilizing role of Islam, which had brought a temporary, tenuous peace between nations that had been engaged in devastating wars less than a century earlier. Indeed, his ability to visit Mongol khanates in Russia, Central Asia, and Persia, newly formed empires in India, and recently converted nations in Africa and Asia was due to the rapid spread of Islam in the previous century. Mecca was not only the spiritual center of this pax-Islamica, serving as the direction of prayer for millions; it was the meeting place of Muslims from Spain to East Africa and Central to Southeast Asia. Although the desert town, with little water or resources, could not support a large year-round population, it was the meeting place for Muslims throughout the world. From here comes the common use of the word 'mecca' to refer to any great confluence of people for a shared purpose. Indeed, Mecca had served this function long before the coming of Islam, as a trading center and a place of truce, where bedouins of different pagan religions put away their swords temporarily.

It was here that, in addition to strengthening his knowledge of Islamic law, Ibn Battuta would meet travelers from most of the countries to which he would later venture and get a sense of the stable relations and vibrant commerce that existed at the time. Likewise, Ibn Battuta discovered in this center of Islamic learning and doctrine that there was a strong demand for trained Islamic scholars in these recently converted regions. While his propensity for travel had been nurtured on his meandering route from Morocco to Mecca, it was here that the world traveler was really born. Thus, it is no surprise that after completing his Hajj and staying in Mecca to study, Ibn Battuta did not take the caravan back to Egypt and his home of Morocco, but headed east instead.

From the Writings of Ibn Battuta

Ibn Battuta's description of the surroundings of Mecca:

(١) هي مدينة كبيرة متصلة البنيان، مستطيلة في بطن واد تحفّ به الجبال (٢) فلا يراها قاصدها حتى يصل إليها. (٣) ولمكّة من الأبواب ثلاثة: باب المُعَلّ بأعلاها، وبابُ الشبيكة من أسفلها ويُعرفُ أيضاً بباب العُمرة، وهو إلى جهة المغرب، وعليه طريق المدينة الشريفة ومصر والشام وجدّة، (٤) وباب المَسفَل، وهو من جهة الجنوب، ومنه دخلَ خالد بن الوليد، رضي الله عنه، يوم الفتح.

He goes on to describe the Great Mosque and the Ka'ba:

(٥) المسجد الحرام في وسط البلد (٦) وهو مُتَسعُ الساحة طولُه من شرق إلى غرب أزيدُ من أربعمائة ذراع (٧) والكعبةُ العظمى في وسطه، ومنظرهُ بديعٌ، ومرآه جميل لا يتعاطى اللسانُ وصفَ بدائعه (٨) وارتفاعُ حيطانه نحو عشرين ذراعاً (٩) والكعبة... هي بَنيّةٌ مربعةٌ (١٠) ومن الجهة الرابعة التي بين الحجر الأسود والركن اليماني تسعٌ وعشرون ذراعاً (١١) وعرض صفحتها التي من الركن العراقي إلى الحجر الأسود أربعةٌ وخمسون شبراً (١٢) وكذلك عرضُ الصفحة التي تقابلها من الركن اليماني إلى الركن الشامي (١٣) ويُفتحُ البابُ الكريمُ في كلّ يوم جمعة بعد الصلاة، ويفتح في يوم مولد رسول الله، صلّى الله عليه وسلّم تسلياً (١٤) وداخلُ الكعبة الشريفة مفروشٌ بالرّخام المجزّع وحيطانُه كذلك (١٥) وستورُ الكعبة الشريفة من الحرير الأسود مكتوبٌ فيها بالأبيض (١٦) ومن عجائبها أنّها لا تخلو من طائف أبداً ليلاً ولا نهاراً (١٧) ولم يَذكر أحدٌ أنّه رآها قطّ دون طائف.

He praises the people of Mecca:

(١٨) لأهل مكّة الأفعالُ الجميلة والمكارمُ التامّة والأخلاقُ الحسنة والإيثارُ إلى الضّعفاء والمنقطعين وحسنُ الجوار للغرباء (١٩) ومن مكارمهم أنهم متى صنع أحدهم وليمةً يبدأ فيها بإطعام الفقراء المنقطعين المجاورين، (٢٠) وأكثرُ المساكين المنقطعين يكونون بالأفران حيثُ يطبخُ الناس أخبازهم، (٢١) فإذا طبخَ أحدهم خبزَه واحتمله إلى منزله يتبعه المساكين فيعطي لكلّ واحد منهم ما قُسِمَ له، ولا يردّهم خائبين، (٢٢) ولو كانت له خُبزة واحدة فإنّه يُعطي ثلثَها أو نصفَها طيّبَ النفس بذلك من غير ضجر. (٢٣) وأهلُ مكّة لهم ظرفٌ ونظافةٌ في الملابس، (٢٤) وأكثرُ لباسهم البياض فترى ثيابَهم أبداً ناصعةً ساطعة (٢٥) ونساءُ مكّة فائقاتُ الحسن بارعاتُ الجمال، ذواتُ صلاح وعفاف.

Vocabulary

مُتصلة (١)	connected, linked
تُحَفّ به (١)	to be surrounded by
العُمرة (٣)	a minor Hajj, a visit to Mecca conducted any time of the year
خالد بن الوليد (٤)	Khalid bin al-Walid (592-642), companion of the Prophet and leader of the Islamic armies
رضي الله عنه (٤)	May God be pleased with him
ذِراع (٦)	cubit; an old unit of measurement (about 206 centimeters)
مرآه (٧)	its sight, scene
شبر (١١)	measure, the span of a hand
مجزّع (١٤)	dappled, grained, spotted
ستور (١٥)	curtains, hangings
طائف (١٦)	one making the circuit around the Ka'ba. Typically done seven times during the Umrah or Hajj
قطّ (١٧)	never, not at all
إيثار (١٨)	unselfishness
المنقطعين (١٨)	homeless people
حسن الجوار (١٨)	good neighborliness
إطعام (١٩)	nutrition, feeding
لا يردّهم خائبين (٢١)	not let them down, not disappoint them
ضجر (٢٢)	annoyance, unease
ظَرف (٢٣)	elegance, style
فائق (٢٥)	supreme, surpassing
ناصعة (٢٤)	clear, pure

Comprehension Exercises

A. Answer the following questions in complete Arabic sentences (numbers refer to the lines in which the information can be found):

١. كم باباً لمدينة مكة؟ ما هي؟ (٣)

_____

_____

_____

٢. مَن فتح مدينة مكة؟ (٤)

_____

_____

_____

٣. متى يطوف الطائفون حول الكعبة الشريفة؟ (١٦–١٧)

_____

_____

_____

٤. ماذا يفعل أهل مكة مع الفقراء والغرباء؟ (١٨–٢٠)

_____

_____

_____

٥. ما عادات أهل مكة في اللِباس؟ (٢٣–٢٤)

_____

_____

_____

B. Find Arabic phrases in the text that approximate the following meanings in English:

1. adorned with:_____

2. among their kind deeds:_____

3. without fuss:_____

4. exceptionally beautiful:_____

5. pious and virtuous:_____

C. Find Arabic synonyms or equivalents in the text for the following words and phrases:

١. منتصف المدينة : _____

٢. أبداً : _____

٣. مروءة كاملة: _____

٤. مائدة : _____

٥. ضيق : _____

D. Find Arabic antonyms or opposites for each of the following words in the text and use each in a complete sentence:

١. منفصلـة: ـ_____

٢. أسفلها : ـ_____

٣. الشــمال : ـ_____

٤. السـواد : ـ_____

Interpreting the Text

١. كيف تحمي الطبيعة الجغرافية[67] مدينة مكة؟ وما أثر ذلك على المدينة؟ (١-٢)

_____

_____

_____

٢. لماذا جاء وصف ابن بطوطة للمسجد الحرام في مكة دقيقاً ومُفصّلاً[68]؟ (٥-١٧)

_____

_____

_____

٣. ما أسماء أركان الكعبة العظمى؟ هل لهذه الأسماء دلالات معينة؟ (١٠-١٢)

_____

_____

_____

67 geographic situation
68 accurate and detailed

٤. ‏‏"أهل مكة شعب كريم ومضياف." ما مدى صحة هذه المقولة؟ (١٨–٢٢)

_____

_____

_____

٥. كيف تعكس[٦٩] طريقة لِباس أهل مكة أخلاقهم وعاداتهم؟ (٢٤–٢٥)

_____

_____

_____

69 reflect

Grammar, Structure, and Context Clues

1. The word قَطّ used in line 17 means 'never,' 'not at all' and comes at the end of a negative statement (typically in the past tense) to stress the absoluteness of the negation. When spelled with a *kasra* instead of a *fatha*, however, the word means 'a male cat.' Even without the vowel, the context will indicate the correct meaning. Notice Ibn Battuta's statement: "لم يَذكر أحد أنّه رآها قطّ دون طائف." The negative لم which is further strengthened by the subject أحد (thus, 'no one...') suggests the absolute negativity of this statement, indicating the reading of قَطّ. Here, he is stressing that the circling of the Ka'ba never ceases.

2. The term طائف in line 16 refers to one making the circuit around the Ka'ba and is a key part of the description of Mecca. With the addition of a *taa marbuta*, the word طائفة indicates a party, group, or sect. This meaning lends itself to the adjective طائفي frequently used in the news to mean 'sectarian,' very often in the negative sense of 'sectarian violence' or 'sectarian conflict.' Careful attention to spelling as well as the general context of the description indicates that Ibn Battuta is not talking about sectarian divides within Mecca, but the presence of pilgrims circling the Ka'ba.

3. In lines 18, 19, and 20, Ibn Battuta makes frequent reference to المنقطعون/ المنقطعين. The word comes from the verb انقطع and means literally 'cut off.' In common use, however, this term has many meanings, all related to something cut off or separated from that around it. In the context of this paragraph, which describes the charity of the Meccans and their giving food to those in need, the appropriate connotation is 'homeless.' In other contexts, however, some of the other meanings of this term include:

مُنقطع إلى ... / لـ = مُتَفَرِّغٌ لِـ =dedicated to, devoted to, exclusively occupied with

مُنقطع النظير = لا مثيل له = beyond comparison

مُنقطع عن = discontinuous

4. In line 25, Ibn Battuta describes the women of Mecca as فائقاتُ
الحسن، بارعاتُ الجمال. This common literary device, the 'false *idaafa*' is
an eloquent way of bestowing praise. As you know, a normal *idaafa*
combines two or more nouns in a possessive relationship (e.g. باب البيت
— 'door of the house). The false *idaafa*, however, uses an adjective
(or a participle) as its first term, as in the cases above: 'surpassing in
fairness,' 'brilliant in beauty.' This usage is similar to English expressions such as 'fair of face,' 'quick of wit,' and so on. As in English, it
has a more poetic, elegant use than everyday connotation. The *idaafa*
is 'false,' not in the sense of being incorrect, but that its meaning is
figurative.

In Arabic grammar, adjectives and participles are classified as nouns.
In the examples above, we see two instances of plural feminine participles in the nominative case. The definite *idaafa*-type structure is made
possible in Arabic due to the fact that generic qualities such as 'beauty,'
'wisdom,' 'purity,' and so on all take the definite article.

5. The word وادٍ in line 1 belongs to a special category of nouns, called
defective nouns. This means the word's root has a و or a ي as its final
radical. The nouns and adjectives derived from this type of root may
drop the final radical, depending on the case. The word وادٍ comes from
such a root, و-د-ي. The full form of this word is وادي. Similar words
include Ibn Battuta's profession—قاضٍ (judge), or the word 'past'
(ماضٍ).

The final ي will be replaced by two *kasras* when the word is indefinite,
as in line 1 of this text. These two *kasras* do not represent the genitive
case in this instance. These two *kasras* will often not be written in
unvoweled texts. The ي will be restored if the noun has الـ attached, has
a suffix attached, or is used in an *idaafa*. It will also be present in the
accusative case. The examples below illustrate:

رأيت وادياً كبيراً—I saw a large valley (accusative case)

تقع المدينة في وادٍ—The city is located in a valley (genitive case)

يسكن في الوادي—He lives in the valley (definite)

رأيت واديه—I saw his valley (possessive suffix)

Writing Exercises

A. Translate the following sentences into Arabic, using vocabulary from this reading. Hints in parentheses indicate which lines to look at for similar structures:

1. A person approaching by car cannot see our house from the street (2):

_____

_____

_____

2. Words cannot describe his good deeds (7, 18):

_____

_____

_____

3. No one ever saw him without his glasses[70] (17):

_____

_____

_____

---

70 نظّارة

4. He completed his work without any fuss (22):

_____

_____

_____

5. The inside of the mosque was surpassing in beauty (25):

_____

_____

_____

B. Rearrange the words below into coherent sentences:

١. يرى حتى لا يصـل المدينة إليها قاصدها

_____

_____

_____

٢. هذه الحسـنة المدينة الأخلاقُ لأهل

_____

_____

_____

٣. منـه أحد طعاماً يعطي منهم جيرانه إذا طبخَ لكلّ

_____

_____

_____

٤. الجبال المدينة بطن وادٍ تحفّ به تقع في

_____

_____

_____

٥. جـدتي كل بعد جمعة أزور يوم الصلاة

_____

_____

_____

Discussion Questions

١. كان لموقع مكة الاستراتيجي المتميز الفضلُ في إمساكها بزمام[71] التجارة بين أطراف[72] شبه الجزيرة العربية في العصور القديمة، وقد كانت محطة[73] للقوافل بين الشمال والجنوب، فهل تحتفظ المدينة حتى اليوم بهذه المكانة و تلك الأهمية؟ لماذا؟

٢. السفر اليوم إلى الحج أقل مشقةٍ[74] مما كان عليه في عصر ابن بطوطة. ناقشوا هذه العبارة مستشهدين[75] على ذلك بما جاء في النص؟

٣. في رأيكم، لماذا ركّز ابن بطوطة على وصف مكارم أخلاق أهل مكة وحسن ضيافتهم وأناقة لباسهم مثلما ركّز على وصف معالم المدينة المقدسة؟

٤. خرج ابن بطوطة من بلده قاصدا الحج. بعد تحقيقه لهدفه، هل يبدو أنه سيعود إلى بلده مباشرة أم سيواصل رحلته؟ ما أدلتكم على ذلك؟

٥. على موقع يوتيوب، شاهدوا فيلم ''رحلة ابن بطوطة إلى مكة'' ثم قارنوا بين أحداث الفيلم وبين ما قرأتموه عن هذه الرحلة.

---

71 control
72 sides, parts
73 station
74 hardship, discomfort
75 citing

Research and Presentation

يبلغ عدد أسماء مكة المكرمة عبر العصور المختلفة أكثر من خمسين اسماً وكنية. ابحثوا في الإنترنت عن بعض هذه التسميات وأسبابها ومعانيها، واكتبوا ملخصا عنها.

8
Baghdad, City of Caliphs

ذكر مدينة بغداد (Baghdad, Iraq, 1327)

Several of Ibn Battuta's side trips are not shown

Baghdad was once the largest and most prosperous city in the world. Founded in AD 762 by the victorious Abbasid Caliphate to be the crowning glory of the world's largest land empire, the meticulously planned city was also the leading center of learning in the world. During their 500-year rule, the

Abbasid caliphs recruited scholars from a wide range of disciplines to fill the libraries and institutes of Baghdad. The famous Bayt al-Hikma (بيـت الحكمـة or 'House of Wisdom'), which was founded by the Caliph Harun al-Rashid (هـارون الرشــيد) as a center for the translation of scholarly works from Persian, Greek, Indian, and even Chinese sources, became the largest repository of books in the world. Tradition holds that the caliph paid the equivalent in gold of the weight of any book translated. While most likely a legend, this speaks to Baghdad's reputation as a center of knowledge.

Ibn Battuta knew Baghdad's glorious past well and his travel narrative begins with effusive praise for the city's reputation. He also knew its more recent history, however, and was not surprised to find the city in ruins when he arrived. The Mongol invasion that had been stopped successfully by the Mamluks in Egypt had fallen full force on Persia and Iraq. In 1258, Genghis Khan's grandson Hulagu had destroyed much of Baghdad and killed most of its inhabitants, including the last Abbasid caliph. The number of books from the famous Bayt al-Hikma that were thrown into the Tigris River were so numerous it is said that it was possible to walk across the river on them. Islamic civilization never completely recovered from the blow. What survived went to Cairo, which became the center of the Islamic world.

The Ilkhanate
Despite having destroyed much of Iraq and Persia, the Mongols quickly set about rebuilding an efficient, if harsh state on the wreckage. The Ilkhanate was one of the four major Mongol kingdoms set up by the descendants of Genghis Khan (the others being in China, Russia, and Central Asia). The Mongol rulers of Iraq and Persia posed something of a puzzle for Ibn Battuta. Although the Mongols had inflicted incalculable harm on the Islamic caliphate, the ilkhan Ghazan publicly converted and made Islam the state religion in 1295, although he privately practiced Shamanism and led wars against the Muslim Mamluks. Like most Mongol leaders, his successors embraced numerous religions as political conditions dictated. Yet as often happened, Ibn Battuta arrived in Baghdad at the right time. The ilkhan at the time, Abu Sa'id (1316–35) was actually a devout Muslim who enforced Sunni Islamic law, sponsored the arts, and did much to revitalize the coun-

try. He also happened to be visiting Baghdad, by now a minor city, at the time Ibn Battuta was there. He took great interest in this visiting scholar of Islamic law and invited him to join his caravan to Persia. Ever the eager traveler, Ibn Battuta went along, by his own account out of curiosity to see what life was like among the Mongol converts.

From the Writings of Ibn Battuta

Ibn Battuta pays tribute to the greatness of Baghdad in Islamic history, but then contrasts that glory with its current condition:

(١) مدينةُ دار السلام. وحضرةُ الإسلام. ذات القدر الشريف. والفضل المُنيف. مثوى الخلفاء. ومقرّ العلماء. (٢) قال أبو الحسين بن جُبير، رضي الله عنه: "وهذه المدينة العتيقة، وإن لم تزل حضرة الخلافة العبّاسيّة، ومثابة الدعوة الإماميّة القرشيّة، فقد ذهب رسمُها، ولم يبقَ إلا اسمُها". (٣) وهي بالإضافة إلى ما كانت عليه قبل إنحاء الحوادث عليها والتفات أعين النوائب إليها كالطلل الدارس، أو تمثال الخيال الشاخص. (٤) فلا حسنَ فيها يستوقف البصر ويستدعي من المستوفز الغفلة والنظر، إلا دجلتها التي هي بين شرقيّها وغربيّها كالمرآة المجلوّة بين صفحتين، (٥) والحُسن الحريميّ بين هوائها ومائها ينشأ.

The western section of Baghdad, once the site of the great Abbasid institutions, had been devastated by the Mongols:

(٦) الجانب الغربي منها هو الذي عُمّر أوّلاً (٧) وهو الآن خراب أكثره، (٨) وعلى ذلك فقد بقي منه ثلاثَ عشرةَ محلّة كلّ محلّة كأنّها مدينة بها الحمامان والثلاثة، (٩) وفي ثمان منها المساجد الجامعة. (١٠) ومن هذه المحلات محلّة باب البصرة، (١١) وبها جامع الخليفة أبي جعفر المنصور، رحمه الله، والمارستان فيما بين محلّة باب البصرة ومحلّة الشارع على الدجلة، (١٢) وهو قصرٌ خَرِبٌ بقيت منه الآثار.

The eastern section of the city, where most of the citizens settled, had fared much better since the Mongol invasion:

(١٣) وهذه الجهة الشرقية من بغداد حافلة الأسواق، عظيمة الترتيب، (١٤) وأعظم أسواقها سوقٌ يُعرف بسوق الثلاثاء، (١٥) كلّ صناعة فيه على حدة، (١٦) وفي وسط هذا السوق المدرسة النظامية العجيبة التي صارت الأمثال تُضرب بحسنها. (١٧)

وفي آخـره المدرسـة المسـتنصريّة، (١٨) وبهـا المذاهـب الأربعـة، لـكلّ مذهـب إيـوانٌ فيـه المسـجد، وموضـع التدريـس (١٩) وفي داخـل هـذه المدرسـة الحـمّام للطلبـة ودار الوضـوء.

Ibn Battuta describes the Muslim Mongol ruler of Iraq:

(٢٠) وهـو السـلطان الجليـل أبـو سـعيد بَهـادُر خـان، وخـان عندهـم الملـك، (٢١) ابـن السـلطان الجليـل محمـد خُذابَنْـدَه، وهـو الـذي أسـلم مـن ملـوك التـتر. (٢٢) وقدّمنـا قصتـه[76]، وكيـف أراد أن يحمـل النـاس لمـا أسـلم عـلى الرفـض، (٢٣) ولمـا مـات ولي الملـك ولـده أبـو سـعيد بهـادر خـان، وكان ملـكاً فاضـلاً كريـماً ملـك وهـو صغيـر السـن، (٢٤) ورأيتـه ببغـداد، وهـو شـامل أجمـل خلـق الله صـورة لا نَبـات بعارضيـه.

Ibn Battuta is invited to join the Mongol sultan's caravan into Persia. As an experienced traveler, he is quite curious to investigate the travel habits of the Mongols:

(٢٥) ثـمّ خرجـت مـن بغـداد في محلّـة السـلطان أبي سـعيد وغـرضي أن أشـاهد ترتيـب ملك العـراق في رحيلـه ونزولـه وكيفيّـة تنقّلـه وسـفره. (٢٦) وعادتهـم أنّهـم يرحلون عنـد طلوع الفجـر وينزلـون عنـد الضحـى، (٢٧) وترتيبهـم أنّـه يـأتي كلّ أمـير مـن الأمـراء بعسـكره وطبولـه وأعلامـه (٢٨) فيقـف في موضـع لا يتعـدّاه قـد عُـيّن لـه إمّـا في الميمنـة أو الميسـرة. (٢٩) وأتـى كلّ أمـير منهـم فسـلّم عـلى الملـك وعـاد إلى موقفه.

---

76   In an earlier narrative not included here.

Vocabulary

مَثوى (١)	dwelling, habitation, home; lodging
أبو الحسين بن جُبير (٢)	Abu al-Husayn Ibn Jubayr (1145–1217), a Muslim geographer from al-Andalus
عتيق (٢)	ancient, old
مثابة (٢)	refuge, resort
قرشيّة (٢)	affiliated with the Quraysh tribe (the tribe of the Prophet Muhammad)
التفات (٣)	attention
طَلَل (٣)	remains of something that has decayed, collapsed, or been destroyed
مُستوفز (٤)	confused, excited
دِجلة (٤)	Tigris River
مَجلوّة (٤)	shiny, polished, gleaming
حريميّ (٥)	characteristic of women
محلّة (٨)	a city quarter or district
الخليفة أبي جعفر المنصور (١١)	Abu Ja'far al-Mansur (AD 714–75), the second Abbasid Caliph
خَرِب (١٢)	decayed, destroyed
حافل (١٣)	full of, loaded with
على حدة (١٥)	separately, has its own place
المدرسة النظامية (١٦)	the Nizamiya school, founded by the Seljuks in 1065, one of the leading Islamic schools of its time
المدرسة المستنصريّة (١٧)	the Muntasariya school, built in 1234, one of the first to feature all four schools of Islamic law

مَذهب (١٨)	a school of thought in Islamic law (there are four in Sunni Islam: Hanafi, Hanbali, Shafi'i, and Maliki, of which Ibn Battuta was a scholar)
إيوان (١٨)	*iwan*, a vaulted alcove off a central courtyard
وضوء (١٩)	the *wudu'*— the Islamic procedure for washing before prayer
الجليل أبو سعيد بَهادُر خان (٢٠)	Abu Sa'id Bahadur Khan (1305-35), sultan of the Mongol Ilkhanate, based in Iran
تتر (٢١)	Tatars
لا نَبات بعارضيه (٢٤)	no growth on his cheeks (i.e. no hair; a reference to his youth)
مَحلّة (٢٥)	*mahalla*, a movable Mongol camp
الضُّحى (٢٦)	forenoon, the part of the day before noon
الميمنة أو الميسرة (٢٨)	the right hand-side or the left hand-side
يتعدّاه (٢٨)	to exceed, go past

Comprehension Exercises

A. Answer the following questions in complete Arabic sentences (numbers refer to the lines in which the information can be found):

١. ماذا حدث للقسم الغربي للمدينة؟ (٦–٧)

_____

_____

_____

٢. ماذا تبقى من قصر الخليفة أبي جعفر المنصور؟ (١١-١٢)

_____

_____

_____

٣. ما أعظم الأسواق الموجودة في القسم الشرقي من مدينة بغداد؟ (١٣-١٤)

_____

_____

_____

٤. كيف وصف ابن بطوطة ملوك التتر الذين حكموا العراق؟ (٢٠-٢١)

_____

_____

_____

٥. ماذا كان غَرَض ابن بطوطة من سفره مع سلطان العراق؟ (٢٥)

_____

_____

_____

B. Find Arabic phrases in the text that approximate the following meanings in English:

1. nothing remains but its name : _____

2. in addition to : _____

3. nothing pleasing to the eye remains : _____

4. youthful : _____

5. teeming with markets : _____

C. Find Arabic synonyms or equivalents in the text for the following words and phrases:

١. مكان : ـــــــــــــــ : _____

٢. القديمـة : ـــــــــــــــ : _____

٣. دمـار : ـــــــــــــــ : _____

٤. منفصلـة : ـــــــــــــــ : _____

٥. يتخطّى : ـــــــــــــــ : _____

D. Find Arabic antonyms or opposites for each of the following words in the text and use each in a complete sentence:

١. رجـالي : ـــــــــــــــ : _____
   _____

٢. الصحـوة : ـــــــــــــــ : _____
   _____

٣. بخيـل : ـــــــــــــــ : _____
   _____

٤. ذهب : ـــــــــــــــ : _____
   _____

Interpreting the Text

١. من وصف ابن بطوطة، ما أبرز صفات مدينة بغداد؟ وكيف تعكس هذه الصفات مكانة هذه المدينة على مر العصور[77]؟ (١-٥)

_____

_____

_____

٢. ما الأدلة على أهمية القسم الغربي للمدينة وكيف غيّرت غزوة التتر من معالم المدينة؟ (٦-١٢)

_____

_____

_____

٣. في المدرسة المستنصريّة كان هناك مسجد وموضع تدريس لكل مذهب من المذاهب الأربعة السُنّية. هل يدل ذلك على التعددية أو الانقسام في الإسلام؟ لماذا؟ (١٦-١٨)

_____

_____

_____

٤. كيف تمت مراسم[78] توديع[79] أمراء المغول للملك عند سفره؟ (٢٥-٢٩)

_____

_____

_____

---

77 throughout the ages
78 ceremony
79 farewell, goodbye

_____

_____

_____

Grammar, Structure, and Context Clues

1.	In lines 1–2, Ibn Battuta makes use of a number of definite *idaafa*s that are meant to convey a special historical significance. Some of these include:

حضرةُ الإسلام—the seat of Islam

مثوى الخلفاء—the home of caliphs

مقرّ العلماء—the place of the ‘ulama (scholars)

Unlike his use of indefinite *idaafa*s in describing other peoples and places (eg. - أهل جهاد 'a people of jihad'), these are meant to signify unique places of honor, reflecting Baghdad's role as the capital of the Islamic state. These absolute terms set a dramatic opening for the contrast he is about to establish when describing the degraded current state of the city.

2.	The word دارس used in line 3 looks like the active participle of the verb دَرَسَ, meaning 'a learner.' It would be easy to mistake the intent here, as Ibn Battuta has just made numerous comments about Baghdad as a former center of education. However, the usage in this case means something erased or forgotten. This reinforces the more familiar word طلل (remains of something destroyed or abandoned), which is commonly used in classical Arabic poetry, typically describing the remains of an abandoned campsite. For that description to be applied to the

80 during

former capital of the Islamic world is especially potent. The combination of the two words adds extra emphasis to Ibn Battuta's description of the city of Baghdad, in which the glories of lines 1 and 2 contrast heavily with the ruin that follows.

3. The verb تُضْرَب in line 16 is in the passive voice, derived from the verb ضَرَبَ. If you consult an Arabic dictionary you will find a long list of meanings for this verb (Hans Wehr, for example, lists close to two pages, worth of meanings for this verb). Thus, context is extremely important for deducing the intended meaning.

Look at the examples below of the verb ضرب in several collocations and try to figure out the meaning intended in line 16 of the text[81]:

ضرب الباب: to knock on the door

ضرب (شخص) بـ (شيء): to hit (s.o.) with (s.th.)

ضرب الأعداد: to multiply numbers

ضرب بـ (شخص / شيء) عرض الحائط: (expression) to ignore/brush off (s.o./s.th.)

يضرب الرقم القياسي : (expression) to break a record

ضرب أخماسا في أسداس: (expression) to rack one's brain in order to find way out, be at wits' end

ضرب موعدا : (expression) to agreed on a time and place for a meeting

يضرب مثلا / مثالا (لـ، على، بـ) : (expression) to say a parable, give an example

---

81 Examples based on the Hans Wehr Dictionary of Modern Written Arabic

4. The compound وإن should not be confused with the particle إِنَّ (verily, indeed). Its meaning, instead of affirming, is 'although,' marking contrast. Ibn Battuta has just given a long list of very laudatory superlatives about the place of Baghdad in Islamic history. وإن marks a shift in tone, as he then turns to lamenting the sad state of the city.

Writing Exercises

A. Translate the following sentences into Arabic, using vocabulary from this reading. Hints in parentheses indicate which lines to look at for similar structures:

1. He was once a powerful king, but nothing remains today except his name (2):

    _____

    _____

    _____

2. There is nothing pleasant in that city except for its main market (4):

    _____

    _____

    _____

3. The great palace has fallen into disrepair (7):

    _____

    _____

    _____

4. The Amir was a favorite even though he was young in age (23):

_____

_____

_____

5. At his birthday, every child approached the father and paid their respects to him (29):

_____

_____

_____

B.: Rearrange the words below into coherent sentences

١.   من لم إلا القديمة المملكة يبقَ اسـمُها

_____

_____

_____

٢.   المدينة حُسْـنَ هذه لا إلاّ مساجدها في

_____

_____

_____

٣.   ماتَ ابنه وُلِّي الملك لما

_____

_____

٤. المدينة حافلة الجهة الشرقية الأسـواق من

_____

_____

_____

٥. الفجـر عند و ينزلون هم طلـوع يرحلون الضحى عند

_____

_____

_____

Discussion Questions

١. كان غزو المغول بمثابة[82] كارثة كبرى للدولة الإسلامية، وبعد مرور حوالي قرن على هذا الغزو، ظهر نوع من الامتزاج[83] بين الثقافتين العربية والمغولية. ما صور وأمثلة هذا الامتزاج في نص ابن بطوطة؟

٢. كانت بغداد أهم مدينة في العالم الإسلامي في عصر خلفاء الدولة العباسية. هل مازالت على نفس القدر[84] من الأهمية في عالمنا المعاصر؟ لماذا؟

٣. ما أوجه الشبه والاختلاف بين تاريخ مدينة بغداد وتاريخ مدينة القسطنطينية؟

٤. في رأيكم، ما أهم المدن في التاريخ الإسلامي؟ إذا نظّمتم رحلة إلى أهم الأماكن في الشرق الأوسط فما المدن التي ستزورونها؟ هل بغداد في قائمتك[85]؟ لماذا نعم أو لا؟

٥. ما أهم التغييرات التي طرأت[86] على ثقافة المغول منذ الغزو؟ وما تأثيرها على الشرق الأوسط وآسيا الوسطى الآن؟

---

82 as
83 blending, intermixing
84 same level of
85 your list
86 happened

Research and Presentation

ابحثوا في الإنترنت أو في مكتبة الجامعة عن موضوع 'التفاعل الثقافي والاجتماعي في العصر العباسي' ثم اكتبوا ملخصا يتضمن أهم نتائج هذا البحث والدروس المستفادة منه.

9

Yemen, the Gateway to East Asia

(Yemen, 1328–30) ذكر سلطان اليمن

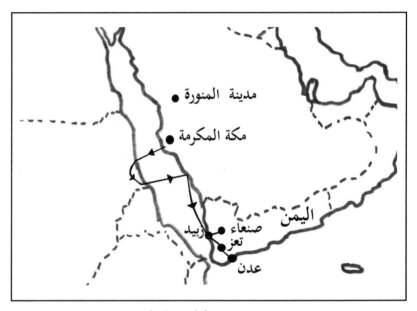

Ibn Battuta's first sea journey

Likely exhausted from traveling the Mongol territories, Ibn Battuta made his second Hajj to Mecca in 1327, and remained there for a year, during which he broadened his study of Islamic law. *Al-Masjid al-Haram*—the Great Mosque—was a center for numerous Muslim teachers, and visitors were welcome to join the teaching circles gathered around a teacher. This was a tremendous opportunity for Ibn Battuta, and he made the acquaintance of jurists and teachers from all schools of Sunni jurisprudence. At the same time, he met travelers from all reaches of the Islamic world, and this no doubt stoked his curiosity for foreign travel.

Ibn Battuta left Mecca in 1328[87] with no plan other than to visit Yemen. His path would take him much farther than that, although his first sea journey did not seem to be a very promising omen. The Red Sea was a particularly treacherous body to cross, with frequent storms, coral reefs, rocks, and changing winds. It is somewhat humorous to read of the epic traveler's unease as he boarded a ship for the first time, departing out of Jeddah. As always, Ibn Batd tuta is not shy about revealing his fear and inexperience. After several unplanned landings on the desert coast, he eventually reached Yemen.

As was often the case on his journey, Ibn Battuta arrived in Yemen at just the right time. The Rasulid dynasty (1229–1454), originally governors dispatched by the Abbasid caliph in Baghdad, had established independence, as Ibn Battuta describes, and ushered in a golden age in Yemeni history. King Mujahid al-Din 'Ali (1322–63), whom Ibn Battuta met in the capital of Ta'izz, had recently suppressed local rebellions and brought much of the country under central control. In the year prior to Ibn Battuta's visit, Mujahid 'Ali had seized the important port of Aden at the junction of the Red Sea and the Indian Ocean. The vigorous international trade brought wealth, knowledge, and travelers from around the world to Yemen, and this could only serve to further fuel Ibn Battuta's desire to travel. Likewise, as much of this trade was facilitated by, and in turn helped to facilitate, the spread of Islam, the need for learned Islamic jurists in faraway lands was only strengthened.

In his description of Yemen, much of Ibn Battuta's talent narrating his travels is evident. He carefully contrasts the nature of the main cities of Yemen: haughty Ta'izz ("as are most cities where kings reside"), cosmopolitan Aden, and hospitable Zabid. He is always interested in the nature of the people, and as a *qadi*, particularly in their religious and moral character. Yet even where he finds that character lacking, he is able to praise the economic or political importance of a town. As one whose record was commissioned by his king, he takes care to note the governing habits—good and bad—of

---

87   The date is not certain in Ibn Battuta's text. It may have been as late as 1330.

leaders he encounters. Here again, as in his record of travel in Egypt, it is questionable whether Ibn Battuta actually visited some of the places he describes. His account of Sanaa' has particularly been challenged by modern scholars. Yet in his age of limited communication, he saw his role also as a collector of reports and stories from others, most of which would never have reached his audience otherwise.

Lastly, it is interesting to note that Ibn Battuta referred to the Indian Ocean as the "Greatest Sea" (البحــر الأعظــم). Although Ibn Battuta's hometown of Tangier lies very close to the Atlantic Ocean, which was of little importance to the Islamic world of the fourteenth century, the Indian Ocean was truly the greatest body of water for maritime trade in his worldview. The sight of this vast expanse, and the stories he heard in its ports stirred his imagination once again, and Ibn Battuta soon put the terror of his first harrowing sea journey aside and headed off for new countries.

From the Writings of Ibn Battuta

Ibn Battuta's first sea journey. Having completed the Hajj, he sets out from Jeddah (in modern-day Saudi Arabia) for Yemen:

(١) ركبنـا البحـر مـن جـدة في مركـب يسـمّونه الجلبـة، (٢) ولم أكـن ركبـت البحـر قبلهـا. وكان هنالـك جملـة مـن أهـل اليمـن قـد جعلـوا أزوادهـم وأمتعتهـم في الجلـب، (٣) وهم متأهّبـون للسـفر. (٤) سـافرنا في هـذا البحـر بالريـح الطيّبـة يومـين، وتغـيّرت الريـح بعـد ذلـك وصدّتـنـا عـن السـبيل التي قصدناهـا، (٥) ودخلـت أمـواج البحـر معنـا في المركـب، (٦) واشتـدّ الميـدُ بالنـاس، (٧) ولم نـزل في أهـوال حتـى خرجنـا في مرسـى يُعـرف بـرأس دوائـر، فيـمـا بـين عيـذاب وسـواكن. (٨) وركبنـا البحـر مـن جزيـرة سـواكن نريـد أرض اليمـن، (٩) وهـذا البحـر لا يُسـافر فيـه بالليـل لكثـرة أحجـاره، (١٠) وإنّـا يسـافرون فيـه مـن طلـوع الشـمس إلى غروبهـا، ويُرسـون وينزلـون إلى الـبر، (١١) فـإذا كان الصبـاح صعـدوا إلى المركـب.

Once in Yemen, Ibn Battuta contrasts the vastly different characters of the inhabitants of its major cities:

(١٢) مدينـة زبيـد مدينـة عظيمـة باليمـن (١٣) وليـس باليمـن بعـد صنعـاء أكـبر منهـا ولا

أغنى من أهلها، (١٤) ولأهلها لطافة الشمائل وحسنُ الأخلاق وجمالُ الصور، (١٥) ولنسائها الحسن الفائق الفائت. (١٦) فتوجّهنا إلى مدينة تَعز حضرة ملك اليمن، (١٧) وهي من أحسن مدن اليمن وأعظمها، (١٨) وأهلها ذوو تجبّر وتكبّر وفظاظة، (١٩) وكذلك الغالب على البلاد التي يسكنها الملوك. (٢٠) ثم سافرت منها إلى مدينة عَدَن مرسى بلاد اليمن على ساحل البحر الأعظم، (٢١) وهي مدينة كبيرة، ولا زرع بها ولا شجر ولا ماء، (٢٢) وهي شديدة الحرّ. (٢٣) وأهل عدن ما بين تجار وحمّالين وصيّادين للسمك، (٢٤) وللتجار منهم أموال عريضة (٢٥) ومع هذا كلّه، فهم أهل دين وتواضع وصلاح ومكارم أخلاق، (٢٦) يحسنون إلى الغريب.

The hospitality of the sultan of Yemen:

(٢٧) وهو السلطان المجاهد نور الدين علي ابن السلطان المؤيّد (٢٨) شُهِرَ جدّه برسول لأن أحد خلفاء بني العبّاسي أرسله إلى اليمن ليكون بها أميراً، (٢٩) وثمّ استقلّ أولاده بالملك. (٣٠) أقمنا بداره في ضيافته ثلاثاً، (٣١) فلمّا كان في اليوم الرابع، وفيه يجلس السلطان لعامّة الناس، دخل بي عليه، فسلّمت عليه. (٣٢) وقعد القاضي عن يمين الملك، وأمرني فقعدت بين يديه، فسألني عن بلادي وعن مولانا أمير المسلمين. (٣٣) وكان وزيره بين يديه، فأمره بإكرامي وإنزالي.

Vocabulary

جلبة (١)	type of boat used in the Red Sea
أزواد (٢)	provisions, supplies
مُتأهّب (٣)	ready to go
صدّتنا عن (٤)	it held us back from, diverted
السبيل (٤)	the path
قصدناها (٤)	we headed for it
المَيدُ (٦)	swaying, shaking
عيذاب (٧)	Aydhab (in Egypt), the main crossing point on the Red Sea between Egypt and Arabia
لطافة (١٤)	friendliness, courtesy
الشمائل (١٤)	characteristics, manners

الحَسَن (١٥)	elegance, beauty
الفائِق (١٥)	superior, surpassing
الفائت (١٥)	the utmost, preeminent
تَجَبَّر (١٨)	to behave arrogantly or proudly
فَظاظة (١٨)	crudeness, harshness, roughness, rudeness
تَكَبُّر (١٨)	lordliness
البحر الأعظم (٢٠)	'the Greatest Sea' — The Indian Ocean
حَمّالين (٢٣)	carriers, porters
عريض (٢٤)	broad, great
تواضع (٢٥)	state of humility, modesty
يُحسِن (٢٦)	treat with kindness, give charity
السلطان المجاهد نور الدين علي (٢٧)	Al-Mujahid Nur al-Din, sultan of Yemen (1322-63), known for his genius in regulating trade and taxes
شُهِر بِـ (٢٨)	to be renowned as
بني العبّاسي (٢٨)	the Abbasid dynasty
استقلّ (٢٩)	to declare independence
ثلاثاً (٣٠)	here, meaning three days, the standard period of hospitality given a guest
عامّة الناس (٣١)	the general public
قعد (٣٢)	to sit down
بين يديه (٣٢)	lit. 'between his hands', an idiom meaning 'before him'
إكرام (٣٣)	performing the duties of a host to a guest
إنزال (٣٣)	lodging or sheltering someone

Comprehension Exercises

A. Answer the following questions in complete Arabic sentences (numbers refer to the lines in which the information can be found):

١.   ماذا وجد ابن بطوطة في المركب عند خروجه من جدة؟ (١-٣)

_____

_____

_____

٢.   كيف وصف ابن بطوطة أهل مدينة زبيد؟ (١٢-١٥)

_____

_____

_____

٣.   ماذا قال ابن بطوطة عن الطبيعة الجغرافية لمدينة عدن؟ (٢٠-٢٢)

_____

_____

_____

٤.   لماذا سُمِيَ جدّ سلطان اليمن 'رسول'؟ (٢٧-٢٨)

_____

_____

_____

٥.   ماذا كان يفعل السلطان عندما زاره ابن بطوطة؟ (٣١-٣٣)

_____

_____

_____

B. Find Arabic phrases in the text that approximate the following meanings in English:

1. which they call:_____

2. of good moral character:_____

3. are arrogant, rude, and self-important:_____

4. dry and barren :_____

5. despite all that :_____

C. Find Arabic synonyms or equivalents in the text for the following words and phrases:

١.   قـــارب :_____

٢.   مُستعِد :_____

٣.   دَوار البحر :_____

٤.   الخصائص :_____

٥.   واسـعة :_____

D. Find Arabic antonyms or opposites for the each of the following words in the text and use each in a complete sentence:

١.   قِلّـة :_____

_____

٢. أفقــر :_____

٣. القُبْـــح :_____

٤. الصعاليـك :_____

Interpreting the Text

١. ما المصاعب والتحديات[88] التي واجهها ابن بطوطة أثناء رحلته إلى جده؟ (٢-١٢)

_____

_____

_____

٢. بماذا وصف ابن بطوطة أهل مدينة تعز وما دلالة قول ابن بطوطة عنهم: "الغالب على البلاد التي يسكنها الملوك"؟ (١٦-١٩)

_____

_____

_____

٣. رسم ابن بطوطة صورة خاصة لمدينة عدن يظهر بها عدد من المتناقضات[89]، فما هي؟ (٢٠-٢٣)

_____

_____

_____

---

88 challenges
89 contradictions

٤. كيف حصل اليمن على استقلاله من الخلفاء العباسيين؟ (٢٧–٣٠)

_____

_____

_____

٥. كيف استقبل السلطان ابن بطوطة عند زيارته له؟ (٣٠–٣٣)

_____

_____

_____

Grammar, Structure, and Context Clues

1. In line 31, Ibn Battuta describes his encounter with the sultan of Yemen, writing "دخل بي عليه". Although the text is not voweled, context dictates the correct reading of the verb دخل. This appears at first glance to be the third person past form (he entered). That does not make sense in the context of the passage, however, and does not account for the two following prepositions بـ and على. Here, the two attached object pronouns, ي (me) and ـه (him) give clues to the intended meaning. 'Me' obviously refers to Ibn Battuta and the 'he' is logically the sultan. The verb, then, is passive, indicating that Ibn Battuta was entered into the sultan's presence.

2. The word ذوو in line 18 is the plural of the word ذو, which means 'possessor of' or 'the one who has.' This is one of a category known as the 'five nouns'[90] (الأسماء الخمسة). These words are unusual in that they take long vowels rather than short vowels for case endings when they precede another noun or an attached suffix. The three cases of ذو are: ذو — nominative, ذا — accusative and ذي — genitive, as shown in these examples:

الرجل ذو الزيَ الأبيض أستاذي—The man with the white outfit is my teacher

رأيت الرجل ذا الزيّ الأبيض—saw the man with the white outfit I

ذهبت إلى الرجل ذي الزيّ الأبيض—I went to the man with the white outfit

ذو is the masculine singular form and the feminine singular form is ذات. Review the different forms of ذو below:

---

90 The other four are: أبو (father), أخو(brother), حمو (father in law), فمو (mouth)

	Singular مفرد	Dual مثنى	Plural جمع
Masculine	ذو / ذا / ذي	ذوا / ذوي / ذوي	ذوو / ذوي / ذوي
مذكر			
Feminine	ذات	ذاتا / ذاتيّ / ذواتا / ذواتيّ	ذوات
مؤنث			

The word ذو is frequently the first term of an *idaafa* (إضافة). Note the following examples:

العمّال ذوو الاحتياجات الخاصة—The workers with disabilities

أصدقائي من الأمريكيين ذوي الأصول العربية—My friends are American of Arabic descent

الشرق الأوسط منطقة ذاتُ أهمية بالغة—Middle East is a region of great importance

مطلوب للعمل: آنسات ذواتُ خبرة في الطهي—Help wanted: women with experience in cooking

3. In Line 28, Ibn Battuta describes the sultan's family history, noting شُهِرَ جَدّه برسول. The verb شهر (to make famous) is most often used in the passive, meaning 'became famous' or 'was well known.' The accompanying preposition ب is very important, filling the role of 'as' in the expression. Here, we learn that the sultan's ancestor was well known as 'the emissary.' The next particle, لأنّ (because) tells us why, in this case because he was sent by an Abbasid caliph as a vassal (أن أحد خلفاء بني العبّاسي أرسله إلى اليمن). Together these words form a fixed expression often used to describe the title or nickname by which someone is known or renowned.

Writing Exercises

A. Translate the following sentences into Arabic, using vocabulary from this reading. Hints in parentheses indicate which lines to look at for similar structures:

1. In Egypt, I traveled in a boat they call a felucca[91] (1):

_____

_____

_____

2. The desert is not traveled during the daytime, due to the intense sun (9):

_____

_____

_____

3. There is no longer river in the world than the Nile (13):

_____

_____

_____

4. Louis XIV was famed as 'The Sun King' (28):

_____

_____

_____

---

91 فلوكة

5. The 'Empty Quarter'[92] is an area of no water and with intense heat (21-22):

_____

_____

_____

B. Rearrange the words below into coherent sentences:

١. من غروبها حتى طلوع سـافرنا الشمس

_____

_____

_____

٢. لأهل هذا الأخلاق حسـنُ البلد

_____

_____

_____

٣. ملكـه الوزير بين يدي كان يجلس

_____

_____

_____

٤. العالم أقدم و أعظمها مدن دمشـق من

_____

_____

_____

٥. إلى الملكة أرسلته ليكون الهند بها حاكماً البريطانية

_____

_____

_____

Discussion Questions

١. هل كان السفر البحري أكثر خطراً من السفر البري في عصر ابن بطوطة؟ ما مزايا السفر بالبحر عن السفر بالبرّ في عصره؟

٢. لماذا وصف ابن بطوطة المحيط الهندي بالبحر الأعظم؟ وماذا كان تأثيره الاقتصادي والسياسي على المنطقة؟

٣. عرفنا من النص أن سلطان اليمن كان يجلس مع الناس بصورة دورية[93]، فهل هذه عادة[94] محمودة[95] للحاكم أو الزعيم؟ وهل يمكن أن تُعدّ أسلوبا مبتكرا[96] للتواصل بين الشعوب وحكامهم اليوم؟

٤. وصف ابن بطوطة عدداً من المدن اليمنية التي زارها، كما تطرّق[97] لذكر أهم سمات أهل كل مدينة على حدة. فما أوجه الشبة والاختلاف فيما بينهم؟

٥. كان اليمن يسمى في الماضي 'بلاد العرب السعيد،' فما سبب تلك التسمية في رأيكم، وهل هذا الاسم مناسبا الآن؟ لماذا؟

Research and Presentation

ابحثوا في الإنترنت عن إحدى الصحف اليمنية واقرؤوا أهم عناوين الأخبار الواردة بها و ترجموا عشرة منها إلى اللغة الإنجليزية.

93 periodically
94 habit
95 commendable
96 innovative
97 discussed

10
The African Coast

(Somalia, Kenya, and Tanzania, 1331–32)

ذكر سلطان مقدَشو

Ibn Battuta's southward journey brought him to the great trading
ports of Mogadishu and Kilwa

Although Islam spread through the Middle East during its first centuries by way of military conquest, its wider spread throughout the medieval period came through merchant trade, reaching all the way to Indonesia in Southeast Asia, down the eastern coast of Africa, and into the lands south of the Sahara. These frontier regions were quite different than the Middle Eastern areas that Ibn Battuta had explored so far. In the latter, Islam was the state religion of land empires, incorporating Arab and Persian culture and forming the central identity of government, law, and culture. In Africa and Asia, Islam spread to ports focused on international trade. In most of those areas, Islam was still a minority religion, only gradually spreading into the hinterlands. The political and economic power of the Islamic caliphate helped facilitate this international trade, as did the uniform code of Islamic sharia law, which could provide a stable set of rules applicable anywhere. The Indian Ocean had become the heart of Islamic maritime trade, the full potential of which struck Ibn Battuta when he visited the strategic port of Aden in Yemen.

It was a time and place of great opportunities for an ambitious young scholar like Ibn Battuta. As Islamic law was being increasingly adopted in these coastal regions of the Indian Ocean, the need for scholars and jurists trained in the great centers of Mecca, Cairo, and Tunis was expanding. Despite his initial jitters about traveling by sea, Ibn Battuta was willing to go nearly anywhere, and was not shy about promoting himself or ingratiating himself with the people in power wherever he went. During his brief stay in the teeming, international port of Aden, he sensed limitless opportunity. While Asia was the most lucrative destination, the seasonal monsoon winds in the Indian Ocean prevented an immediate departure in that direction. Never hesitant to act, Ibn Battuta used this time to travel to East Africa.

Mogadishu and Kilwa
Although its more recent history has been shadowed by tragedy, Mogadishu (in modern-day Somalia) was the richest and most powerful trading port on the East African coast in Ibn Battuta's day. Two hundred years earlier, Muslim traders had begun to build up the small fishing village into an international trading port, trading ivory and gold from the African mainland for goods from China, India, and the Persian Gulf to the East. While local Afri-

can languages predominated in the town, Arabic provided a *lingua franca* for trade, law, and religion.

Ibn Battuta's description of the East African coast is the only eye witness account from the time period, and as such, is a very valuable historical document. Upon his arrival in Mogadishu—apparently unexpected—Ibn Battuta identified himself as a Muslim legal scholar and was quickly brought to the sultan, who put him in the company of other scholars. Although speaking the Somali dialect among themselves, all were able to communicate in Arabic. Ibn Battuta notes well the distinctive practice of assigning local escorts to foreign traders as evidence of the business savvy that made Mogadishu such a strong economic player.

Ibn Battuta then traveled on to Zanzibar and Kilwa (off the coast of Tanzania), which was rapidly emerging as the chief rival to Mogadishu. Founded by a Persian prince in AD 1000, the Sultanate of Kilwa would eventually control the entire East African coast until its conquest by Portugal in the 1500s. The mixture of Persian, Arab, and Bantu language and culture created the distinctive identity referred to as 'Swahili' (from 'coastal' in Arabic). Ibn Battuta praised the local architecture and the sultan's dedication to *jihad* on the mainland in Africa. As always, he takes care to note the character and governing styles of the leaders he met, sharply contrasting the generous former sultan with the recent arrival on the throne who made no secret of his miserliness. Although Ibn Battuta was clearly fascinated by the unique culture and abundant riches of the East African ports, the changing monsoon winds cut his visit short and compelled him to head back to Arabia.

From the Writings of Ibn Battuta

Ibn Battuta arrives in Mogadishu, at the time a great trading port, and describes the distinctive trading practices of the city:

(١) وصلنا مَقْدَشُوْ، وهي مدينة متناهية في الكبر، (٢) وأهلُها لهم جمال كثيرة ينحرون منها المئين في كلّ يوم، ولهم أغنام كثيرة، (٣) وأهلها تجار أقوياء، وبها تصنع الثياب المنسوبة إليها التي لا نظير لها، ومنها تحمل إلى ديار مصر وغيرها، (٤) ومن عادة أهل

هـذه المدينـة أنّـه متى وصـل مركب إلى المرسى تصعـد الصنابـق، وهي القـوارب الصغـار إليـه، (٥) ويكـون في كـلّ صنبـوق جماعـة مـن شبّـان أهلهـا، (٦) ولا ينـزل التاجـر مـن المركب إلّا إلى دار نزيلـه مـن هـؤلاء الشبـان (٧) فـإذا نـزل عنـد نزيلـه بـاع لـه مـا عنـده واشترى له، ومـن اشتـرى منـه ببخـس أو بـاع منـه بغيـر حضـور نزيلـه فذلـك البيـع مـردود عندهم، (٨) ولهـم منفعـة في ذلـك.

Upon arriving in Mogadishu, Ibn Battuta is honored as a guest:

(٩) ولمـا صعـد الشبّـان إلى المركـب الـذي كنـت فيـه جـاء إليّ بعضهـم فقـال لـه أصحابي: "ليـس هـذا بتاجـر، وأنّـما هـو فقيـه." (١٠) فقـال لي: "إنّ العـادة إذا جـاء الفقيـه أو الشريف أو الرجـل الصالـح لا ينـزل حتى يـرى السلطـان." (١١) فذهبـت معهـم إليـه كـما طلبـوا. (١٢) وسـلطان مَقْدَشـوْ، إنـما يقولـون لـه الشيخ، واسمـه أبـو بكـر ابن الشيـخ عمـر، (١٣) وهـو في الأصـل مـن البربـرة، وكلامـه بالمقدشي، ويعـرف اللّسـان العـربي. (١٤) وأتينـا الجامـع، فصلّينـا خلف المقصـورة، (١٥) فلـما خـرج الشيـخ مـن بـاب المقصـورة فرحّـب وتكلّـم بلسـانهم مـع القـاضي ثـمّ قـال باللسـان العـربي: "قدمـتَ خيـرَ مقـدَم، وشرّفـتَ بلادَنـا وآنسـتنا."

Ibn Battuta then travels to the Sultanate of Kilwa (in present-day Tanzania), the great rival of Mogadishu:

(١٦) ثـمّ ركبنـا البحـر مـن مدينـة مقدشـو متوجّهـاً إلى بـلاد السـواحل قاصـداً مدينـة كُلْـوَا مـن بـلاد الزنـوج، (١٧) فوصلنـا إلى جزيـرة مَنْبَسـى. (١٨) وركبنـا البحـر إلى مدينـة كُلْـوَا، وهـي مدينـة عظيمـة ساحليّـة أكثـر أهلهـا الزنـوج المستحكمـو السـواد، (١٩) ولهـم شَرَطـاتٌ في وجوهـم. (٢٠) ومدينـة كُلْـوا مـن أحسـن المـدن وأتقنهـا عـمارة (٢١) وكلهـا بالخشـب، وسقـف بيوتهـا الدّيـس، (٢٢) والأمطـار بهـا كثيـرة (٢٣) وهـم أهـل جهـاد لأنّهـم في بـرّ واحـد متّصـل مـع كفّـار الزنـوج، (٢٤) والغالـب عليهـم الديـن والصـلاح، (٢٥) وهـم شافعيّـة المذهـب.

Ibn Battuta contrasts the character of past and present sultans of Kilwa:

(٢٦) كان سـلطانها في عهـد دخـولي إليهـا أبـو المظفـر حسـن، (٢٧) ويكنـى أيضـاً أبـا المواهـب لكثـرة مواهبـه ومكارمـه (٢٨) وكان كثيـر الغـزو إلى أرض الزنـوج يُغيـر عليهـم ويأخـذ الغنائـم، (٢٩) ويُخـرج خمسـها ويصرفـه في مصـارف المعيّنـة في كتاب الله تعـالى. (٣٠) ولمـا تـوفي هـذا السـلطان الفاضـل الكريـم، رحمـة الله عليـه، وُلِّي أخـوه داود فكان على الضـدّ مـن ذلـك، (٣١) إذا أتـاه سـائل يقـول: "مـات الـذي كان يعطـي، ولم يـترك مـن بعـده مـا يُعطـى."

Vocabulary

يَنْحر (٢)	to slaughter
المئين (٢)	hundredths
المنسوبة (٣)	belonging to, associated with
الصنابق (٤)	small boats
نزيل (٦)	visitor, guest
بخس (٧)	cheap, very low
مردود (٧)	rejected, turned down
منفعة (٨)	benefit, profit
شريف (١٠)	high-ranking, honored
صالح (١٠)	devoted, honest, pious
البربرة (١٣)	Barbary, from the African coast
لسان (١٣)	tongue, here meaning language
المقصورة (١٤)	private room, compartment
السواحل (١٦)	the Swahili coast of East Africa
مَنْبَسى (١٧)	Mombasa (in modern-day Kenya)
كُلْوَا (١٨)	Kilwa, great city state (in modern-day Tanzania)
مستحكم (١٨)	intense, severe
شَرَطاتٌ (١٩)	incisions
الدّيس (٢١)	bulrush
الزنوج (٢٣)	people of the Zanj (African interior)
شافعيّة (٢٥)	the Shafi'i school of Sunni Islam
يُكنّى (٢٧)	to call, to nickname
مواهب (٢٧)	aptitudes, talents
يُغير على (٢٨)	to attack, invade, make a raid into
على الضدّ (٣٠)	contrary to, opposite of

Comprehension Exercises

A. Answer the following questions in complete Arabic sentences (numbers refer to the lines in which the information can be found):

١.   كيف كان يُرحّب أهل مقدشو بالزوار الأجانب؟ (٤-٨)

_____

_____

_____

٢.   ما عادة أهل مقدشو عند وصول فقيه أو شريف إلى المدينة؟ (١٠)

_____

_____

_____

٣.   كم لغة كان يتكلم بها سلطان مقدشو؟ (١٢-١٥)

_____

_____

_____

٤.   كيف وصف ابن بطوطة أهل مدينة كلوا؟ (١٩)

_____

_____

_____

٥.   ماذا كان يفعل سلطان كلوا بالغنائم التي كان يحصل عليها من غزواته؟ (٢٧-٢٨)

_____

_____

_____

B. Find Arabic phrases in the text that approximate the following meanings in English:

1. which has no equal :_____

2. whenever a boat arrives :_____

3. they benefit from that :_____

4. he was the opposite :_____

5. he was called ... because of :_____

C. Find Arabic synonyms or equivalents in the text for the following words and phrases:

١. يذبحـون :_____

٢. العُـرف :_____

٣. على النقيـض :_____

٤. بجانب :_____

٥. يسـمّى :_____

D. Find Arabic antonyms or opposites for each of the following words or phrases in the text and use each in a complete sentence:

١. مدينـة صغـيرة جـداً :_____

_____

٢.   كان بخيـلاً : _____

_____

٣.   البلد تعـاني مـن الجفـاف : _____

_____

٤.   يسكنون بعيداً عـن : _____

_____

Interpreting the Text

١.   ما دور النزيل في النظام التجاري في مقديشو؟ (٥-٨)

_____

_____

_____

٢.   لماذا قال السلطان للفقيه ابن بطوطة "شرّفتَ بلادَنا وآنستنا"؟ (١٥)

_____

_____

_____

٣.   ما الخَصْلَة[98] الدينية التي مدحها ابن بطوطة في أهل مدينة كلوا؟ (٢٣)

_____

_____

_____

٤.   كيف اختلف عصر سلطان كلوا أبو المظفر حسن عن أخيه السلطان داود؟ (٢٦-٣١)

_____

_____

---

98 habits and customs, social behavior

Grammar, Structure, and Context Clues

1. The sultan of Mogadishu is referred to here as being of "أصل البربرة".
   This term and its related forms had several uses in Ibn Battuta's time.
   The term is related to the words 'barbaric,' 'Barbary,' and 'Berber' and
   derives from the Greek term *barbaros*, the sound of which was meant
   to mimic the murmuring of an unintelligible language. The Greeks
   generally used this term to refer to any non-Greek, but the Arabs
   adopted it in reference to a number of non-Muslim peoples. Most
   familiar are the Berbers of North Africa, but here it refers to Barbara, a
   region in Somalia.

2. The other major demographic group Ibn Battuta identifies are the زنوج
   (sing.– زنج). The term was often used to refer to Negroid peoples in
   general, and its use today can be considered offensive. Here, it refers
   specifically to the region of southeast Africa, along the Swahili coast,
   known as the Zanj. This same word is at the root of the name 'Zanzibar.' Ibn Battuta describes them as "deep black" in color (line 18 —
   المستحكمو السواد, with مستحكم being 'profoundly,' or 'deeply'). The Zanji
   territory began south of Mogadishu, which is where Ibn Battuta's narrative shifts to a description of the Zanji. Ibn Battuta identifies them
   as a clearly pagan people (كفّار الزنوج), and the Muslim inhabitants of

---

99 ideal model

Kilwa as أهل جهاد (line 23) for their proximity to them. Thus, in his narrative, he justifies the numerous raids conducted against the Zanji.

3. In line 27, Ibn Battuta uses another of his favorite constructs when he notes the sultan was:

$$يُكنى أيضاً أبا المواهب لكثرة مواهبه$$

The verb كنّى means to be called by a *kuniya* (the pattern of calling someone familiarly 'the father of…' or 'the mother of…' normally followed by the name of the oldest child; e. g. أبو صالح or أم جاسم). Here, however, the person is named as 'the father of' a quality or thing, in this case, gifts (مواهب). As such, it signifies high respect for the leader. The second part of the construct, لِ (for) indicates why the person is so named, in this case for his many gifts to the people. This practice appears throughout Ibn Battuta's writings to show how various famous people were perceived. Ibn Battuta only reports, but does not endorse this practice, which is considered offensive by many strict Muslims as only God can be the 'Father' of such qualities.

4. Notice the difference in meaning between these two words which share the same root غ-ن-م:

a) in line 2, أغنام = sheep or livestock

b) in line 28, غنائم = loot taken from the enemy after war; profits, spoils, prizes of war

Writing Exercises

A. Translate the following sentences into Arabic, using vocabulary from this reading. Hints in parentheses indicate which lines to look at for similar structures:

1. Alexandria is a port with no equal in the Middle East (3):

_____

_____

_____

2. No foreigner enters the city, except to visit the sultan (6):

_____

_____

_____

3. The people of China benefitted from the silk trade (8):

_____

_____

_____

4. He was of Indian origin, but his speech was Arabic (13):

_____

_____

_____

5. My wife loves to travel, but I am the opposite of that (30):

_____

_____

_____

B. Rearrange the words below into coherent sentences:

١.   الأصل يعرف اللّسان البربرة ولكنه في العربي السلطان

_____

_____

_____

٢.   البلد وجوهم شَرَطاتٌ في أهل هذا عندهم

_____

_____

_____

٣.   البحر الهند من عـدن متوجّهاً مدينة إلى بلاد ركبت

_____

_____

_____

٤.   ابنه لما السلطان ولي توفي الصغير

_____

_____

_____

٥.   الضـدّ كان ذلك الملك جداً أخـوه ولكن كان على من كريماً

_____

_____

_____

Discussion Questions

١. يُعدّ النظام التجاري متعدد الأطراف¹⁰⁰ الوسيلة المثلى¹⁰¹ لتسهيل حركة التجارة وتحقيق التنمية الاقتصادية. اشرحوا هذه العبارة في ضوء ما ذكره ابن بطوطة عن العادات التجارية لأهل مقدشو.

٢. عرض لنا ابن بطوطة صورة لمدينة مقدشو في الماضي، فماذا تعرفون عن صورة المدينة في عصرنا الحاضر؟

٣. هل توافق ابن بطوطه في نعته¹⁰² لسلطان كُلْوا بالفاضل والكريم؟ لماذا؟

٤. هل شخصية سلطان كلوا تضاهي¹⁰³ شخصية بعض الزعماء التاريخيين أو المعاصرين الذين تعرفونهم؟ من هم؟

٥. من وجهة نظركم، هل كان للعرب تأثير على الأوضاع السياسية والثقافية في مقدشو في العصور الوسطى الإسلامية؟ كيف؟

Research and Presentation

ابحثوا في الإنترنت واكتبوا مقالا قصيرا عن مدينة كلوا وأهميتها التاريخية والجغرافية.

---

100 multilateral
101 idealist
102 his characterization, description
103 match

11
Travels along the Arabian Gulf

(Oman, Bahrain, and Saudi Arabia, 1330)
من الصحراء إلى البحرين

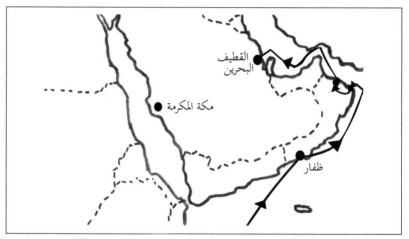

The small land portion of this journey (through modern-day Oman)
proved the most treacherous

Along with his descriptions of important monuments and great leaders, Ibn Battuta provides many anecdotes of hardship and adventure and records the curious practices of different peoples he encountered. His travel back from East Africa to Arabia to embark on another Hajj provides many of these examples. Some of his accounts provide an air of authenticity to his travel record, while others have the opposite effect. It is clear that many of his stories are secondhand reports he picked up along the way, and while they may have seemed to his audience at least as plausible as the wonders he actually did witness, today they stand out as inaccurate. It is, therefore, important to bear the context in mind when judging his reports.

Ibn Battuta's description of pearl harvesting in the Arabian (Persian) Gulf is an example of this tendency. He correctly notes the importance of the pearl industry to the Gulf. Up until the discovery of oil in the twentieth century, pearl diving was the principle economic activity of Gulf cities like Bahrain. The very act of divers retrieving pearls from shellfish in the sea would have been fascinating enough to readers in Morocco, who may have only seen the final product. Yet his description of the actual process of diving, with accounts of divers holding their breath for two hours, obviously has some problems. It is easy to understand, however, why such details would be believable to those who, like Ibn Battuta himself, never attempted the activity.

Ibn Battuta's travels across the Omani desert after landing from Africa offer a clearer delineation of eyewitness and secondhand reporting. The treacherous crossing, which he preferred to the dangers of a sea journey around the coast of southern Arabia, nearly cost Ibn Battuta his life once again. He describes conditions in which the winds and heat threatened all travelers, and many survived by robbery. In the rather lawless territory, he was ambushed by a desert bandit, yet successfully defended his party with a spear. He is careful to contrast this adventure with a story he heard about a noble bandit of the desert, who repented of his crimes and whose grave became a pilgrimage site. Here, his mix of firsthand report and storytelling clearly demonstrate the harsh conditions of the southern desert, far from the control of rulers to the north.

While these areas today constitute some of the richest and most developed in the world, the Arabian Gulf and southern Arabia appear in Ibn Battuta's accounts as undeveloped hinterlands. In his time, they had little natural resources to offer, and what international trade did occur was by sea. While coastal ports could prosper, the desert behind them was largely barren. The contrast bears evidence to how radically the discovery of oil has changed the region.

From the Writings of Ibn Battuta

A treacherous crossing of the desert:

(١) اكترينا دوابّ من التركمان، وهم سكّان تلك البلاد، ولا يُسافَرُ فيها إلاّ معهم لشجاعتهم ومعرفتهم بالطرق، (٢) وفيها صحراء مسيرة أربع أيام يقطعُ بها الطريق لصوص الأعراب (٣) وتهبّ فيها ريحُ السَّموم في شهري تمّوز وحزيران فمن صادفته فيها قتلَته، (٤) ولقد ذُكر لي أنّ الرجل إذا قتلته تلك الريح وأراد أصحابُه غسله ينفصل كلّ عضو منه عن سائر الأعضاء، (٥) وبها قبورٌ كثيرة للذين ماتوا فيها بهذه الريح، (٦) وكنّا نسافر فيها باللّيل، فإذا طلعت الشمس نزلنا تحت ظلال الأشجار من أمّ غيلان.

Ibn Battuta describes a noble bandit of the Persian Desert:

(٧) كان جمال اللُّك من أهل سِجستان، أعجميّ الأصل، واللُّك معناه الأقطع، وكانت يدُه قُطعت في بعض حروبه، (٨) وكانت له جماعةٌ كثيرة من فرسان الأعراب والأعجام يقطع بهم الطرق، (٩) وكان يبني الزوايا ويطعمُ الوارد والصادر من الأموال التي يسلبها من الناس، (١٠) ويقال إنّه كان يدعو ان لا يُسلّط إلاّ على من لا يزكّي مالَه، (١١) لا يقدر عليه ملك العراق ولا غيره، (١٢) ثمّ تاب وتعبّد حتى مات، وقبرُه يُزار ببلده.

From the hardship of the desert to the hardship of the sea, observing pearl diving in the Arabian Gulf:

(١٣) كان شهر إبريل وشهر مايه تأتي القوارب الكثيرة فيها الغوّاصون وتجّار فارس والبحرين والقطيف، (١٤) ويجعل الغوّاص شيئاً يكسوه من عظم الغَليم، وهي السَّلَحُفاة (١٥) ويصنع من هذا العظم أيضاً شكلاً شبه المِقراض يشدّه على أنفه، (١٦) ثمّ يربط حبلاً في وسطه، ويغوص، (١٧) ويتفاوتون في الصبر في الماء، فمنهم من يصبر الساعة والساعتين فما دون ذلك، (١٨) فإذا ضاق نفَسُه حرّك الحبل، فيحسّ به الرجل المسك للحبل على الساحل، فيرفعه إلى القارب (١٩) فتؤخذ منه المخلاة ويُفتحُ الصدف، فيوجد في أجوافها قطعُ لحم تُقطعُ بحديدة، (٢٠) فإذا باشرت الهواء جمدت فصارت جواهر، (٢١) فيجمع جميعها من صغير وكبير فيأخذ السلطان خمسه والباقي يشّريه التجّار الحاضرون بتلك القوارب.

Vocabulary

اكترى (١)	to grant or take on lease, hire
دوابّ (١) (sing.–دابة)	any animal used for riding such as horses, donkeys, camels, etc.
التركمان (١)	a Turkic people located primarily in Central Asia, in the states of Turkmenistan, Afghanistan, Iran, Northern Pakistan, Syria, Iraq, and North Caucasus
مسيرة (٢)	distance
الأعراب (٢)	Arabs of the desert, Bedouins
السَّموم (٣)	a hot wind of the desert, sand-storm
سِجِستان (٧)	Sijistan, a region of Eastern Iran
أعجميّ (٧)	foreigner, non-Arab
الأقطع (٧)	amputee, one-armed person
وارد وصادر (٩)	arriving and departing passengers
سَلَبَ (٩)	to loot
يُزكّي (١٠)	pay *zakat* (charity) for poor people
تَابَ (١٢)	to forsake (his ways), repent
قوارب (١٣) sing.–(قارب)	boats
غوّاص (١٣)	diver
فارس (١٣)	Fars, Persia
القطيف (١٣)	Qatif, a coastal region in Saudi Arabia
عَظْم الغَليم (١٤)	the bones of a small turtle
سلَحْفاة (١٤)	turtle
مِقراض (١٥)	clipper, scissors
الصبر (١٧)	patience, here refers to holding breath
يحسّ (١٨)	to realize, feel, perceive by sense

تُؤخذ (١٩)		to be taken by
مِحلاة (١٩)		bag
صدف (١٩)		seashell
باشر (٢٠)		exposed to
جَمَد (٢٠)		to solidify

Comprehension Exercises

A. Answer the following questions in complete Arabic sentences (numbers refer to the lines in which the information can be found):

١. لماذا يعبر المسافرون الصحراء بصحبة[104] التركمان؟ (١)

_____

_____

_____

٢. لماذا يطلق لقب[105] اللُّك على اللص جمال؟ (٧)

_____

_____

_____

٣. ممَّن تتكوّن جماعةٌ جمال اللُّك؟ وما عمل تلك الجماعة؟ (٨)

_____

_____

_____

---

104 accompanied by
105 nickname

٤. كيف كان اللُّك يتصرف[106] في الأموال التي يحصل عليها من الناس؟ (٩)

_____

_____

_____

٥. ما الأدوات التي كان يستخدمها الغواصون لصيد اللؤلؤ؟ (١٤-١٦)

_____

_____

_____

B. Find Arabic phrases in the text that approximate the following meanings in English:

1. to happen upon by chance :_____

2. to separate :_____

3. to attack, set upon :_____

4. run short of breath :_____

5. takes his fifth :_____

C. Find Arabic synonyms or equivalents in the text for the following words and phrases:

١. استأجرنا :_____

٢. فـارسي :_____

---

106 deal with

٣.   هـواء شـديد : _____

٤.   باقـي : _____

٥.   يــسرق : _____

D. find Arabic antonyms or opposites for each of the following words in the text and use each in a complete sentence:

١.   عـربي: _____
_____

٢.   غابـت : _____
_____

٣.   يطفـو : _____
_____

٤.   ســالت : _____
_____

Interpreting the Text

١.   ما أخطار السفر عبر الصحراء التي ذكرها ابن بطوطة وكيف حَمَى نفسه من تلك الأخطار؟ (١-٦)

_____

_____

_____

٢.   ما التغييرات التي طرأت على سلوك[107] جمال اللُّك؟ ولماذا اهتم ابن بطوطة بذكرها في كتابه؟ (٧-١٢)

_____

107   behavior

٣. هل تظنون أن ابن بطوطة شَهِد طريقة استخراج اللؤلؤة بنفسه أم سمع عنها فقط؟ لماذا؟ (١٣-٢١)

٤. ما حِصة[108] السلطان من تجارة اللآلئ؟ (٢١)

٥. كيف أسسّ اللُك استراحة للمسافرين عبر الصحراء؟ (١٢-٧)

---

108   share, portion

Grammar, Structure, and Context Clues

1. As you may know, there are three different systems for naming months
    in Arabic. Interestingly, Ibn Battuta makes use of all three in his narra-
    tive, which complicates dating the events he describes. In this passage,
    for example, he uses different calendar references in lines 3 and 13.
    The choice is generally based on the people about whom he is talking.

    The months of the Gregorian calendar (that familiar to us in the
    West), are referred to either by a set of names based on the Roman
    names, or by a set of names based on the Aramaic versions of the
    Babylonian calendar. In the chart below, the names that sound close
    to the English equivalents (الميلادي) are those used commonly in Egypt,
    Yemen, and North Africa. The second set (السرياني) are those based
    on the Babylonian and are commonly used in Iraq and the Levant.
    The third calendar is the Islamic calendar (الهجري), which is a lunar
    calendar and does not match the dates of the Gregorian, but is used
    frequently by Ibn Battuta.

The Gregorian Calendar		
	Name	Number of Days
1	كانون الثاني / يناير	31
2	شباط / فبراير	28/29
3	آذار / مارس	31
4	نيسان / أبريل	30
5	أيار / مايو	31
6	حزيران / يونيو	30
7	تموز / يوليو	31
8	آب / أغسطس	31
9	أيلول / سبتمبر	30
10	تشرين الأول / أكتوبر	31
11	تشرين الثاني / نوفمبر	30
12	كانون الأول / ديسمبر	31

2. The word مَسِيرة in line 2 has many meanings in Arabic and is used in a large number of idioms. Context is very important for determining the intended meaning in a given phrase. Here are some examples of the numerous functions of مَسِيرة:

مسيرة السفر: a distance traveled, a route, direction

مسيرة السلام: the peace process

مسيرة وطنية: a national rally, march, demonstration

3. The word سائر in line 4 is related to مسيرة, as both come from the same root س-ي-ر, which has the basic meaning of 'to head, to move' and may be best known to you from the word سيّارة (car). While سائر is the active participle (اسم فاعل) of the first measure verb سار, and logically refers to one who travels, the word has many other idiomatic uses. Like the word مسيرة, the corresponding passive participle (اسم مفعول) usage depends a great deal on context.

The word سائر thus performs many functions, as seen in the examples below:

سائر الناس: All/the rest of the people

سائر الأعضاء: All/the rest of the members or organs

مَثَلٌ سائر: a common proverb

رجلٌ سائر: a pedestrian man

طلبٌ سائر: a current demand

These distinctions are very important, as Ibn Battuta's narrative includes many descriptions of travel, as well as descriptions of common people and their habits. In line 4, for example, despite the fact that Ibn Battuta is talking about a path of travel through the desert, a close reading of the context will indicate that the word is being used in this case to refer to "all" the other body parts.

4. The two occurrences of the word صدف in lines 3 and 19 provide another example of the importance of reading for context. This word, when written without vowels, can actually be two different words with two different and unrelated meanings. The verb صَدَفَ can mean 'to avoid' or, as in this case, 'to come across unexpectedly.' The noun صَدَف , however, refers to seashells or oysters. From the context, it is clear that the two instances of صدف in lines 3 and 19 are two different words with different meanings. In line 3, Ibn Battuta is talking about the fate of one who runs into the *simoom* sandstorm. Line 19 is a description of pearl diving.

Writing Exercises

A. Translate the following sentences into Arabic, using vocabulary from this reading. Hints in parentheses indicate which lines to look at for similar structures:

1. No one travels to that island except by boat (1):

_____

_____

_____

2. We traveled only by day and stopped whenever the sun went down (6):

_____

_____

_____

3. It is said that he knew the only route through the desert (10):

_____

_____

_____

4. He made a shape that resembled a cross from a bone[109] (15):

_____

_____

_____

5. He repented of his crime[110] and gave his money to charity (9, 12):

_____

_____

_____

B. Rearrange the words below into coherent sentences:

١. الصيف في السَّموم ريحٌ في تهبّ فصل الصحراء

_____

_____

٢. بـِ البحر الجزيرة ماتوا قبورٌ كثيرة للذين هذه في

_____

_____

---

109 صليب
110 جريمة

٣.   سيارة يدُه في حادث قُطعت

_____

_____

٤.   لا بالجبال المنطقة هذه إلاّ معه لمعرفته في يُسافَرُ

_____

_____

٥.   لا المدينة ملك ولا غيره أن يُسيطِر يَقدر هذه على الصين

_____

_____

Discussion Questions

١.   كيف اعتمد ابن بطوطة على خبرة الأهالي المحليين في سفره؟ وعلامَ[111] تعتمدون الآن في سفركم؟

٢.   هل يوجد في نص ابن بطوطة إشارات[112] تدل على مدى تقديره[113] لقوة الصحراء الطبيعية وأخطار السفر فيها؟ كيف تغيرت هذه الأخطار منذ ذلك العصر؟

٣.   كيف أظهرت حكاية جمال اللُّكَ أخلاقيات أهل الصحراء وكيف تختلف عن أخلاقيات أهل المدن؟

٤.   كيف تغير اقتصاد الخليج العربي ومصادره منذ عصر ابن بطوطة حتى الآن؟

٥.   عرض ابن بطوطة تقريرا مفصلا عن كيفية صيد اللؤلؤ من الخليج، فما الجوانب السلبية[114] والإيجابية[115] التي وردت في هذا التقرير؟

---

111 على ماذا
112 signals
113 his assessment
114 negative
115 positive

Research and Presentation

اكتبوا مقالا بعنوان مَتاعب المهنة[116] تتناولون فيه أكثر المِهَن والحِرَف مشقة وأعلاها خطورة على حياة الإنسان.

---

116 professional difficulties

12

The Golden Horde of Mongol Russia

ذكر السلطان محمد أوزبك خان (Russia, 1332–33)

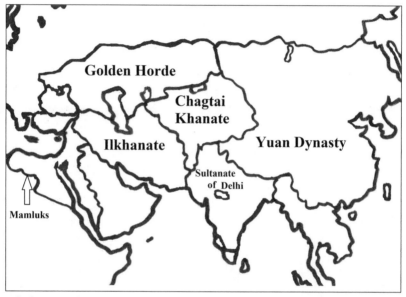

The four Mongol empires and the Mamluk and Delhi Sultanates. Along with Marinid Morocco, these constitute the seven 'great empires' of Ibn Battuta's text

After his travels through East Africa and the Arabian Gulf, Ibn Battuta made his third Hajj to Mecca, where he remained to study Islamic law. By this time, he had begun to distinguish himself as a *qadi* and scholar. While not in the same league as the renowned Islamic teachers who established themselves in the major centers of learning, he was certainly more than willing to take his expertise abroad and offer his services to the many kingdoms into which Islam was spreading. About this time, Ibn Battuta learned that the powerful sultan of Delhi, in India, was one such ruler who invited learned

Muslim jurists to come to his court. With the general intent of seeking such opportunity in India, yet nonetheless wanting to see as many new lands as possible, he headed north through Turkey and Central Asia on the inland route to India. This route would take him through the territory of Mongol-controlled Russia, later dubbed the land of the 'Golden Horde.'

The Golden Horde
After Genghis Khan's death, his vast land empire was divided into four parts to be ruled by his descendants. So large were each of these parts that Ibn Battuta lists all four of them in his enumeration of the 'seven great kingdoms' of his day (the other three being his own kingdom of Morocco, Mamluk Egypt, and his future employer, the Sultanate of Delhi). Ibn Battuta had already visited one of these four Mongol kingdoms, the Ilkhanate of Persia and Iraq. There, he found a state that was rapidly adopting Islamic law and Persian culture. From there he passed into the land of the Kipchak (later known as the 'Golden Horde'), that controlled much of southern Russia and Ukraine, but which at its greatest extent stretched from Poland to China. In this steppe country, the Mongols retained most of their nomadic culture.

As so often the case, timing favored Ibn Battuta's visit. For their first seventy years of rule, the Mongols of the Golden Horde practiced the Shamanist religion of their homeland. Uzbek Kipchak Khan, who ruled from 1313–41 and was in power during Ibn Battuta's visit, had recently imposed Islam as the state religion and vigorously promoted the Islamicization of the kingdom. Uzbek Khan also established good relations with the Mamluk Sultanate in Egypt and the Ilkhanate to the south. For a traveling Muslim jurist who had studied in the great centers of Islamic learning, it was a good time to be welcomed into this rapidly Islamicizing state.

Ibn Battuta devotes great attention to the status of women in that society. While he may have exaggerated somewhat in registering his surprise (noting sarcastically that a husband of a rich woman could easily be mistaken for one of her servants), the role of women was certainly more prominent and powerful than that in his homeland. In particular, the *khatuns*, or wives of the ruler, held significant power, and he would often find himself dealing with a powerful khatun rather than an amir.

It was, in fact, one of these powerful *khatuns*—the third wife of Sultan Uzbek and daughter of the Byzantine emperor—who provided the opportunity for the next leg of Ibn Battuta's journey—as he accompanied her on to Constantinople, the greatest city of the eastern Christian world.

From the Writings of Ibn Battuta

The Mongol khan, one of the 'Seven Great Rulers' of the world:

(١) واسمه محمد أوزبَك، ومعنى خـان عندهـم السلطان، (٢) وهـذا السـلطان عظيم المملكة، شـديد القـوّة، كبـير الشـأن، رفيـع المكان، (٣) قاهـر لأعـداء الله أهـل قسطنطينيّة العظمـى، (٤) مجتهـد في جهادهـم، وبلادهـم متسـعة ومدنهـا عظيمـة، (٥) منهـا التكفـار والقِرَم والماجَـر وأزاق وسـرداق وخـوارزم، (٦) وحضرتـه السـرا، وهـو أحـد الملوك السـبعة الذيـن هـم كـبراء الدنيـا وعظماؤهـا، (٧) وهـم مولانـا أمـير المؤمنـين ... أيّـد الله أمـره وأعـزّ نصـره، (٨) وسـلطان مصـر والشـام، وسـلطان العـراق، وسـلطان أوزبـك هـذا، وسـلطان بـلاد تركسـتان ومـا وراء النهـر، وسـلطان الهنـد، وسـلطان الصـين.

Ibn Battuta marvels at the role of women in Turkish society:

(٩) ورأيـتُ بهـذه البـلاد عجبـاً مـن تعظيـم النسـاء عندهـم. (١٠) وهـنّ أعـلى شـأناً مـن الرجـال. (١١) فأمّـا نسـاء الأمـراء فكانـت أوّل رؤيتـي لهـنّ عنـد خروجـي مـن القِـرَم، (١٢) رؤيـة الخاتـون زوجـة الأمـير سـلطية في عربـة لهـا، (١٣) وكلّهـا مجلّلـة بالملـف الأزرق الطيّـب، وطيقـان البيـت مفتوحـةٌ وأبوابـه (١٤) وأمـا نسـاء الباعـة والسـوقة فرأيتُهـن، (١٥) واحداهـن تكـون في العربـة والخيـل تجرهـا، وبـين يديهـا الثـلاث والأربـع مـن الجـواري يرفعـن أذيالهـا وعـلى رأسـها البَغطـاق وهـو أقـروف مرصـع الجوهـر (١٦) وتكـون طيقـان البيـت مفتّحـة، وهـي باديـة الوجـه لأن نسـاء الأتـراك لا يحتجبـن (١٧) وربـما كان مـع المـرأة منهـن زوجُهـا فيظنّـه مـن يـراه بعـض خدّامهـا، (١٨) ولا يكـون عليـه مـن الثيـاب إلاّ فروةٌ مـن جِلـد الغنـم.

Ibn Battuta commends the generosity of the Turks:

(١٩) ولأهـل تلـك البـلاد اعتقـادٌ حسـن في الفقـراء (٢٠) وفي كلّ ليلـة يأتـون إلى الزاويـة بالخيـل والبقـر والغنـم ويـأتي السـلطان ويأتـي الخواتـينُ لزيـارة الشـيخ والتـبرّك بـه، (٢١) ويجزلـون الإحسـان ويُعطـون العطـاء الكثـير، وخصوصـاً النسـاء فإنّهـنّ يكثـرن الصدقـة ويتحرّيـن أفعـال الخـير.

Vocabulary

محمد أوزبَك (١)	Muhammad Uzbek (ruled 1313–41), longest ruling khan
أهل قسطنطينيّة العظمى (٣)	people of Greater Constantinople, i.e. Byzantines
متسعة (٤)	vast, wide
التكفار والقِرَم والماجَر وأزاق وسرداق وخوارزم (٥)	regions of southern Russia and Crimea, Machar, Azaq, Sudak, Khwarizm
أيّد (٧)	to support, bless
أمر (٧)	condition, situation
أعزّ (٧)	to reinforce, strengthen
نَصُر (٧)	victory, conquest
ما وراء النهر (٨)	Oxus, region in Central Asia (today in Uzbekistan)
الخاتون (١٢)	*khatun*, title of a wife of the sultan
مُجَلَّلة (١٣)	wrapped, covered up
طيقان (١٣)	arches, window openings
(sing. –ذيل) أذيال (١٥)	lower parts, ends, tails
(تاج للزينة) البَغطاق (١٥)	*bughtaq*, a conical crown
أقروف (١٥)	consumer jewelry
بادية (١٦)	visible, exposed
يحتجب (١٦)	covered, veiled
فروةٌ (١٨)	fur, animal skin
اعتقادٌ (١٩)	firm belief without proof
التبرُّك بـ (٢٠)	asking the blessing of
يَجزِل (٢١)	to donate and give with generosity
عَطاء (٢١)	gift
يتحرّى (٢١)	seek

Comprehension Exercises

A. Answer the following questions in complete Arabic sentences (numbers refer to the lines in which the information can be found):

١.   ما المقصود بكلمة "خان" في لغة المغول؟ (١)

_____

_____

_____

٢.   مَن الملوك السبعة الذين قال عنهم ابن بطوطة "كُبراء الدنيا"؟ (٦–٨)

_____

_____

_____

٣.   لماذا يُعَدّ دور النساء في هذا المجتمع غريباً عجيباً؟ (٩)

_____

_____

_____

٤.   مَن "الخاتون" وما علاقتها اللغوية بكلمة "خان"؟ (١٢)

_____

_____

_____

٥.   كيف يتعامل أهل هذه البلاد مع الفقراء؟ (١٩–٢١)

_____

_____

_____

B. Find Arabic phrases in the text that approximate the following meanings in English:

1. great in power : _____

2. high in status : _____

3. of more importance : _____

4. do not veil themselves : _____

5. anyone who sees him would think : _____

C. Find Arabic synonyms or equivalents in the text for the following words and phrases:

١. مهـم جـداً : _____

٢. قديــر : _____

٣. منتـصر عـلى : _____

٤. يبـدو أنـه : _____

٥. عقيــدة : _____

D. Find Arabic antonyms or opposites for each of the following words or phrases in the text and use each in a complete sentence:

١. ضعيــف: _____

_____

٢. تصغـير: _____

_____

٣. مــن المستحيل: _____

_____

٤. مُحِبّـات: _____

_____

٥. يبخلون عـلى: _____

_____

Interpreting the Text

١. لماذا يذكر الكاتب ملك المغرب أولاً في قائمة زعماء العالم ويُلقّبه بـ "أمير المؤمنين"؟ (٧)

_____

_____

_____

٢. ماذا رأى ابن بطوطة في رجال هذا البلد؟ (٩–١٢)

_____

_____

_____

٣. كم ملكاً من الملوك السبعة العُظماء التقى ابن بطوطة شخصياً؟ مَن منهم الأعظم، من وجهة نظره؟ (٧-٨)

_____

_____

_____

٤. وصف ابن بطوطة الخان بصفات عديدة، فما هي؟ وهل لكم مآخذ[117] على ما ذكره؟ (١٢-١٣، ٢٠-٢١)

_____

_____

_____

٥. كيف تختلف مكانة المرأة ومرتبتها[118] عن الرجل في هذا البلد المسلم؟ (٩-١٨)

_____

_____

_____

---

117   criticisms, objections
118   her rank

Grammar, Structure, and Context Clues

1. In his description of the khan, particularly in line 2, Ibn Battuta makes frequent use of the 'false *idaafa*' (إضافة غير حقيقية) construction which was discussed earlier.[119] This construct, although taking the same form as an *idaafa*, is different in the sense that its first term is an adjective, rather than a noun. The usage in line 2 is a very typical function of the false *idaafa*, that is, to impart a sense of greatness or importance to the thing described. Notice the qualities Ibn Battuta attributes to the khan:

    عظيم المملكة

    شديد القوّة

    كبير الشأن

    رفيع المكان

    In each case, the adjective conveys some type of intense importance or power, and the nouns that follow are all attributes of the job of a ruler. This construction is similar to English expressions like 'mighty in power' 'sure of foot,' and so on. Notice how it conveys a stronger impression than just saying هو قوي جداً, for example, yet falls short of a superlative, such as أعظم or أكبر. As Ibn Battuta has identified Uzbek Khan as *one* of the seven great rulers of the world, he cannot ascribe absolute superlatives to him, but this construction certainly emphasizes his power and greatness more so than a normal adjectival construction.

2. In describing the Mongol treatment of women in line 9, Ibn Battuta uses the word تعظيم. This form is easily recognizable as the *masdar* (مصدر) of a measure II verb (تفعيل). As you likely remember, the most common use of this measure is to cause something to be or have the basic meaning of the root. The *masdar* then is the act of doing this. You can also easily recognize that the root here ع-ظ-م means 'great' as in the adjective عظيم. In many contexts, however, this form implies the

---

119   See Lesson 7 for more discussion

act of giving something a quality it would not necessarily have. When used in this sense, it does not necessarily mean the Mongol women are inherently great, but that they are being treated as such, and this is what he finds curious. Look at the other examples of تفعيل words below and notice that some can have a negative connotation.

تكبير – (enlarging, but also exaggerating) from 'large' كبير

تصغير – (shrinking, but also to minimize, belittle) from 'small' صغير

تبسيط – (simplifying, sometimes oversimplifying) from 'simple' بسيط

3. Ibn Battuta uses a special comparative to describe the position of women and men in Mongol society in line 10: أعلى شأناً من. This con-struction is known as the *tamyiiz* (تمييز). The first word 'higher (أعلى)' and the third word 'than (من)' look like the normal comparative form. Here, however, Ibn Battuta wants to distinguish how Mongol women are higher than men, specifically in regard to importance or influence. To do this, he uses the noun in the accusative form. This same pattern could be applied to any of the statements of praise Ibn Battuta used in the first excerpt. Following the example, try to turn these statements into comparatives using the *tamyiiz* (تمييز) construction:

great in power شديد القوّة (٦) – أشدّ قوّةً ←

كبير الشأن (٦) ← _____

رفيع المكان (٦) ← _____

4. The hypothetical sentence in line 17, "ربّما كان مع المرأة منهن زوجُها فيظنّه من يراه بعضَ خدّامها", is an excellent example of the importance of referent pronoun suffixes in understanding a complex text. You can identify the subject of this sentence as زوجُها from the case ending or from the context. This subject then appears twice more in the sentence in the form of attached object pronouns — at the end of يراه and فيظنّه. One

of these means 'see him' and the other 'think that he.' Notice that the word order of this sentence is very different from its English translation: 'Sometimes the husband was with of one of these women and anyone seeing him would think him one of her servants.' The attachment of the pronoun suffixes makes this order possible in Arabic, while still keeping the meaning clear. Note how awkward a literal translation into English would sound.

Writing Exercises

A. Translate the following sentences into Arabic, using vocabulary from this reading. Hints in parentheses indicate which lines to look at for similar structures:

1. He was once a man of high position (2):

_____

_____

_____

2. Their city is vast and its buildings are great (4):

_____

_____

_____

3. I found it interesting how these people glorified their scholars[120] (9):

_____

_____

_____

120 علماء

4. The merchants are of greater importance in that city than the teachers (10):

_____

_____

_____

5. The people of this country hold a belief in the importance of the family (19):

_____

_____

_____

B. Rearrange the words below into coherent sentences:

١.   هو الخمسة الأساتذة العربية الذين يدرّسون اللغة أحد

_____

_____

_____

٢.   من يرى يظنّه رجل بسيط الملك

_____

_____

_____

٣. البلاد اعتقادٌ بالنسـبة لي[121] عجيبٌ تلك لأهل

_____

_____

_____

٤. إلى كلّ يأتـون الناس في الزاوية لزيارة الشـيخ ليلة

_____

_____

_____

٥. أعلى الملك من الوزير شـأناً

_____

_____

_____

Discussion Questions

١. في رأيكم، ما صفات الزعيم المثالي اليوم؟ كيف تختلف هذه الصفات عن صفات سلطان روسيا؟

٢. وصف ابن بطوطة السلطان بأنه "أحد الملوك السبعة الذين هم كبراء الدنيا وعظماؤها"، فمن هم "كبراء الدنيا وعظماؤها" في عالمنا المعاصر؟ ولماذا؟

٣. هل مازال لتاريخ المسلمين والأتراك أثراً في الثقافة الروسية. كيف تغيرت أحوال المسلمين في روسيا في العصر الحديث؟

٤. للمرأة دور مهم في تنمية المجتمع وتطوره، فما الصورة المثلى التي يجب أن تكون عليها لكي تقوم بهذا الدور على أكمل وجه[122]؟

121 بالنسبة لي — in my opinion
122 perfectly

٥. ناقشوا بعض المعتقدات والسلوكيات التي يرفضها مجتمعنا المعاصر؟ ورأيكم فيها؟

Research and Presentation

ابحثوا في الإنترنت عن ثلاث مقالات على الأقل تناقش موضوع 'العلاقات الروسية التركية قديها وحديثا،' واكتبوا مقالة تحليلية ناقدة عن وجهات النظر المختلفة التي وردت في هذه المقالات.

13
Constantinople, Capital of the Byzantine Empire

(Constantinople, 1332)

ذكر مدينة القسطنطينية والكنيسة العظمى

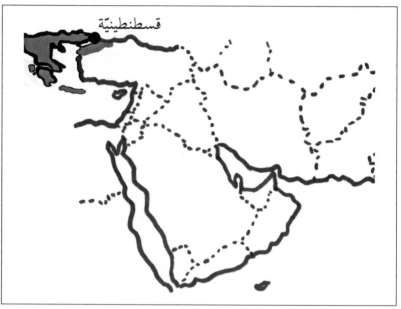

قسطنطينيّة

Constantinople and what remained of the once-great Byzantine Empire

Constantinople (modern-day Istanbul, Turkey) had once been for Christendom what Baghdad was for the Islamic world. Planned and designated by a powerful emperor as the new capital of the largest empire of its day, it was the largest city in the world for centuries, and the most renowned center of the arts, commerce, and religion. Named by Emperor Constantine after himself when he chose it as the new capital of the Eastern Roman Empire, Constantinople would remain the center of the Eastern Orthodox Church and the Byzantine Empire long after the fall of Rome. The great Hagia Sofia of Constantinople was the world's largest cathedral for nearly a thousand years.

Also like Baghdad, Constantinople's golden years were behind it by Ibn Battuta's time. The Byzantine Empire had been gradually reduced by the expanding territory of the Seljuk (and later Ottoman) Turks until little remained outside of Constantinople. Constantinople had also been sacked in the 1200s and its great library destroyed, but in this case, it had been European Crusader forces, not Mongols, who inflicted the damage. Having enjoyed something of a renewal in the period between that inglorious takeover and the final Ottoman conquest in 1453, Constantinople when Ibn Battuta visited it was enjoying a period of stability and good relations with its neighbors. It was as a direct result of these relations that Ibn Battuta would make his first journey outside the realm of Islam into the once-great center of Christendom.

Having ingratiated himself into the company of the Mongol khan of Russia, as was his habit, Ibn Battuta quickly recognized the sway that the *khatuns*, or wives of the khan held. He won the favor of the third *khatun*, Bayalun, who was something of an outsider herself, actually being the daughter of the Byzantine emperor. When he heard that she was planning to return to Constantinople for the birth of her child, Ibn Battuta joined the caravan, which included some five thousand people and two thousand horses.

In this atmosphere of reduced tensions, the traveling Muslim jurist in the company of Mongols was greeted by the Byzantine emperor and visited the largest Christian church in the world before heading off to serve in India. Although he refused to enter the interior of the cathedral, Ibn Battuta observed the habits of the Christian worshippers with curiosity and recorded them for his readers. In particular, he took note of the Christian tendency to venerate relics with a religious connection, something that would have struck a strict Muslim as idolatry. He notes the requirement for worshippers to bow before a cross they claimed to be made from remnants of the wood from the Crucifixion.

From the Writings of Ibn Battuta

Ibn Battuta arrives in Constantinople, capital of the Byzantine Empire and once the greatest city on earth. He describes the section of the city given the name 'Istanbul':

(١) هـي متناهيـة في الكـبر، منقسـمة قسـمين، (٢) بينهـا نهـرٌ عظيـم المـدّ والجـزر، (٣) وكانـت عليـه فيـما تقـدّم قنطـرةٌ مبنيّـة فخربـت، وهـو الآن يُعـبَرُ في القـوارب (٤) وأحـد القسـمين مـن المدينـة يسـمّى أصْطَنْبُـول، وهـو بالعـدوة الشـرقيّـة من النهر (٥) وفيه سُكنى السـلطان وأربـاب دولتـه وسـائر النـاس، وأسـواقه وشـوارعه مفروشـة بالصفـاح، متّسـعةٌ (٦) وأهـلُ كلّ صناعـة علـى حِدة لا يشـاركهم سـواهم، (٧) وعلى كلّ سـوق أبـوابٌ تسـدّ عليـه بالليـل، (٨) وأكثـر الصنّـاع والباعـة بهـا النسـاء.

The other main division of the city, today Galata:

(٩) وأمّـا القسـم الثـاني منهـا فيسـمّى الغَلَطـة، وهـو بالعـدوة الغربيّـة مـن النهر شـبيهٌ برباط الفتـح في قريـة مـن النهـر، (١٠) وهـذا القسـم خـاصّ بنصـارى الإفرنـج يسـكنونه (١١) وهـم أصنـاف: فمنهـم الجنويـون والبنادقـة وأهـلُ روميـة وأهـلُ فرنسـة (١٢) وجميعهـم أهـلُ تجـارة، ومَرسـاهم مـن أعظـم المَراسي (١٣) وأسـواق هـذا القسـم حسـنة إلّا أنّ الأقـذار غالبـة عليهـا، (١٤) ويشـقّها نهـرٌ صغيـر قَـذِرٌ نَجِـس، وكنائسـهم لا خيـرَ فيهـا.

Ibn Battuta's description of the Hagia Sofia, the largest Christian church in the world of his day:

(١٥) إنّـما نذكـر خارجَهـا، وأمـا داخلهـا فلـم أُشـاهده، (١٦) وهـي تسـمّى عندهـم أيا صُوفيـا، (١٧) ويُذكـر أنّهـا مـن بنـاء آصَـف بـن برخيـاء، وهـو ابـن خالـة سـليمان، عليـه السـلام، (١٨) وهـي مـن أعظـم كنائـس الـروم، وعليهـا سـور يُطيـف بهـا، فكأنّهـا مدينـة، وأبوابهـا ثلاثـة عـشر بابـاً (١٩) ولهـا حـرم هـو نحـو ميـل، عليـه بـابٌ كبـير، ولا يمنـع أحـد مـن دخولـه، وقـد دخلتـه مـع والـد الملـك.

Ibn Battuta further describes the practices of the Christian worshippers:

(٢٠) وعلـى بـاب الكنيسـة سـقائف يجلسُ بهـا خدّامُهـا الذيـن يقمّـون طرقَهـا ويوقـدون سُرُجَهـا، ويغلقـون أبوابهـا، (٢١) ولا يدعـون أحـداً بداخلهـا حتـى يسـجد للصليـب الأعظـم عندهـم، الـذي يزعمـون أنّـه بقيّـة مـن الخشـبة التـي صُلـبَ عليهـا شـبيهُ عيسـى، عليـه السـلام، (٢٢) وهـو علـى بـاب الكنيسـة مجعـول في جعبـة ذهب طولُهـا نحـو عـشرة أذرع، وقـد عرضـوا عليهـا جعبـة ذهب مثلهـا حتـى صـارت صليبـاً.

Vocabulary

مُنقسم (١)	divided
قنطرةٌ (٣)	building with a curved top and straight sides supporting a bridge
عُدوة (٤)	riverbank, side
أرباب (٥)	lords, officials
صُفّاح (٥)	thin paving stones
يشارك (٦)	to share
سوى (٦)	except, only
تُسَدّ (٧)	to be closed up, blocked
شبيهةٌ (٩)	similar
الإفرنج (١٠)	Westerners, Europeans
الجنويون، البنادقة، الرومية (١١)	people of Genoa, Venice, Rome
مَرسى، مراسي (١٢)	harbor, seaport
أقذار (١٣)	garbage, junk, trash
نَجِس (١٤)	filthy, extremely unclean
يُشُقّ (١٤)	to cleave, split
أيا صُوفيا (١٦)	Aya Sofi (Hagia Sofia, lit 'Holy Wisdom' in Greek) Cathedral
آصف بن برخياء (١٧)	Asaph son of Berechiah, legendary builder of Hagia Sofia
يُطيف (١٨)	to encircle, surround
حرم (١٩)	a sacred territory or space
سقائف (٢٠)	booths, sheds
يقُمّ (٢٠)	to sweep
يُوقد (٢٠)	to enkindle, light
سُرُج (٢٠)	lamp, light
يزعُم (٢١)	to claim, allege
شبيهُ عيسى (٢١)	one who resembles Jesus (a reference to the Islamic belief that Jesus himself was not crucified)
مجعول (٢٢)	had put
جُعبة (٢٢)	case, frame
أذرُع (٢٢) (sing. _ذراع)	cubit — a unit of measurement about the length of an arm

Comprehension Exercises

A. Answer the following questions in complete Arabic sentences (numbers refer to the lines in which the information can be found):

١.   ما القسمان الرئيسان لمدينة القسطنطينية؟ (٤، ٩)

_____

_____

_____

٢.   مَن يسكن في قسم الغَلَطة؟ (١٠)

_____

_____

_____

٣.   هل دخل ابن بطوطة الكنيسة؟ (١٥)

_____

_____

_____

٤.   كم باباً للكنيسة؟ (١٨)

_____

_____

_____

٥.   ماذا يفعل المسيحون عند دخولهم الكنيسة؟ (٢١)

_____

_____

_____

B. Find Arabic phrases in the text that approximate the following meanings in English:

1. in older times, in past days :_____

2. they are of many types :_____

3. unpleasant, dingy :_____

4. it is said, it is claimed :_____

5. none may enter...until :_____

C. Find Arabic synonyms or equivalents in the text for the following words and phrases:

١ . معظـــم :_____

٢ . وسخ :_____

٣ . فقــط :_____

٤ . الأوربيــون :_____

٥ . يقولون :_____

D. Find Arabic antonyms or opposites for each of the following words or phrases in the text and use each in a complete sentence:

١. مُتحـدة : _____

٢. عُمِّرَت : _____

٣. بعضهـم : _____

٤. رديئة : _____

٥. مفتوح لعامـة النـاس : _____

Interpreting the Text

١. ما الأدلة على تدهور مدينة القسطنطينية في نص ابن بطوطة؟ (١-٤)

_____

_____

٢. ما أبرز نقاط الخلاف بين عقائد ابن بطوطة وعقائد المسيحيين في هذا النص. (٢١-٢٢)

_____

_____

٣. لماذا تعدّ أيا صوفيا من أعظم كنائس العالم؟ اذكروا الدليل من تقرير ابن بطوطة؟ (١٥-١٩)

_____

٤. لم يشاهد ابن بطوطة الكنيسة من الداخل أثناء زيارته لمدينة القسطنطينية، فما سبب ذلك؟ (١٥)

_____

_____

_____

٥. لماذا انقسمت مدينة القسطنطينية إلى قسمَيْن؟ وما مدى التأثير الذي يمكن أن يحدثه هذا الإنقسام على العلاقات الاجتماعية والاقتصادية في هذا البلد؟

_____

_____

_____

Grammar, Structure, and Context Clues

1. At several places in his text, Ibn Battuta uses the term أهل — 'a people' — in an *idaafa* (إضافة) construct to characterize the residents of a place (see lines 6, 7, 11, and 12 for examples). This is one of his most common idioms to characterize the nature of a population, and indicative of the kind of study Ibn Battuta made of the common members of the societies he visited, rather than just the rulers of the day. This term, when paired with a definite noun, refers to a specific, recognized group of people such as:

أهل الكتاب — People of the Book (Jews, Christians, and Muslims)

أهل السنة — People of the Sunna (Sunni Muslims)

أهل البيت — Members of the House of the Prophet

As used here, with an indefinite noun, it signifies 'a people' and is thus indicative of a general quality he observed, and not exclusive to one group. In Africa (see Lesson 10), for example, he uses the term أهل جهاد — a people of *jihad*, to refer to those living in close proximity to infidels. They are not singled out as *the* people of *jihad* – i. e., the exclusive keepers of *jihad*. Here, the citizens of Constantinople are singled out primarily as 'people of' various crafts and arts, indicative of the high level of civilization remaining in the declining city, as well as 'people of' various foreign nationalities:

أهلُ تجارة — people of commerce (line 12)

أهلُ فرنسة — people of France (line 11)

2. Ibn Battuta refers to the inhabitants of the Galata section of Constantinople collectively as الإفرنج (line 10). The term means 'Franks' and originally referred to the Germanic tribes that established the first empires in medieval Europe. During the Middle Ages, however, it was common to use the term to refer to Western Europe as a whole, particularly among Muslim and Eastern Orthodox writers. Ibn Battuta further identifies in this category a number of groups from all over Western Europe – أهل فرنسة، الجنويون، البنادقة (French, Genoans, and Venetians). Interestingly, the latter term is the plural of البندقية, the name for Venice, although these two words also refer to a 'crossbow,' or 'pellet bow', and today 'rifle,' both in singular and plural, for the resemblance of the bullet to a بندق or hazelnut.

3. In line 15 of his description of the Hagia Sofia church, as in many other places in his text, Ibn Battuta uses the construction أ...أمّا...ف.... This very common construct, sometimes called the 'topic — comment' sentence, is much more prevalent in Arabic than its equivalent in English. The first term, أمّا means 'as for...' and introduces a topic or thing. The second term, the particle ف, as it does in many constructions, introduces the result, or information clause of a two-part construction.

The particle ﻓ would not normally be translated in English, but in similar statements, its function is typically carried by a comma:

أمّا...ﻓ... (as for... , ...)

The function of this construct is to highlight and isolate for consideration what comes between أمّا and ﻓ. Observe Ibn Battuta's usage in line 15:

أما داخلها فلم أُشاهده — as for the inside, I did not see it

Here, Ibn Battuta, before describing the exterior of the marvelous Hagia Sofia church in great detail, makes a point of emphasizing that he did not go inside, for clearly implied religious reasons. By using this construct, he manages to shift the topic from his description of the outside of the church, drawing a strong conceptual boundary between describing the outside of a building and entering an active place of worship.

4. In line 6, Ibn Battuta uses a favorite phrase when he applauds the artisans of Constantinople:

أهلُ كلّ صناعة على حِدة لا يشاركهم سواهم

They are described as a people of every craft, to the extent that "لا يشاركهم سواهم". The word سوى (equally,' 'the same as) is often used in a negative construct with لا, as here, to mean 'none but.' The verb شارك is familiar as meaning 'to share.' The artisans of Constantinople are craftspeople of a level shared with none but themselves. The word سوى can be combined with a suffix (as here) or in an *idaafa* (إضافة) in this way to mean 'no one but (him, her, etc.).' Ibn Battuta often uses this construct in his description of cities—each of which he seems to find unique in some way—in the construct لا...سواها, with the feminine singular suffix referring to the city.

Writing Exercises

A. Translate the following sentences into Arabic, using vocabulary from this reading. Hints in parentheses indicate which lines to look at for similar structures:

1. Yemen was divided into two parts; one was called North Yemen, the other South Yemen (1, 4, 9):

   _____

   _____

   _____

2. The city of Baghdad is divided by the Tigris[123] River (14):

   _____

   _____

   _____

3. I visited Egypt last summer; as for Tunisia, I have never visited it (15):

   _____

   _____

   _____

4. That city is overtaken with filth; there is nothing good there (13, 14):

   _____

   _____

---

123 دجلة

5. No one is allowed to enter the church except by the eastern door (21):

_____

_____

_____

B. Rearrange the words below into coherent sentences:

١. قِسمين مدينة نهرٌ مُنقسمة بينها باريس السين[124]

_____

_____

٢. للمسيحين[125] القديمة كان مدينة هناك قسم القدس خاصّ في

_____

_____

٣. المدينة، وأما أزره داخلها فلم شاهدتُ الخارج من

_____

_____

٤. من العالم مسجد محمد علي[126] مساجد أعظم

_____

---

124 the Seine
125 Christians
126 the Muhammad Ali Mosque (Cairo)

٥. هي القسطنطينية الآن إسطنبول مدينة

Discussion Questions

١. مدينة القسطنطينية وإمبراطورية الروم كانت تحت تهديد الأتراك في عصر ابن بطوطة. ماذا حدث للقسطنطينية بعد قرن من زيارته لها؟

٢. ظلت مدينة القسطنطينية (إسطنبول) وعلى مدى عدة عصور من أهم المدن الثقافية والسياسية والاقتصادية. فما العوامل التي ساعدت على ذلك؟ وهل حافظَ[127] مجتمع هذه المدينة على هذه السِمة[128] حتى الآن ؟

٣. أفْرَدَ[129] ابن بطوطة في هذا النص وغيره تقارير مُفصّلة عن أسواق المدينة. لماذا تُعدّ الأسواق الشعبية مرآة تعكس جلياً[130] ثقافة المجتمع وعاداته ؟

٤. هل أبدى[131] ابن بطوطة احتراماً واضحا للدين المسيحي وعقائده في النص؟ لماذا؟

٥. ما أهمية مفهوم وفكرة 'حوار الأديان' في تحقيق السلام العالمي والتقريب بين الشعوب؟

Research and Presentation

قوموا بتصميم كُتَيّب[132] مُصوّر يتضمن معلومات تاريخية وثقافية وسياحية عن مدينة اسطنبول.

---

127 continue, adhere to
128 characteristic
129 allocated
130 clearly
131 expressed
132 brochure

14
The Sultan of India

ذكر ملك الهند (Delhi, India, 1334–41)

At long last, Ibn Battuta reached Delhi, capital of a growing Islamic Sultanate

While Egypt had become the first center of Islamic power in the 1300s, In-dia was rapidly emerging as the second. Throughout its history, India had been subject to waves of conquerors from Central Asia to the north, most of whom settled into the existing culture and, in the long run, blended into Indian civilization. Ibn Battuta had the fortune to have been born during one such period, following the widescale Mongol conquests of the 1200s and before the devastating invasion of Tamerlane at the end of the 1300s. As he encountered in Iraq, Persia, and Central Asia, Ibn Battuta would find in India an Islamic dynasty, founded by former Turkic invaders, that had brought stability, a resumption of cross-border trade and travel, and, most importantly for Ibn Battuta, a need for trained scholars.

The Sultanate of Delhi
When Turkish Muslims (calling themselves the Mamluks after the success-ful state in Egypt) seized the city of Delhi and turned it into a capital in 1206, India had not been unified for some eight centuries. By the time of Ibn Battuta's arrival in 1334, the Tughluq sultan Muhammad had brought most of India under his control. He successfully held off several Mongol at-tempts at invasion, and by the time Ibn Battuta arrived, had built profitable, if very tenuous, relations with the Mongol states around him. At the same time, India occupied the eastern shore of the very active Islamic Indian Ocean trade, the riches of which Ibn Battuta had seen firsthand in Yemen and Africa. Although Muslims were still a minority, they occupied the upper levels of power, while the long-established Hindu social and administrative system continued at the lower levels.

While in Egypt and the trading ports of Yemen, Ibn Battuta likely heard of the career opportunities available for trained scholars from the Arab heart-land. Although he had embarked on a journey as far down the East African coast as possible, then back up through Asia, his ultimate destination was the court of the Sultanate of Delhi. There, he would not be disappointed. He was welcomed with lavish gifts and signed a contract to serve in India. He would serve seven years in India as a judge and administrator, attending to such sensitive matters as tax collection during the famine that struck the country. Indeed, had it not been for political intrigues in the sultan's court, he may have stayed much longer, perhaps to the end of his days. Here, Ibn Battuta showed the qualities that made him such a successful and sought-af-ter *qadi*. He could be very harsh in his punishments for infractions of Islam-ic law, and very exacting in collecting the taxes that were of concern to the sultan, while at the same time encouraging charity in the name of God for those who were suffering.

Sultan Muhammad, however, emerges even in the highly flattering accounts of Ibn Battuta as a somewhat dangerous character. Like many great rulers of the time, he was capable of impressive victories, monumental building projects, as well as extreme paranoia and cruelty. He spent much of his time suppressing rebellions—real or imagined—and punishing the disloyal. It was Ibn Battuta's misfortune to wind up on the sultan's list of enemies, and at one point, he fully expected to die. Given his position and his own tendency to work for his own interests, it may be surprising that Ibn Battuta lasted as long as he did in Delhi.

From the Writings of Ibn Battuta

Ibn Battuta's description of Sultan Muhammad Tughluq:

(١) هـذا الملـك أحـبّ النـاس في إسـداء العطايـا وإراقـة الدمـاء، (٢) فـلا يخلـو بابـه عـن فقـير يَغنـى أو حـيّ يُقتـل، (٣) وقـد شُـهِرَت في النـاس حكاياتُـه في الكـرم والشـجاعة وحكاياتُـه في الفتـك والبطـش بـذوي الجنايـات، (٤) وهـو أشـدّ النـاس مـع ذلـك تواضعـاً وأكثرُهـم إظهـاراً للعـدل والحـقّ.

Ibn Battuta is appointed to the service of the sultan and receives lavish hospitality:

(٥) وصلتنـا ضيافـة السـلطان، (٦) فأعطـاني بَدرتـين كلّ بَـدرة مـن ألـف دينـار دراهـم (٧) وأعطـاني خِلعـة مـن المرعـز، وكتـبَ جميعَ أصحـابي وخدّامـي وغلـماني، وجُعِلـوا أربعـة أصنـاف: (٨) فالصنـفُ الأوّل منهـا أعطـي كل واحـد منهـم مائتـي دينـار، والصنـفُ الثـاني أعطـي كلّ واحـد منهـم مائـةً وخمسـين دينـاراً، (٩) والصنـفُ الثالـث أعطـي كل واحـد مائـة دينـار، والصنـفُ الرابـع أُعطـي كلّ واحـد خمسـةً وسـبعينَ دينـاراً (١٠) وفي أثنـاء مقامـي أمـرَ السـلطان أن يعيّـن لي مـن القـرى مـا يكـون فائـدة خمسـة آلاف دينـار في السـنة.

The sultan orders a cruel punishment upon a sheikh who defied his authority:

(١١) بعـثَ إليـه السـلطان بطعـام مـع مخلـص الملـك فأبَـى أن يـأكل، (١٢) وقـال: "قـد رُفِـعَ رزقـي مـن الأرض، ارجـع بطعامـك إليـه." (١٣) فلـمّا أخـبرَ بذلـك السـلطان أمـرَ عنـد ذلـك أن يطعـم الشـيخ خمسـة إسـتار (أسـاتير) مـن العَـذِرة، (١٤) وهـي رطـلان ونصـف مـن أرطـال المغـرب، (١٥) فأخـذ ذلـك الموكلـون بمثل هـذه الأمـور، وهـم طائفة

من كفّار الهنود، (١٦) ومدّوه على ظهره وفتحوا فمه بالكلبتين، وحلّوا العَذِرة بالماء، وسقوه ذلك.

Ibn Battuta's text abounds with accounts of the killings ordered by the sultan:

(١٧) وكان مرّةً عيّنَ حصّةً من العسكر تتوجّه مع الملك يوسف بغرة إلى قتال الكفّار ببعض الجبال المتّصلة بحوز دهلي. (١٨) فخرَجَ يوسف. وخرَجَ معه معظم العسكر، (١٩) وتخلّفَ قومٌ منهم، فكتب يوسف إلى السلطان يُعلمه بذلك، (٢٠) فأمرَ أن يُطاف بالمدينة، ويُقبض على من وُجد من أولئك المتخلّفين، ففُعِلَ ذلك، (٢١) وقُبِضَ على ثلاثمائة وخمسين منهم فأمرَ بقتلهم أجمعين، فقُتلوا.

Vocabulary

إسداء (١)	giving, granting
العطايا (١) – (.sing) عطية	something received as a gift
إراقة الدماء (١)	killing without good reason
الفَتْك (٣)	violence, cruelty
البَطْش (٣)	annihilation, execution
مع ذلك (٤)	although, in spite of all that
بَدرة (٦)	sum of money, purse
خِلعة (٧)	a robe given as a reward
المِرعز (٧)	cashmere
غِلمان (٧)	servant boys, slaves
صنف (٨)	group, rank
قِرى (١٠)	hospitality, receiving as a guest
أبَى (١١)	to refuse
العَذِرة (١٣)	human excrement
رطل (١٤)	unit of weight, approx. half a kilogram
الموكّلون (١٥) (.sing) – موكّل	assignees, those charged
الكلبتين (١٦)	pliers, pincers
سقى (١٦)	to give (someone) to drink

حِصَّةً (١٧)	group, unit
يُطاف (٢٠)	to patrol, circle
أجمعين (٢١)	all together

Comprehension Exercises

A. Answer the following questions in complete Arabic sentences (numbers refer to the lines in which the information can be found):

١.   ما أهم صفات السلطان تُغلق التي ذكرها ابن بطوطة؟ (١–٤)

_____

_____

_____

٢.   ماذا أعطى السلطان لابن بطوطة وأتباعه[133]؟ (٦–١١)

_____

_____

_____

٣.   ماذا فعل السلطان مع الشيخ؟ (١٢–١٧)

_____

_____

_____

٤.   بماذا أمر السلطان عسكره؟ (١٨–٢١)

_____

133 followers

_____

_____

٥. هل أطاع العسكر أوامر السلطان؟ وماذا كانت نتيجة ما فعلوه؟ (١٩-٢١)

_____

_____

_____

B. Find Arabic phrases in the text that approximate the following meanings in English:

1. his gates were never free from:_____

2. stories circulated:_____

3. during my stay:_____

4. whomever:_____

5. once:_____

C. Find Arabic synonyms or equivalents in the text for the following words and phrases:

١. الهدايـــا :_____

٢. أولاد :_____

٣. النوع :_____

٤. رفــض :_____

٥. يــأكل :_____

D. Find Arabic antonyms or opposites for each of the following words in the text and use each in a complete sentence:

١. الكَـرم : _____

_____

٢. تواضع : _____

_____

٣. أعطــى : _____

_____

٤. رديئة : _____

_____

٥. الأرض : _____

_____

Interpreting the Text

1. "وهو أشدّ الناس مع ذلك تواضعا وأكثرهم إظهارا للحق" لماذا يصفّ ابن بطوطة السلطانَ بهذه الكلمات؟ وما دلالة عبارة: "مع ذلك"؟ (٤)

_____

_____

_____

٢. كيف صنّفَ السلطان ابن بطوطة ورفاقه عندما كانوا في ضيافته؟ (٥-١٠)

_____

_____

_____

٣. كيف عاقَبَ السلطان الشيخَ الذي رفض الطعام، وما رأيكم في هذه العقوبة؟ (١١-١٦)

_____

_____

_____

٤. ما فحوى[134] الرسالة التي أرسلها يوسف للسلطان؟ (١٧-٢١)

_____

_____

_____

٥. أمر السلطان بقتل بعض العسكر لأنهم _____ .
_____ اختلفوا مع الملك يوسف _____ كانوا متخلّفين ذهنيا
خالفوا أوامر السلطان _____ كانوا مختلفين عن باقي العسكر

Grammar, Structure, and Context Clues

1. In line 3, Ibn Battuta cites the sultan's ruthless punishment: "بذوي
   الجنايات." The second word refers to serious crimes in Islamic law. The
   particle ذو, which is used in an *idaafa* (إضافة) with it, is one of the most
   important and tricky particles in Arabic. We discussed this particle
   earlier, in Lesson 9. In that instance, it was being used in the nominative case and had a و ending. As mentioned earlier, the meaning of the
   particle is 'possessor of' or 'one having' and here refers to 'those who
   have [i.e. have guilt for] crimes.' ذو is one of the 'five nouns' in Arabic,
   noted for their quality of taking long vowel case endings (when
   singular and followed by another noun in an *idaafa* construct or a pronoun suffix). Here, the word has a ي because it is in the genitive case
   as a result of being the object of the preposition ب. The middle و vowel
   indicates that it is plural. The particle ذو (and its feminine counterpart)
   are used in a large number of compounds, including:

---

134 synonym of مضمون, content of the message

ذو المال — rich, wealthy

ذو الشأن — important, powerful

ذو الصحة — healthy

2. Several words in Arabic can be confused in unvoweled texts. Since few books, other than the Quran, include full voweling, it is important to use context to determine the intended meaning. These passages include several examples of words which could easily be confused for more common, similarly spelled words:

In line 6, Ibn Battuta notes that the sultan sent him two —
بَدرة: فأعطاني بَدرتين كلّ بَدرة من ألف دينار دراهم

The word بَدرة intended here means 'sum of money' or 'money case,' while بُدرة would mean 'powder.'

In line 10, Ibn Battuta is assigned:

القرى ما يكون فائدة خمسة آلاف دينار في السنة

The word قُرى is the plural of قرية (village), while قِرى can be something given to a guest, such as a lavish reception. While both could make sense in terms of the sultan's generosity, the description of annual revenues indicates these are villages.

In line 7, the sultan gives Ibn Battuta a خِلعة or 'robe.' With the voweling خُلعة , it would refer to a divorce at the insistence of the wife.

In the very bizarre narrative of the sultan's cruelty, the word العَذِرة (excrement) is key to understanding the story. This rather obscure word is easily mistaken for the more common العُذرة (virginity) which does not make sense in the contex. This is further made difficult by the use of the verb حلّ (see below).

3. The verb حلّ has many related meanings, which creates challenges for understanding. It can mean to 'solve,' 'break down,' 'happen,' and 'analyze,' among its many meanings. Here, in describing the manure or excrement that was used in the torture, it means to dilute with water. This is related to the idea of solving or breaking down, in the sense that the English word 'solvent' or 'dissolve' refers to breaking something down. The wide range of uses, however, makes context extremely important in understanding the intended meaning.

4. Arabic has three grammatical cases, which is fewer than many Western languages. Therefore, the نصب case, although normally translated as 'accusative,' actually performs the functions of several different cases that may be familiar from other languages. The accusative case is normally defined as identifying the direct object of a verb. While the نصب case performs this function, it is also used to indicate how, when, and where an action takes place, as well as identifying adverbs and indirect objects. An example of the multiple functions of النصب can be found in line 17, which begins:

وكان مرّةً عيّنَ حصّةً من العسكر تتوجّه

The first instance—مرّةً—tells us when something happened (once). The second—حصّةً—is the object of the verb عيّنَ (a portion of the army was charged). Here, the same case ending has two different functions.

5. Ibn Battuta's description of the sultan makes use of several stylistic devices. In line 4, he describes the sultan as:

هو أشدّ الناس مع ذلك تواضعاً

The superlative أشدّ (most intense) is used in compounds with indefinite nouns of character as a very emphatic type of superlative statement. Here, it is paired with تواضعاً to mean "the most [intensely] humble of people." The case ending on the noun is the indicator of what is being intensified. The phrase مع ذلك which is interposed is thus an added modifier. It means 'in spite of' and here refers back to the preceding description of the sultan's fame: "He was, in spite of all that, the most humble of people."

Writing Exercises

A. Translate the following sentences into Arabic, using vocabulary from this reading. Hints in parentheses indicate which lines to look at for similar structures:

1. His house was never without guests (2):

_____

_____

_____

2. Tales of the King's mercy became famous throughout the kingdom (3):

_____

_____

_____

3. When I heard the news of her death, I became very sad (13):

_____

_____

_____

4. He was appointed the amir's ambassador[135] (10):

_____

_____

_____

5. He once refused the sultan's hospitality (5, 11, 17):

_____

_____

_____

B. Rearrange the words below into coherent sentences:

١. من دينار الملك مئة أعطاه بَدرة

_____

_____

_____

٢. الحكمة في البلد في حكاياتُها شُهِرَت

_____

_____

_____

٣. زيارتي أثناء بالخبر أخبرتُه

_____

_____

سفير 135

٤. بيته من يخلو الزائرين لا

_____

_____

_____

٥. هي كرامةً أشدُّ النساء

_____

_____

_____

Discussion Questions

١. ما تصوّركم للعلاقة بين ابن بطوطة والسلطان؟

٢. في رأيكم، هل كان ابن بطوطة مؤيدا لسياسات السلطان؟

٣. ما العُمْلات التي ذكرها ابن بطوطة، وهل مازالت مستخدمة في بعض البلدان إلى الآن؟

٤. هل يمكن للديكتاتورية أن تحقق نوعا من العدل والكرامة في المجتمع؟

٥. هناك حكمةٌ عربيةٌ مأثورة تقول: "اللهُ يَنْصُرُ الدَّوْلَةَ الْعَادِلَةَ وَإِنْ كَانَتْ كَافِرَةً وَلَا يَنْصُرُ الدَّوْلَةَ الظَّالِمَةَ وَإِنْ كَانَتْ مُؤْمِنَةً"، ما رأيكم في هذه المقولة وهل هناك أمثلة لهذه الدول في عالمنا المعاصر؟

Research and Presentation

اكتبوا مقالا تحليلياً بعنوان: 'تأثير رحلة ابن بطوطة إلى الهند على العلاقات العربية الهندية فيما بعد، وبعض أوجه التشابه بين الحضارتين.'

15
Delhi, Capital of Islamic India

ذكر مدينة دهلي (Delhi, India. 1334–41)

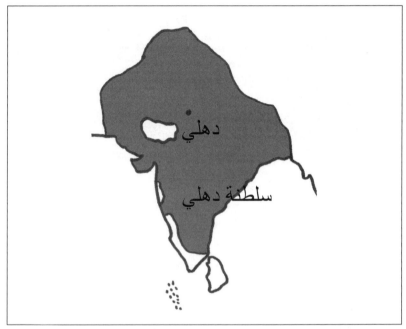

The Islamic Sultanate of Delhi, Ibn Battuta's adopted home for six years

Ibn Battuta's stay in India turned out to be a story of high adventure. While in Delhi, he describes the erratic behavior of Sultan Muhammad Tughluq, who at one moment could be shooting coins from a catapult mounted on an elephant into a crowd, and the next moment imposing bizarre acts of torture on those suspected of disloyalty. Thus, Delhi itself could be a place of constant surprises, a sharp contrast to the more stable, well-established Islamic capitals in North Africa and Arabia, a point the writer was keen to record for his patron, the sultan of Morocco.

Having successfully negotiated his way from a position of suspicion and near execution, Ibn Battuta realized he needed to leave Delhi before his fortunes turned again. His intent was to make another Hajj, a rather natural choice for a Muslim scholar of his renown. Yet here again, the extravagance of the sultan and Ibn Battuta's own propensity for seizing opportunity led to what would be his most famous of journeys.

Envoy to China

Sultan Muhammad Tughluq, who had established profitable relations with the Mongol kingdoms bordering his own land, desired to extend those relations to the most lucrative of the four Mongol khanates, the 'great' khanate in China. In 1341, Muhammad Tughluq assembled a huge caravan of gifts, including some 200 slaves, guarded by a thousand soldiers, as an offering to the khan of China. To lead such an expedition, there was no better choice than Ibn Battuta, who had already distinguished himself on sea and land journeys of impressive length, and whose political skill the sultan knew first hand. Ibn Battuta found himself in the honored position as ambassador to the court of the khan, and beyond the honor, recognized the opportunity to get himself out of Delhi.

Despite the size of the convoy and its protection, this would prove to be Ibn Battuta's most dangerous and least successful journey. Attacked by Hindu rebels on the land crossing and shipwrecked on the sea journey, he found himself washed ashore with nothing. The trepidation with which Ibn Battuta had greeted his first sea journey over a decade earlier seems to pale in comparison to this perilous trip. Though, afraid to return to Delhi and the cruel sultan Muhammad Tughluq, and unable to continue his diplomatic journey to China, Ibn Battuta was still the opportunist. He made a most unexpected detour to the tiny island kingdom of the Maldives, which, like many of his stops, was a recently converted Islamic territory in need of scholars such as himself.

From the Writings of Ibn Battuta

The sultan displays both extravagant generosity on his arrival to Delhi:

(١) ركبَ السلطان لدخول حضرتـه وركبنا في مقدّمتـه مـع صـدر الجـهان (٢) وزُيِّنَت الفيلـة أمـام السلطان، وجُعلـت عليهـا الأعـلام (٣) وجُعل عـلى بعـض الفيلـة رعـاداتٌ صغـار، (٤) فلـمّا وصـلَ السلطان إلى قـرب المدينة رمـي في تلـك الرعـادات بالدنانـير والدراهـم مختلطة (٥) والمشـاةبـينَ يـدي السـلطان وسـواهم ممّـن حـضرَ يلتقطـون ذلـك .

...and his paranoia and harshness in his personal dealings:

(٦) ذهبـتُ يومـاً لزيـارة الشيـخ شـهاب الديـن ابـن الشيـخ الجـام بالغـار الـذي احتفـرَه خـارج دهـلي، وكان قصـدي رؤيـة ذلـك الغـار، ولـما أخذه السـلطان سـأل أولاده عمّـن كان يـزوره فذكـروا ناسـاً أنـا مـن جملتهـم، (٧) فأمـرَ السلطان أربعـةً مـن عبيـده بملازمتي بالمشـور. وعادتُه أنّه متـى فعـلَ ذلـك مـع أحـد، قلّـما يتخلـص. (٨) فألهمَني الله تعـالى إلى تـلاوة قولـه: "حسـبُنا الله ونعـمَ الوكيـل،" فقرأتهـا ذلـك اليـوم ثلاثةً وثلاثـين ألـف مـرّة، (٩) وتخلصتُ بعـد قتـل الشيـخ والحمـدُ لله تعـالى.

From a position of suspicion, Ibn Battuta is elevated to be the sultan's emissary to China:

(١٠) بعـثَ إليّ السـلطان خيـلاً مسرَجـة وجـواري وغلمانـاً وثيابـاً ونفقـةً، فلبسـتُ ثيابـه وقصَدتُـه، وكانـت لي جبّـة قطـن زرقـاء مبطنـة لبستهـا أيّـام اعتكافـي، (١١) ولـمّا وصـلتُ إلى السلطان زادَ في إكرامي عـلى مـا كنتُ أعهـده، (١٢) وقال لي: "إنـما بعثـتُ إليـك لتتوجّـه عنـي رسـولاً إلى ملـك الصيـن، فـإني أعلـم حبّـك في الأسـفار والجَـوَلان، (١٣) فجهّـزني بـما أحتـاجُ لـه.

Ibn Battuta learns the reasons for his historic mission to China:

(١٤) كان ملـك الصيـن قـد بعـثَ إلى السـلطان مائـةَ مملـوك وجاريـة وخمسـائة ثـوب مـن الكمخـا منهـا مائـة مـن التـي تُصنـع بمدينـة الزيتـون، و مائـة مـن التـي تصنـع بمدينـة الخنسـاء (١٥) وخمسـة أمنـان مـن المسك، وخمسـة أثـواب مرصّعـة بالجوهـر، وخمسـة مـن التراكـش مزركشـة، وخمسـة سيـوف، (١٦) وطلـبَ مـن السـلطان أن يـأذنَ لـه في بنـاء بيـت الأصنـام الـذي بناحيـة جبـل قراجيـل المتقـدّم ذكـرُه (١٧) وإليـه يحجّ أهـل الصيـن، وتغلّـب عليـه جيـش الإسـلام بالهنـد فخربـوه وسـلبوه. (١٨) فلـمّا وصَلـت هـذه الهديّـة إلى السـلطان كتـبَ إليـه بـأن هـذا المطلـب لا يجـوز في ملّـة الإسـلام إسعـافه، ولا يبـاح بنـاء كنيسـة بأرض

المسلمين إلّا لمن يُعطي الجزية، (١٩) فإن رضيتَ بإعطائها أبحنا لك بناءه، والسلام على من اتّبع الهُدى. (٢٠) وكافأه على هديّته بخير منها.

Vocabulary

صدر الجهان (١)	Sadr al-Jihan, the Grand *Qadi* of Delhi
رعّاداتٌ (٣)	catapults
سِواهم (٥)	others
احْتفَر (٦)	to dig
من جُملتهم (٦)	among them
مُلازمة (٧)	accompanying, guarding
قلّما (٧)	rarely, seldom
يتخلّص (٧)	be freed from, cleared of
ألْهَم (٨)	to be inspired to
مُسرَّجة (١٠)	saddled
نفقة (١٠)	a sum of money for expenses
جُبّة (١٠)	jubbah, a loose outer garment
اعتكاف (١٠)	isolation, retreat
الكمخا (١٤)	velvet
مدينة الزيتون (١٤)	Hangchou, a city in China
أمنان (١٥)	unit for measuring weight
قراجيل (١٦)	the Himalaya Mountains
سَلبَ (١٧)	to loot, sack
إسعافُ (١٨)	complying with, granting
يُباح (١٨)	to be allowed, authorized
الجِزية (١٨)	the *jizya*, a poll tax paid by non-Muslims living in an Islamic state

Comprehension Exercises

A. Answer the following questions in complete Arabic sentences (numbers refer to the lines in which the information can be found):

١. لماذا وضع السلطان الرعّادات على الفيلة؟ (٤)

_____

_____

_____

٢. ماذا حدث للشيخ الذي زاره ابن بطوطة؟ (٦-٩)

_____

_____

_____

٣. كم مرة قرأ ابن بطوطة قول: "حسبُنا الله ونعمَ الوكيل"؟ ولماذا؟ (٨)

_____

_____

_____

٤. إلى من بعث السلطان ابن بطوطة رسولاً؟ (١٢)

_____

_____

_____

٥. ماذا طلب ملك الصين من سلطان دهلي؟ (١٦)

_____

_____

_____

B. Find Arabic phrases in the text approximate the following meanings in English:

1. and others :_____

2. I was among them :_____

3. very rarely escaped :_____

4. inspired me :_____

5. more than I was accustomed to :_____

C. Find Arabic synonyms or equivalents in the text for the following words and phrases:

_____ : قذف . ١

_____ :نيّتـي . ٢

_____ : كنتُ مـن بينهـم . ٣

_____:بـ لا يُسمح . ٤

_____ : ينجـو . ٥

D. Find Arabic antonyms or opposites for each of the following words or phrases in the text and use each in a complete sentence:

١. خَلْفـه : _____

٢. أجـاب : _____

٣. في الأغلب : _____

٤. هَـدْم : _____

٥. يأخـذ : _____

Interpreting the Text

١. ما أهم الصفات الشخصية للسلطان التي يمكن استنباطها[136] من صورة موكبه[137]؟ (١-٤)

_____

_____

_____

٢. لماذا ارتاب[138] السلطان في ولاء ابن بطوطة؟ (٦-٩)

_____

_____

_____

٣. كيف أظهرت تصرفات ابن بطوطة بعد زيارته للشيخ قوة عقيدته وإيمانه بالله؟ (٨-٩)

---

136 elicitation
137 caravan
138 distrust

٤ . ما أبرز نقاط الجدل التي دارت بين[139] ملكي الصين ودهلي؟ (١٤–٢٠)

٥ . هل تُعدُّ الهدية التي أرسلها ملك الصين للسلطان رِشوة[140]؟ لماذا؟ (١٤–٢٠)

Grammar, Structure, and Context Clues

1. In line 18, the sultan responds to the request from the ruler of China
    to repair a shrine within his territory saying: "هذا المطلب لا يجوز في ملّة
    ملّة, Here" .الإسلام إسعافُه، ولا يباح بناء كنيسة بأرض المسلمين إلاّ لمن يُعطي الجزية
    refers to a religious community or nation, rather than the term دين ,
    for religion. Under Islamic law, religious minorities in Islamic states
    were granted a considerable degree of freedom and autonomy within
    their own communities. This practice would later be formalized in the
    Ottoman Empire as the 'Millet system,' based on the word used by Ibn
    Battuta above, yet was nonetheless quite important in his time as well.
    The word الجزية refers to the tax that those religious minorities paid to
    the Islamic state. In giving this answer, which the sultan entrusted to
    his veteran diplomat and legal scholar, Ibn Battuta, the sultan avoids
    a religious condemnation of the request, instead citing established

---

139 took place between
140 bribe

legal constraints that prevent construction of a non-Islamic shrine in territory under Islamic control.

2. Ibn Battuta gives little amplification to the terrifying incident recounted in lines 6–9 that nearly cost him his life. Several clues in his narrative, however, point to the nature of the conflict. The man he visited is identified as a شيخ (*shaykh*), a typical title for a Sufi figure. While some Sufi orders were well integrated with the political powers of their day, others made a point of distancing themselves from official rulers and mainstream society. Nonetheless, they often had strong followings. Such a situation would not have sat well with the paranoid ruler Muhammad Tugluq. The likelihood of this possibility is support-ed by the fact that Ibn Battuta visited the *shaykh* in a غار (cave), خارج دهلي (outside of Delhi), الذي احتفرَه (that the *shaykh* had dug himself). Further, Ibn Battuta claims in his defense that the only purpose of his visit was رؤية ذلك الغار and after the *shaykh*'s arrest, the sultan demand-ed to know who his recent visitors were "سأل أولاده عمّن كان يزوره". This would all suggest that the cave was wellknown and well-frequented, such that it would warrant a visit from Ibn Battuta, the curious traveler, without implying that he was a follower of the *shaykh*.

3. In line 7, after being placed under guard by the sultan, Ibn Battuta notes, "عادتُه أنّه متى فعلَ ذلك مع أحد، قلّما يتخلص". The first part of the sentence tells us that typically, when this happens to someone, "قلّما يتخلص" ("rarely is one spared"). The word قلّما (rarely) is an adverbial phrase formed by adding ما to the verb قلّ (to be rare, few). Similar phrases made from other verbs that specify qualities or quantities include:

طال (to be or last long) طالما ← (often, how long)

قَصُرَ (to be short) قصر ما ← (briefly, for a short time)

كَثُرَ (to be numerous) كثر ما ← (how much)

4. In his answer to the ruler of China, the sultan notes that building a shrine both يجوز إسعافهُ Vand يباح Y. The first verb—"to be permissible" takes the subject إسعافهُ (indicated by the *damma*), "its compliance." The second is the passive form of the verb 'to permit' (clear from the *alif* in the present tense). Seeking not to offend the recipient, the sultan manages to keep himself entirely out of the statement, either as a subject or object, by stressing the restrictions of the law. Nonetheless, he uses both an active and passive verb in parallel and in quick succession to repeat this message, keeping his own agency out of the equation in both cases. The combination of the two different verb voices to convey the same meaning is an eloquent way of stressing the immutable power of the law.

Writing Exercises

A. Translate the following sentences into Arabic, using vocabulary from this reading. Hints in parentheses indicate which lines to look at for similar structures:

1. When the king's caravan arrived close to the city, the people cheered[141] (4):

   _____

   _____

   _____

2. The president's car was decorated with many flags (2):

   _____

   _____

   _____

---

141 هتف بـ

3. My purpose in visiting the city was to see the mosque (6):

_____

_____

_____

4. The amir sent a thousand dinars of gold to the king before his visit (14):

_____

_____

_____

5. They asked the sultan for permission to build a new church in the city (16):

_____

_____

_____

B. Rearrange the words below into coherent sentences:

١.   الخيول بعض جُعلت الأعلام على

_____

_____

_____

٢.   المدينة وصلنا شاهدنا إلى قرب فلمّا القصر

_____

_____

٣. الأمير لزيارة بقصره ذهبتُ يوماً

_____

_____

_____

٤. طلبَ يأذنَ المدينة السلطان أن لهم بناء أهل جسر من جديد بـ

_____

_____

_____

٥. الكتاب هذا هذه السنة مرّات ثلاث قرأتُ

_____

_____

_____

Discussion Questions

١. كانت بلاد الهند الشمالية في عهد زيارة ابن بطوطة دولة مسلمة قوية. فما التغييرات التي طرأت على الوضع السياسي والديني في الهند وآسيا الجنوبية الآن؟

٢. استخدم السلطان سلاح المال ليضمنَ ولاء شعبه من ناحية و لِيأمَنَ[142] غَدْر[143] أعدائه من ناحية أخرى. هل هناك من زعماء هذا العصر من يتبع هذا المبدأ[144]؟

٣. ما مَغْزى[145] اختيار السلطان لابن بطوطة ليكون رسولا له في بلاد الصين من وجهة نظركم؟

---

142 feel secure
143 treachery
144 precept
145 significance

٤.   بعث سلطان دهلي هدايا كثيرة وفاخرة إلى نظيره في الصين. هل مازالت هذه
البروتوكولات[146] تُمَارَس في الحياة الدبلوماسية اليوم؟

٥.   ناقشوا مفهوم 'العلاقات الدولية،' وما أهم العوامل المؤثرة فيها؟

Research and Presentation

ابحثوا في الإنترنت عن أهم سلاطين الهند المسلمين واكتبوا مقالا تفصيليا عن أحدهم.

---

146 protocols

16
Judge in the Maldives

ذكر ذِيبة المهل (جُزُر المالديف) (The Maldives, 1343)

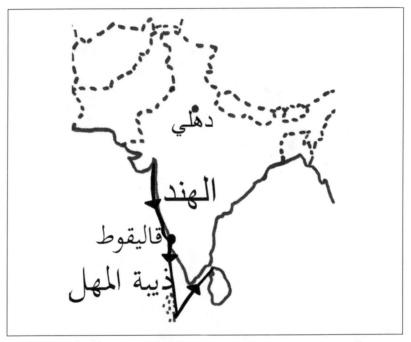

The tiny island kingdom of the Maldives provided Ibn Battuta a welcome refuge.

One of the most unusual episodes in Ibn Battuta's travels was his nine-month term as Islamic judge or *qadi* (قاضٍ) of the tiny island nation of the Maldives. This brief period reveals much about the spread of Islam into Asia and the mixing of traditional and Islamic cultures. Equally intriguing are the attitudes of a prominent Muslim jurist from the Arab world to these newly converted areas and Ibn Battuta's capacity for political intrigue.

Located in the Indian Ocean, southwest of India, the Maldives consist of over 1,000 islands that average just over one meter above sea level. Ibn Battuta, on the run from several vengeful rulers in India and reeling from the disastrous loss at sea of his China-bound fleet, decided to make a voyage to this tropical nation with a reputation as a natural paradise. Ibn Battuta would soon find that his own reputation as a prominent Muslim jurist would put him in great demand in this recently converted nation (despite his insistence to the contrary, Ibn Battuta likely did a great deal to court this attention). Previously a Buddhist state, the Maldives had converted to Islam in the twelfth century due to the influence of Muslim traders arriving on the islands. Ibn Battuta, himself from Morocco, attributed the conversion to a Moroccan trader, Abu al-Barakat, but the truth is not clear in the historical records. In any case, the islands were still struggling to adapt the Maliki legal school of Sunni Islam to local lifestyles, and as a renowned judge of the Maliki school, Ibn Battuta was a natural choice to become chief *qadi* of the islands. Marrying at least six times in nine months for political reasons, enmeshing himself in local power struggles, and publicly clashing with the ruler, Ibn Battuta soon found himself on a departing ship, although his fondness for the islands would later lead him to consider a military expedition to seize control.

Ibn Battuta found the local customs to be puzzling, particularly on the subject of gender relations, and he was frustrated by his inability to change them. Foremost among these was the rule of a woman, Sultana Khadija (although he noted that the real holders of power were the male *wazirs* behind her). Ibn Battuta also noted that women customarily went around unclothed above the waist, and even though they made sure to cover up in his presence, he found the practice scandalous. Likewise, the habit of divorced men keeping their former wives in their houses shocked him. Not lacking in vehemence, Ibn Battuta instituted public beatings for violating moral laws to include infractions like missing prayer, but was frustrated at his inability to change in a matter of months what two centuries of adaptation had not yet altered. Nonetheless, despite his harsh words for some of the customs of the islands, Ibn Battuta described the local population in positive and affectionate terms, praising their religious sincerity as well as their gentle nature.

From the Writings of Ibn Battuta

Ibn Battuta describes the gentle and pious nature of the inhabitants of the islands (الجزائر here means 'the islands,' and does not refer to Algeria):

(١) أهـل هـذه الجزائـر أهـل صـلاح وديانة وإيـمان صحيح ونيّـة صادقـة، أكلُهـم حـلال، ودعاؤهـم مُجـاب. (٢) وأبدانُهـم ضعيفـة ولا عهـدَ لهـم بالقتـال والمحاربـة، وسـلاحُهم الدعـاء. (٣) وفي كلّ جزيـرة مـن جزائرهـم المسـاجد الحسـنة (٤) وهـم أهـل نظافـة وتنـزّه عـن الأقـذار، وأكثرُهـم يغتسلون مرّتـين في اليـوم.

Ibn Battuta describes his attempts to change the local customs on women's dress:

(٥) نساؤها لا يغطّيـنَ رؤوسهنَّ، ولا سلطانتُهنَّ تغطّي رأسَها. (٦) ولا يَلبَس أكثرُهـنَّ إلّا فوطـةً واحـدة تسترُها مـن السـرّة إلى أسـفل، وسائرُ أجسـادهنَّ مكشـوفةٌ،(٧) وكذلـك يمشيـنَ في الأسـواق وغيرهـا. (٨) ولقـد جهدتُ لمّـا وليتُ القضـاء بهـا أن أقطعَ تلـك العـادة وآمرهـنَّ باللبـاس فلـم أسـتطع ذلـك.(٩) فكنـتُ لا تدخـل إليّ منهـنَّ امـرأة في خصومـة إلّا مستترة الجسـد (١٠) ومـا عـدا ذلـك لم تكـن لي عليـه قـدرة.

While in the islands, Ibn Battuta contracts a number of marriages for political purposes:

(١١) في الثانـي مـن شـوّال اتفقتُ مـع الوزيـر سليمان مانايـك عـلى تـزوّج بنتـه. (١٢) وحضرَ النـاس، وأبطأ الوزيـر سليمان. (١٣) قـال لي الوزيـر سـرّاً: "إن بنتـه امتنعـتْ، وهـي مالكـة أمـرَ نفسـها، (١٤) والنـاسُ قـد اجتمعـوا، فهـل لـك أن تـزوّج بربيبـة السـلطان زوجـة أبيهـا" (١٥) فقلـتُ لـه: "نعـم!" (١٦) فكانـت مـن خيـار النسـاء. (١٧) وتزوجـتُ أيضـاً زوجـةً أخـرى بنت وزيـر (١٨) ثـمّ تزوّجـتُ زوجـةً كانـت تحت السـلطان شهاب الديـن.

As chief judge, Ibn Battuta enforces strict adherence to religious law:

(١٩) لمّـا وليـت اجتهـدتُ جهـدي في إقامـة رسـوم الشـرع، وليسـت هنالـك خصومـات كـما هـي بـبلادنـا، فـأوّل مـا غـيّرت مـن عوائـد السـوء مكـثَ المطلقـات في ديـار المطلقيـن. (٢٠) فحسـمتُ علّـة ذلـك. (٢١) وأتي إليّ بنحـو خمسـة وعشريـن رجـلاً ممّـن فعـلَ ذلـك، وضربتُهـم وشـهّرتُهم بالأسـواق، وأخرجـت النسـاء عنهـم. (٢٢) ثـمّ اشتددتُ في إقامـة الصلـوات وأمـرت الرجـالَ بالمبـادرة إلى الأزقّـة والأسـواق اثـرَ صـلاة الجمعـة، فمـن وجـدوه لم يصـلّ ضربتـه وشـهرته.

Vocabulary

سليمان مانايك (١١)	Suleiman Manayk (a minister or counselor of the islands)
شهاب الدين (١٨)	Shihab al-Din (former sultan)
أبدان، أجسام (sing.بدن) (٢)	bodies
دعاء (١)	call, prayer, supplication
تنزّه (٤)	to keep away / far above
أقذار (٤)	filth
سائر (٦)	all
سُرّة (٦)	navel
تستُرُ (٦)	to cover, veil
وليتُ (٨)	I administered, governed
خصومة (٩)	lawsuit
شوّال (١١)	the Islamic month of Shawwal
أبطأ (١٢)	to be slow, to hesitate
امتنع (١٣)	to decline
ربيبة (١٤)	stepdaughter
خَيار (١٦)	the finest
رسوم الشرع (١٩)	guidelines of the *sharia* law
مكث (١٩)	residing, remaining
عوائد (sing.عادة) (١٩)	custom
حسم (٢٠)	to put an end to
شهّر (٢٢)	to publicly expose, denounce
مبادرة (٢٢)	initiative
الأَزِقة (sing.زُقاق) (٢٢)	alleys, side streets, lanes

Comprehension Exercises

A. Answer the following questions in complete Arabic sentences (numbers refer to the lines in which the information can be found):

١. كيف صوّر ابن بطوطة أهل جُزُر المالديف في كتابه؟ (١-٤)

_____

_____

_____

٢. ماذا طلب ابن بطوطة من الوزير سليمان؟ وماذا كانت نصيحة الوزير سليمان له؟ وما رأيُك فيها؟ (١١)

_____

_____

_____

٣. لماذا حاول ابن بطوطة تغيير عادات نساء هذه الجُزُر في الملابس؟ وهل نجح في ذلك؟ (٥-٦)

_____

_____

_____

٤. كم مرةً تزوّج ابن بطوطة في هذه القصة؟ (١٤-١٧-١٨)

_____

_____

_____

٥ . هل كان ابن بطوطة قاضياً عادلاً[147] أم حازماً[148]؟ لماذا؟ (٢٢)

_____

_____

_____

B. Find Arabic phrases in the text that approximate the following meanings in English:

1. their weapon is prayer :_____

2. she is in charge of herself :_____

3. she was one of the best women :_____

4. she first thing I changed :_____

5. whomever was found having not prayed :_____

C. Find Arabic synonyms or equivalents in the text for the following words and phrases:

١ .   نـــاس : _____

٢ .   رفضـــتْ : _____

٣ .   بيـــوت : _____

٤ .   بعد : _____

٥ .   حـــوالي : _____

---

147 fair
148 firm, tough

D. Find Arabic antonyms or opposites for each of the following words in the text and use each in a complete sentence:

١.   حـلال : _____

_____

٢.   ضعيفـة : _____

_____

٣.   يغطـي : _____

_____

٤.   صادقـة : _____

_____

٥.   مُطلّـق : _____

_____

Interpreting the Text

١. لماذا وصف ابن بطوطة أهل هذه الجزر بالصلاح والإيمان؟ (١-٤)

_____

_____

_____

٢. ما رأيك في أزياء نساء هذه الجُزُر؟ وهل لهذا الزيّ أبعاد[149] ثقافية؟ (٥-١٠)

_____

_____

_____

---

149 dimensions

٣. لماذا لم يستطع الوزير أن يُجْبِر ¹⁵⁰ ابنته على الزواج من ابن بطوطة؟ (١١-١٣)

---

٤. ما أبرز عادات الطلاق التي ذكرها ابن بطوطة وكيف تعامل معها؟ (١٩-٢٢)

---

٥. بماذا تفسر زيجات ابن بطوطة المتعددة خلال فترة قصيرة؟ (١١-١٨)

Grammar, Structure, and Context Clues

1. In the last part of line 22 "فمن وجدوه لم يصلّ ضربته وشهرته" the word مَن
    carries the familiar meaning of 'who,' although here it is not used as a
    question word, but rather as synonymous with الذي 'whom, that, which.'
    Note also that in such a clause, Arabic requires a pronoun with each verb
    to refer back to the person or thing in question. In English, we would say
    'whomever was found not having prayed, I beat and displayed publicly.'
    In Arabic, the three instances of the pronoun suffix ـهُ are all required,
    but not translated into English. Literally, this would read "whomever *he*
    was found having not prayed, I beat *him* and I displayed *him*."

2. This text involves extensive use of the feminine plural, both in verbs
    and pronouns, since one of Ibn Battuta's chief concerns is the behav-
    ior of the women of the islands. As you read the text, pay particular
    attention to:

---

150 to force, compel

- the possessive suffix هُنَّ (their), feminine equivalent of هُم

- the direct object pronoun هُنَّ (them), similar to above, using context to determine which use is intended

- the verb conjugation يفعلنَ, feminine equivalent of يفعلون

With these in mind, how would you translate the following:

–أَكثرُهنَّ: _____

(What is the word to which هنَّ is attached? أَكثرُ means 'most,' and thus, we have an *idaafa* meaning, 'most of them)

– آمرهنَّ: _____

(Here, the first word is a verb 'to command,' thus, هنَّ is an object pronoun — 'command them)
Try this sentence:

–لا يغطّينَ رؤوسهنَّ: _____

3. Ibn Battuta's general description includes many *idaafa* constructions and nominal sentences. This means there are often no verbs to use as clues to separate phrases. The repetition or omission of words, as well as the case endings, helps to identify the phrases. Take the first sentence as an example:

أهلُ هذه الجزائر أهلُ صلاح وديانة وإيمان صحيح ونيّة صادقة

The ٗ case ending on أهلُ and the definite article on الجزائر indicate that this is an *idaafa*. The noun أهلُ following it indicates that the first أهلُ is being equated to the second. Without the case endings, context could also help. The repetition of أهل indicates that the definite أهل is being equated to (and described as) the indefinite أهل (the people of these islands are a people of…). Everything after the first three words is a long *idaafa*. Start with the first two words in the *idaafa*, أهلُ صلاح (a people of righteousness) to this are added all the other things describing this people (religion, true faith, and good intentions).

4. The word عهد in line 2 refers to a 'custom' or 'acquaintance.' In the phrase "لا عهد لهم", remember that ل can mean 'belonging to' (like عند) and that in Arabic expressions of possession, the thing possessed is the subject. Here this would be rendered as, '(there is) no custom belonging to them,' a phrase meaning 'they have no custom of,' 'no knowledge of,' or 'habit of,' and so on. In this case, what is it of which the inhabitants of the Maldives have no custom regarding? How has that endeared them to Ibn Battuta, despite their shortcomings in *sharia* law?

5.   The phrase "ما عدا" in line 10 means 'besides' or 'except.' As used in the sentence: "ما عدا ذلك", it has the meaning of 'except for that' or 'other than that' and is used to qualify a negative statement, as in this case"لم تكن لي عليه قدرة" (I did not have the ability). Coming after his preceding description of requiring women to cover themselves when coming to see him, it acknowledges he had no further success.

6.   The preposition ل is among the most flexible of words. In line 14, after the wazir's daughter has declined to marry Ibn Battuta, the *wazir* asks "هل لك أن تتزوّج", a very casual phrase asking "how about marrying…" (literally, "is it with you to marry"). The intent of this choice of phrase, in a recollection written long after the event, is to convey the casual, off-hand nature of the suggestion, rather than using هل تفضل or هل تريد or something more formal.

7. Ibn Battuta uses the verb تنزّه to mean 'keep away, keep far above' in line 4. This verb can also be used to mean 'to promenade, stroll' as in "تنزّه الولد في الحديقة مع أسرته". The context in each case is the best clue as to the intended meaning.

Writing Exercises

A. Translate the following sentences into Arabic, using vocabulary from this reading. Hints in parentheses indicate which lines to look at for similar structures:

1. The people of this city are a people of hospitality[151] (1):

    _____

    _____

    _____

2. He has no knowledge of (acquaintance with) failure (2):

    _____

    _____

    _____

3. He was one of the best of friends (16):

    _____

    _____

    _____

4. How about going to the cinema this evening? (14):

    _____

    _____

    _____

ضيافة 151

5. Whomever arrived late, didn't enter (22):

_____

_____

_____

B. Rearrange the words below into coherent sentences:

١. الجزائر أهل أهل نظافة وضيافة هذه

_____

_____

_____

٢. يغير الجزائر يستطع بطوطة أن ابن عوائد أهل لم

_____

_____

_____

٣. الوزير رفضتْ ابن الزواج بطوطة بنت من

_____

_____

_____

٤. اجتمع حفلة زواج الناسُ بطوطة ليشاهدوا ابن

_____

_____

_____

٥. سلطانة جداً امرأة كانت قوية الجزائر

_____

_____

_____

Discussion Questions

١. في رأيك، هل نجح ابن بطوطة في تغيير عادات أهل هذه الجزائر؟

٢. هل زواج المصلحة [152] ظاهرة منتشرة في عالمنا المعاصر؟

٣. ما أسباب الصراع/ التصادم بين التعاليم الدينية والأعراف الثقافية وتأثيره على المجتمع؟

٤. كيف أثرت عزلة هذه الجزائر في المحيط الهندي على أسلوب أهلها وطريقة معيشتهم؟

٥. هل تلعب التجارة الدولية دورا مهما في نشر الأفكار الثقافية والدينية؟ كيف؟

Research and Presentation

ابحثوا في الإنترنت عن تاريخ وصول الإسلام إلى جزائر الملديف واكتبوا مقالاً عن هذا التاريخ.

---

152   marriage for reasons other than love

17

The Rich Kingdom of China

ذكر أهل الصين (Quanzhou, China, 1345)

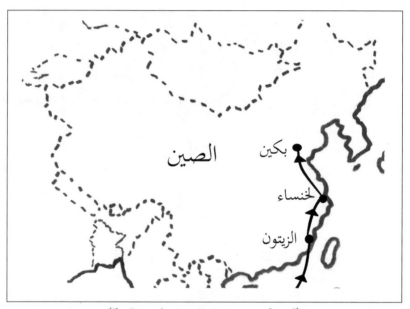

(Ibn Battuta's trip to Beijing is unconfirmed)

Although Ibn Battuta is best known in the Western world as the Arab travel-er who reached China—prompting frequent comparisons to Marco Polo—he actually spent very little of his time in China. Some scholars have even questioned whether Ibn Battuta actually visited all the places and witnessed all the sights in China that he mentioned in his memoirs. His descriptions sound exaggerated to modern readers, no doubt, but nonetheless offer a valuable picture of how a distinguished Muslim scholar of the medieval period viewed the distant kingdom. China was, at the time, the only true rival to Islamic civilization in terms of political power, wealth, culture, and learning, and Ibn Battuta's observations show both tremendous admiration and amusement at the achievements of this civilization.

As in his visits to India and Southeast Asia, the distinguished Muslim jurist remarks on the religious habits of the people he observed. While clearly labeling the Chinese as كفّار (non-believers), and pointing out their eating habits, his overall tone is one of awe. Ibn Battuta is keen to point out that Muslims in China were well treated. The majority of his text, however, centers not on religious issues, but economic ones. The picture of Chinese society that emerges from his description is one of incredible wealth in which gold and silver abound.

Ibn Battuta's journey from the Maldives to China was long and frequently disrupted . Having left the island paradise under pressure, and lost his official caravan, he still desired to see the most distant kingdom. His travels landed him in present-day Indonesia, Malaysia, and finally Vietnam, where he boarded a ship to China. He arrived at the major port of Quanzhou, known to Muslim traders as الزيتون (the Olive), a city known as the start of the 'Maritime Silk Road,' the counterpart to the famous land route through Central Asia. The Arabic name of the city, in fact, provides the origin of the word 'satin,' referring to the fabric. Accordingly, the traveler marveled at the abundance of silk and the ease of its production, making the ironic observation that cotton (the famous export commodity of Islamic Egypt) was of far greater value in China than the silk, which was treasured in the Middle East and Europe. While Ibn Battuta spent much of his time in the trading ports of coastal China, he also describes a visit to Beijing. Based on the vagueness of his report and its inaccuracies, however, the trip to Beijing may actually have been the re-telling of secondhand stories.

At the time of Ibn Battuta's visit, China was under the control of the Yuan (Mongol) Dynasty (1271–1368). Despite the devastation that the Mongols had caused in the Arab world, by the time of Ibn Battuta's visit, the Mongol Dynasty had brought stability to China, while encouraging the entry of foreigners to the country. The dynasty would collapse shortly after Ibn Battuta's visit, but he had the good fortune to arrive when conditions for a foreign and particularly a Muslim visitor were at their most favorable. In fact, the Mongol khan, Kublai, had appointed Sayyid Ajjal Shams al-Din Omar al-Bukhari, a Muslim from the Central Asian city of Bukhara as governor of the province of Yunnan.

Ibn Battuta's stay in China was very brief, perhaps six months in length. His official mission as an ambassador of the sultan of Delhi had failed, but he nonetheless got to see the country as a tourist. By the end of 1346, Ibn Battuta left China with no particular destination in mind, but likely intending to make another Hajj journey.

From the Writings of Ibn Battuta

Ibn Battuta describes the religious habits of the people of China:

(١) أهلُ الصين كفّار يعبدون الأصنام ويحرقون موتاهم كما تفعل الهنود. (٢) وكفّار الصين يأكلون لحوم الخنازير والكلاب ويبيعونها في أسواقهم.

Ibn Battuta's notes on the conditions of Muslims in China:

(٣) في كلّ مدينة من مدن الصين مدينة للمسلمين ينفردون بسكناهم، ولهم فيها المساجد لإقامة الجمعات وسواها. (٤) وهم معظمون محترمون.

The wealth of China, especially its silk industry:

(٥) وهم أهلُ رفاهية وسعة عيش إلاّ أنهم لا يحتفلون في مطعم ولا ملبس. (٦) وترى التاجر الكبير منهم الـذي لا تحصى أمواله كثرة، وعليه جبة قطن خشنة. (٧) وجميعُ أهل الصين إنما يحتفلون في أواني الذهب والفضّة. (٨) والحرير عندهم كثيرٌ جدّاً لأنّ الـدود تتعلّق بالثمار وتأكلُ منها (٩) فلا تحتاج إلى كثير مؤنة (١٠) ولذلك كثر، وهو لباس الفقراء والمساكين بها (١١) ولولا التجار لما كانت له قيمة (١٢) ويباع الثوب الواحد من القطن عندهم بالأثواب كثيرة من الحرير.

Ibn Battuta's admiration for the artistic talents of the Chinese:

(١٣) وأهلُ الصين أعظمُ الأمم إحكاماً للصناعات أشدّهم إتقاناً فيها (١٤) وذلك مشهورٌ من حالهم، قد وصَفه الناس في تصانيفهم فأطنبوا فيه (١٥) وأمّا التصويرُ فلا يُجاريهم أحدٌ في إحكامه من الرـوم ولا من سواهم، (١٦) فإن لهم فيه اقتداراً عظيماً.

Ibn Battuta relates an amusing anecdote as evidence of the artistic skill of the Chinese:

(١٧) ومن عجيب ما شاهدت لهم من ذلك اني ما دخلتُ قطّ مدينة من مدنهم ثمّ عـدتُ إليها إلاّ ورأيتُ صورتي وصور أصحابي منقوشةً في الحيطان والكواغـد، موضوعةً في الأسـواق. (١٨) ولقـد دخلـتُ إلى مدينة السلطان فمررتُ عـلى سـوق النقّاشين ووَصَلتُ إلى قصر السلطان مـع أصحابي (١٩) ونحنُ عـلى زيّ العراقيـين (٢٠) فلمّا عـدت مـن القـصر عشيّاً مـررتُ بالسـوق المذكورة فرأيتُ صـور صـورتي وصـور أصـحابي منقوشـةً في كاغـد قد ألصقوه بالحـائط (٢١) فجعل كلّ واحـد منّا ينظرُ إلى صورة صاحبه لا تخطـئ شيئاً من شبهه

Vocabulary

يَنفَرِد (٣)	to be unique, to be segregated
سِوى (٣)	except, other
رفاهية (٥)	luxury
يحتفلون (٥)	to celebrate, be interested in
تُحصى (٦)	to be counted, be calculated
خَشِنة (٦)	rough
تَعلّق بـ (٨)	to hang on
ثِمار (٨)	fruits
مَؤنة (٩)	supply
أطْنب (١٤)	to exaggerate
التصويرُ (١٥)	making a picture (modern usage — photography)
قَطّ (١٧)	never, under no circumstance
كواغد (.sing—كاغد) (sing.) (١٧)	sheets of paper
عشيّاً (٢٠)	in the evening
ألصق (٢٠)	to stick, affix
تُخطِئ (٢١)	to make a mistake

Comprehension Exercises

A. Answer the following questions in complete Arabic sentences (numbers refer to the lines in which the information can be found):

١. ما ديانة أهل الصين في رأي ابن بطوطة؟ (١)

_____

_____

_____

٢. كيف وأين كان يسكن مسلمو الصين في عهد ابن بطوطة؟ (٣-٤)

_____

_____

_____

٣. ماذا كانت قيمة الحرير بالنسبة لقيمة القطن في الصين؟ (١٢)

_____

_____

_____

٤. ماذا يلبس الفقراء في الصين؟ (١٠)

_____

_____

_____

٥. ماذا رأى ابن بطوطة في السوق؟ (٢٠)

_____

_____

_____

B. Find Arabic phrases in the text that approximate the following meanings in English:

1. uncountable:_____

2. the greatest in the world :_____

3. no one can equal them :_____

4. any one of their cities :_____

5. a flawless representation :_____

C. Find Arabic synonyms or equivalents in the text for the following words and phrases:

١ . يُقدّس : _____

٢ . رَغَـد : _____

٣ . الفواكه : _____

٤ . يُنافِس : _____

٥ . بَدْلــة : _____

D. Find Arabic antonyms or opposites for each of the following words in the text and use each in a complete sentence:

١ . يشتري : _____

_____

٢. مُحْتَقَـرون : _____

٣. ناعمـة : _____

٤. مغمـور : _____

٥. الأغنيـاء : _____

Interpreting the Text

١. كيف تختلف عادات ومعتقدات أهل الصين عن تعاليم الإسلام، ولماذا اعتبرهم ابن بطوطة كفاراً؟ (١-٤)

_____

_____

_____

٢. كيف كانت الأحوال المعيشية للمسلمين في الصين إبّان[153] هذه الفترة؟ (٤)

_____

_____

_____

٣. . لماذا كان الحرير رخيصاً ووفيراً في الصين؟ (٥-١١)

_____

_____

---

153 during

٤. هل عَدَّ ابن بطوطة الصينَ من البلاد الغنية التي زارها؟ ما الأدلة على ذلك؟ (٥-١١)

_____

_____

_____

٥. كيف وصف ابن بطوطة إتقان أهل الصين للصناعات المختلفة وكيف قارَنَ بينهم و بين
غيرهم في هذا المجال؟ (١٣-١٦)

_____

_____

_____

Grammar, Structure, and Context Clues

1. In discussing the silk industry, in line 11, Ibn Battuta notes: "لولا التجار
لما كانت له قيمة". The first term, لولا, a compound of the counterfactual
'if' and 'not,' means 'if not for...' the item following it, in this case,
'the merchants.' This construction is common in classical writing, and
can be made using a pronoun suffix (such as لولاه, 'if not for him'). The
second part of the sentence, the 'then' clause, is introduced by ل, here
stating that 'it (silk) would have no value.' As with other uses of لو, the
result clause is in the perfect tense, although the result is clearly hypothetical, and has not taken place.

2. In describing the habits of the Chinese, Ibn Battuta makes several
uses of the verb احتفل بـ (see lines 5–9). This verb is most commonly
used to mean 'to celebrate,' as in: نحتفل بعيد الاستقلال. A second use of
the verb, with the same following preposition—بـ—is used to mean
'concern oneself with.' That is the meaning intended here:

لا يحتفلون في مطعم ولا ملبس (5) — They do not concern themselves with
food or clothing

يحتفلون في أواني الذهب والفضّة (7) — They concern themselves with gold and silver vessels

3. In line 17, Ibn Battuta notes: "ما دخلتُ قطّ مدينة من مدنهم"(I never entered any of their cities) without returning later to find a picture of himself. The word قَطُّ here is not related to the verb 'to cut' (قَطَّ) or the word for a male cat (قِطّ), but rather is used to add an emphatic 'ever' to a statement, or, as in this case of a negative assertion, 'never.' As is the case here, it is typically used with negative sentences.

4. The particle ما can be a tricky word, as it has many usages, particularly in classical writing. Note the use of ما twice in line 17. Additionally, both instances are followed by past-tense verbs. One of these, however, means 'what' and the other is a negating particle. Ibn Battuta begins by saying it was 'amazing' (من عجيب), with ما شهدتُ, here to be translated as "what I saw." The next instance, ما دخلتُ , means "I did not enter." The following قطّ (see above) further renders this "I never entered…" This sentence provides a good example of how context and surrounding idioms indicate the correct reading of the two phrases.

Writing Exercises

A. Translate the following sentences into Arabic, using vocabulary from this reading. Hints in parentheses indicate which lines to look at for similar structures:

1. The inhabitants of this country worship idols (1):

_____

_____

_____

2. The Muslims were mostly respected in China (4):

_____

_____

_____

3. He would often revel in his wealth (7):

_____

_____

_____

4. If not for the silk trade, the city would be poor (11):

_____

_____

_____

5. No one could equal his skill in music (15):

_____

_____

_____

B. Rearrange the words below into coherent sentences:

١. مدينة في ممتاز مدن سورية في من سوق كلّ

_____

_____

_____

٢. أهلُهم ملبس مطعم لا يحتفلون في ولا

_____

_____

_____

٣. يُجاريه الفنّ إحكامه فلا أحدٌ في أمّا

_____

_____

_____

٤. ما قطّ من مدن مسجداً وسط مصر إلاّ ورأيتُ دخلتُ جميلاً في المدينة مدينة

_____

_____

_____

٥. لولا لما مساعدة الامتحان نجحتُ في أستاذي

_____

_____

_____

Discussion Questions

١. لخّصوا[154] الإيجابيات والسلبيات التي ذكرها ابن بطوطة عن أهل الصين؟

٢. كيف تختلف فنون أهل الصين عن الفنون الإسلامية؟ وما العوامل التي قد تؤثر على تطوّرها وتنوّعها؟

٣. هل يوجد في وصف ابن بطوطة لأحوال أهل الصين ما يدّل على اتباعهم لمبدأ التسامح الديني من أجل تحقيق فكرة التعايش[155] الإنساني؟ كيف؟

٤. يعد مفهوم "الزُهد[156]" من السُنن[157] الإسلامية المحمودة. كيف ظهرت بعض صور الزهد في مجتمع أهل الصين على اختلاف ديانتهم وعقائدهم، وما دلالة ذلك من وجهة نظركم؟

٥. قانون 'العَرض والطَلب'[158] هو أحد القوانين الأساسية في علم الاقتصاد ويلعب دوراً رئيسياً في تحديد الأسعار وتثمين السلع[159] وتشكيل[160] الأسواق، فهل هناك أمثلة لهذا القانون مما قرأتم في هذا النص؟

Research and Presentation

ابحثوا في الإنترنت عن أحوال المسلمين في الصين اليوم واكتبوا مقالا مقارناً بين الوضع الحالي وبين الوضع في عصر ابن بطوطة.

---

154 summarize
155 coexistence
156 asceticism
157 norms
158 supply and demand
159 goods
160 formation

18
Islamic Spain (al-Andalus)

ذكر البلاد الأندلُسيّة (Spain, 1350)

All that remained of Islamic Spain was the Emirate of Granada.

Among the events that shaped Ibn Battuta's worldview, the decline of Islamic Spain was certainly one of the most profound. Growing up in Morocco, he lived a safe distance from the Mongol and Turkic invasions that had devastated Iraq and kept the Levant on alert. The kingdom that once unified Morocco and Spain, however, had some great centers of Islamic learning rivaling those in Baghdad and Cairo. The more-than-700-year campaign by which Islamic cities in Iberia fell to Christian European armies (culminating in the fall of Granada in 1492) was nearing its final stages by Ibn Battuta's day. Great Islamic cities like Toledo, Zaragoza, and the capital of Cordoba had fallen and their scholars were forced to flee to Morocco and Tunis, while the sole remaining Islamic emirate in Granada was in retreat.

al-Andalus

When Islamic armies first crossed into Iberia in AD 711 under Umayyad general Tariq Ibn Ziyad (طـارق بـن زيـاد), for whom Gibraltar (جبـل طـارق) is named, the region was ruled by the Visigoths. The Arabic term for the area, al-Andalus (الأندلـس) is derived from the Vandals, who had previously controlled it. The Spanish language did not exist at the time, and indeed Spanish identity largely grew out of the campaign against the Islamic states. Some of the greatest medieval Muslim and Jewish scholars, including Ibn Rushd, Ibn Sina, and Moses Maimonides worked in Arabic in al-Andalus.

Ibn Battuta, himself from the coastal city of Tangier on the straits of Gibraltar, was very concerned about developments in al-Andalus. Upon returning to Morocco, he traveled to the city of Ceuta (سَـبتة), the main port of entry for those fleeing from al-Andalus. Here, he was to hear disturbing reports of the fighting in Spain. In Ibn Battuta's long absence, the Moroccan king Abu al-Hassan (ruled 1331–51) had launched a military campaign to reverse the Spanish Reconquista, scoring several impressive ground and sea victories. Despite Ibn Battuta's effusive praise for the king's efforts at *jihad*, the Islamic force was decisively defeated in 1340 and rather than dreams of conquest, the king spent the rest of his reign in fear of a Spanish invasion. When Ibn Battuta returned to his home, the situation in Spain was perilous. The armies of Castilian king Alfonso XI were besieging the gateway of Gibraltar, threatening to cut off the remaining Islamic state in Europe.

Having been a traveler, diplomat, and judge, Ibn Battuta now eagerly signed up to be a warrior. He joined a Moroccan military expedition and set sail for Gibraltar to fight the advancing Castilians. By the time he arrived, however, the Black Plague had killed off Alfonso XI and much of his force and put an end to military operations. Possessed of a remarkable constitution, Ibn Battuta again survived the epidemic and took the opportunity to return to his favorite activity—traveling.

As in many of his travels, he would find his trip to al-Andalus disappointing. The glories of the past were gone, and he now found a besieged state fighting for its existence. Even more bitter than the demise of Baghdad, the decline of al-Andalus hit much closer to home. Ironically, however, although Ibn Battuta did not get to meet any of the great leaders or scholars of the type he managed to find in far-off corners of the world, he did have a brief encounter with a young writer who was to have a much greater impact on his legacy. Ibn Juzayy, a minor poet from Granada, who would later move to Morocco, would be commissioned to write the story of Ibn Battuta's travels. It is Ibn Juzayy's version that we study today.

From the Writings of Ibn Battuta

Hearing of the attacks by Castilian King Alfonso, Ibn Battuta travels to join in the defense of Islamic Spain:

(١) أردتُ أن يكونَ لي حظٌّ من الجهـاد والرّبـاط، (٢) فركبتُ البحـرَ مـن سَبتة في شَطّي لأهـل أصيـلا. (٣) فوصَلـتُ إلى بـلاد الأندلـس، حَرَسَها الله تعـالى، حيـثُ الأُجـر موفورٌ للسـاكن، (٤) والثـوابُ مذخـورٌ للمقيم والظاعـن، (٥) وكان ذلك إثـرَ مـوت طاغيـة الـروم الفونس، (٦) وحصاره الجبل عـشرةَ أشهر، (٧) وظنّـه أنّـه يستولي عـلى مـا بقي مـن بـلاد الأندلـس للمسلمين، (٨) فأخـذه الله مـن حيـثُ لم يَحتَسِب، (٩) وماتَ بالوبـاء الـذي كان أشـدّ النـاس خوفـاً منـه.

Despite the end of King Alfonso's threat, Ibn Battuta finds that Spain is still very much beset with conflict:

(١٠) وَجـدتُ بهـا جماعـة مـن الفرسـان متوجهـين إلى مالقـة، (١١) فـأردتُ التوجّـه في صحبتهـم، (١٢) ثـمّ إنّ الله تعـالى عصَمني بفضلـه، (١٣) فتوجهـوا قبـلي فـأُسروا في الطريـق، وخرجـتُ في أثرهـم، (١٤) فلـمّا جـاوزت حـوز مربلـة ودخلـتُ في حـوز سُـهيل (١٥) ثـمّ تقدّمـتُ إلى دار هنالـك فوجـدتُ فرسـاً مقتـولاً، (١٦) فبينـما أنا هنالـك سمعتُ الصيـاح مـن خلفي وكنـتُ قـد تقدّمـتُ أصحابي، (١٧) فعـدتُ إليهـم (١٨) فوجـدتُ معهـم قائـد حصن سُـهيل فأعلمني أن أربعة أجفـان للعـدوّ ظهـرَت هنالـك (١٩) ونـزل بعـض عمارتهـا إلى البـرّ، ولم يكـن الناظـور بالبـرج، (٢٠) فمـرّ بهـم الفرسـان الخـارجون من مربلـة، وكانـوا اثنـى عـشر، (٢١) فقتل النصـارى أحدهـم وفـرّ واحـدٌ وأُسِـرَ العـشرة، وقُتِـلَ معهـم رجـلٌ حـوّات، وهـو الـذي وجـدت قفّتـه مطروحـة بـالأرض، (٢٢) فبـتُ عنـده

بحصن الرّابطة المنسوبة إلى سهيل، (٢٣) والأجفان المذكورة مرساةٌ عليه.

Arriving at the seat of Islamic Spain, Granada:

(٢٤) سافرتُ منها إلى مدينة غرناطة قاعدة بلاد الأندلس وعروس مدنها، (٢٥) وخارجُها لا نظيرَ له في بلاد الدنيا، (٢٦) وهو مسيرة أربعينَ ميلاً يخترقه نهر شَنِّيل المشهور وسواه من الأنهار الكثيرة والبساتين والجنان والرياض (٢٧) والقصورُ والكرومُ محدقة بها من كلّ جهة. (٢٨) ومن عجيب مواضعها عينُ الدمع، (٢٩) وهو جبل فيه الرياض والبساتين لا مثيلَ له بسواها. (٣٠) وكان ملك غرناطة في عهد دخولي إليها السلطان أبو الحجّاج يوسف ابن السلطان أبي الوليد إسماعيل (٣١) ولم ألقه بسبب مرضٍ كان به، (٣٢) وبعثَتْ إليّ والدتُه الحرّة الصالحة الفاضلة بدنانير ذهب.

Vocabulary

حظّ (١)	chance, fortune
سَبتة (٢)	Ceuta, a city in northern Morocco across the straits from Gibraltar, now controlled by Spain
أصيلا (٢)	Asila, fortified town on the Moroccan coast, close to Ceuta
الأندلس (٣)	al-Andalus, the name for Islamic Spain
مذخور (٤)	is provided, stored
ظاعن (٤)	transitory
طاغية (٥)	tyrant
الفنش (٥)	King Alfonso XI of Castile from 1325–50
الجبل (٦)	the mountain, here meaning Gibraltar
وباء (٩)	epidemic, plague
مالقة (١٠)	Malaga, coastal city of Spain
عصمني الله (١٢)	God protected/saved me
حوز (١٤)	enclosure

مَربلة (١٤)	Marbella, a city in Spain close to Malaga
سُهيل (١٤)	city in Spain, now called Fuengirola
صِياح (١٦)	shouting, yelling
أجْفان (١٨) (.sing جَفن)	scabbards, sheaths
ناظور (١٩)	observer, watcher
النصارى (٢١)	Christians
حوّات (٢١)	fisherman
قُفّة (٢١)	basket
غِرناطة (٢٤)	Granada, city and Emirate in Southern Spain
شَنّيل (٢٦)	Genil River, tributary of the Guadalquivir
جِنان (.sing جنّة) (٢٦)	paradises
رياض (.sing روضة) (٢٦)	meadows, gardens
السلطان أبو الحجّاج يوسف (٣٠)	Yusuf I, sultan of Granada from 1333-1354
الحرّة (٣٢)	meritorious

Comprehension Exercises

A. Answer the following questions in complete Arabic sentences (numbers refer to the lines in which the information can be found):

١.   لماذا سافر ابن بطوطة إلى الأندلس؟ (١)

_____

_____

_____

٢.   ماذا كان هدف الملك الفونس عندما حاصر الجبل؟ (٧)

_____

_____

_____

٣. ماذا حدث للفرسان الاثني عشر الذين خرجوا من مربلة؟ (٢٠–٢١)

_____

_____

_____

٤. لماذا لم يلتق ابن بطوطة بسلطان غرناطة؟ (٣١)

_____

_____

_____

٥. ماذا بعثتْ أم السلطان إلى ابن بطوطة؟ (٣٢)

_____

_____

_____

B. Find Arabic phrases in the text that approximate the following meanings in English:

1. there are abundant rewards for one who lives there : _____

2. that was immediately after : _____

3. what remained of : _____

4. when I reached : _____

5. it has no parallel : _____

C. Find Arabic synonyms or equivalents in the text for the following words and phrases:

١. نصيب : ــ

٢. حماها الرّب : ــ

٣. ديكتاتور : ــ

٤. أردتُ أن أسافر برفقتهم : ــ

٥. صراخ : ـــ

D. Find Arabic antonyms or opposites in the text for each of the following words and phrases and use each in a sentence:

١. مُغادريـن : ـــ
ــ

٢. هاجمني : ـــ
ــ

٣. أفرجوا عنهـم : ـــ
ــ

٤. هنـاك الكثـير مثلُهـا : ـــ
ــ

٥. اجتمـع معـه : ـــ
ــ

Interpreting the Text

١. كيف وصف ابن بطوطة بلاد الأندلس؟ (٣-٥)

_____

_____

_____

٢. لماذا قال ابن بطوطة عن الملك الإسباني إنه "طاغية الروم"؟ وما دلالة هذا الوصف؟ (٥)

_____

_____

_____

٣. مَن كان 'العدو' بالنسبة لابن بطوطة في هذا النص؟ كيف عرفتم ذلك؟ (١٠-٢٢)

_____

_____

_____

٤. ما أبرز آثار ومعالم مدينة غرناطة التي رآها ابن بطوطة عند زيارته؟ (٢٥-٣٠)

_____

_____

_____

٥. ما الدور الذي قامت به أم سلطان غرناطة خلال فترة مرض السلطان وما مدى أهميته من وجهة نظركم؟ (٣٢)

_____

_____

_____

Grammar, Structure, and Context Clues

1. Ibn Battuta's term for Christians, 'النصارى' — collective of نصراني —
   comes from the name 'Nazareth,' referring to the birthplace of Jesus. It
   is the term used in the Quran (see Quran 2:62), and one used mostly
   by Muslims. The other familiar term, مسيحي (plural مسيحيون) is derived
   from the meaning 'Messiah' and is used primarily by Christians.

2. The Christian king of Castile, Alfonso XI—an enemy of the Muslims
   in al-Andalus—is referred to as "طاغية الروم" (the Tyrant of Rome).
   Alfonso was king of Castile in Spain, of course, and not of Rome. The
   term as it is used here refers to Christendom in general, and is the
   same one Ibn Battuta uses—in a much more positive sense—for the
   emperor of the remaining Byzantine Empire. The word is used more
   often in Islamic historical writing to refer to Byzantines and Orthodox, but can also refer to Rome and the Catholic Church in general.
   Here Ibn Battuta clearly wants to identify Alfonso as the leader in the
   forcible expansion of Catholicism and Christendom.

3. In line 16, Ibn Battuta uses the compound word بينما to describe when
   he heard a scream behind him. This compound, formed from بين and
   ما is used in this case to mean 'while,' or 'during,' with بين (between)
   giving the sense of 'in the middle of' something. The same compound
   can also mean 'whereas,' or 'however,' used to contrast two things. The
   context will tell which of these different meanings is intended:

   بينما كنتُ نائماً سرق اللص الكنز — *While* I was asleep, the thief stole the
   treasure

   توقعت أن الطقس سيكون بارداً بينما وجدته جميلاً — I expected the weather to be
   cold, *however*, I found it pleasant

   In this text, as the word is followed by أنا هنالك (I was there), it indicates that the 'while' meaning is intended.

4. At several points in the text, Ibn Battuta uses the demonstrative pronoun هنالِك to mean 'there' (for example, lines 15, 16, and 18). While this term carries the same general meaning as هناك, classical grammarians distinguished between three levels of proximity: near, middle, and far. The term هنا indicates closeness, or 'here,' while هناك indicates the middle distance, or 'there,' and the word هنالك refers to the farthest distance, similar to 'over there' in English. Ibn Battuta uses it here consistently to refer to distant places he was passing through.

Writing Exercises

A. Translate the following sentences into Arabic, using vocabulary from this reading. Hints in parentheses indicate which lines to look at for similar structures:

1. I wanted to have the good fortune to travel to the Middle East (1):

_____

_____

_____

2. While I was on the road to Damascus, I heard the army approaching (16):

_____

_____

_____

3. 3. I visited Delhi, seat of power in India, and the greatest of its cities (24):

_____

_____

_____

4. The city of Cairo has no equal in all the world (25):

_____

_____

_____

5. I did not meet the king during my visit due to the political crisis[161] in the country (31):

_____

_____

_____

B. Rearrange the words below into coherent sentences:

١. الفرسان إلى جماعة من بالطريق متوجهين المدينةَ وجدتُ

_____

_____

_____

٢. إلى مصر القاهرة قاعدة مدينة بلاد سافرتُ

_____

_____

_____

٣. لم زيارتي السلطان ألقَ بسبب مرضه خلال

_____

_____

أزمة 161

٤.   السيارة سمعتُ كنتُ في المدينة صوت حادث بينها

٥.   حسن[162] المغرب في عهد إليه الملك ملك كان سفري

Discussion Questions

١.   هل تضاربت[163] رغبة ابن بطوطة في الجهاد والقتال مع شَغَفه[164] وحبه الأبَديّ[165] للسفر
     والترحال؟ كيف؟

٢.   ماذا كانت أهمية مدينة غرناطة بالنسبة للخلافة الإسلامية في هذه الفترة؟ ولماذا أراد ابن
     بطوطة أن يشارك في الدفاع عنها؟

٣.   كان ابن بطوطة يُظْهِر دائما احتراما وتقديرا لمعظم زعماء بلاد العالم التي زارها سواء أكانوا
     من المسلمين أم من غير المسلمين، فلماذا كان موقفه[166] مغايرا[167] عند ذِكْره للملك الإسباني
     ألفونس؟

162   a name, Hassan
163   conflict
164   his passion
165   eternal
166   his attitude
167   different

٤. ما أخطر الأوبئة[168] المنتشرة هذه الأيام من وجهة نظركم، وما أفضل الطرق لعلاجها والحدّ من انتشارها؟

٥. كانت حضارة الأندلس الإسلامية من أعظم حضارات التاريخ الإنساني. كيف أثرت –في رأيكم– هذه الحضارة على الثقافة الأوربية الحديثة؟

Research and Presentation

ابحثوا في الإنترنت ثم اكتبوا مقالا تفصيليّاً عن أسباب تأثُّر اللغة الإسبانية باللغة العربية ومظاهر هذا التأثير[169] في المفردات والأبنية[170] اللغوية.

---

168 the plural of وباء
169 influence
170 structures

19
Return Home

(Damascus, Syria; Tangier and Fez, Morocco, 1348–50)
الوصول إلى طنجة

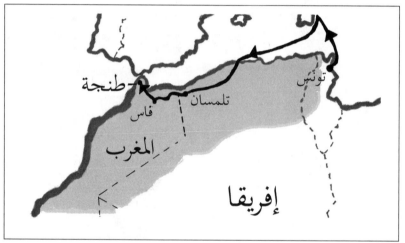

Upon his return, Ibn Battuta's home state had expanded

Ibn Battuta's twenty-year journey to the far corners of his known world had not been a deliberately planned one. Neither was his decision to return home. His service as a judge and ambassador had been rewarding and he showed no inclination toward ending that career when he reached the farthest point of his travels, in China. Yet just as favorable conditions had facilitated his continuing travels, unfavorable changes in the world were rendering his adopted homes inhospitable. As he headed back westward, he found the locations that had charmed him a few years earlier falling apart, one after another.

The Black Plague

No force shook Ibn Battuta's world more deeply that the plague that ravaged Asia, Europe, and Africa in the mid-fourteenth century. From 1346–53, the plague killed between a third and a half of Europe's population. The Middle East was devastated as well, with nearly 40 percent of Egypt's population dying. The plague is believed to have originated in Central Asia from fleas and spread along the Silk Road and maritime trade routes into Europe and the Middle East, with the first major reported outbreaks occurring the year Ibn Battuta left China. As he fled westward from the destruction, the panf demic was chasing him the entire year. The medieval world understood little of infectious diseases, generally believing the attacks to be the hand of God. Thus, Ibn Battuta was both shocked and puzzled to find no relief from the spreading calamity, no matter how far he traveled.

The plague also produced economic and political collapse in many of the places that once welcomed the traveler. On his eastward journey, Ibn Battuta had benefitted in many cases by unusually good relations between nations and particularly strong central leaders who respected Islamic law. His final summation of his travels gives a very succinct rundown of those who impressed him most. But these conditions were somewhat precarious to begin with, and the plague inspired persecution and isolation instead.

Ibn Battuta landed in India, his former home for six years, but the Sultanate of Delhi was beset by rebellion. He continued on to Persia, and found the once-mighty Ilkhanate falling apart, the pious Sultan Abu Sa'id murdered in the internal fighting. He then went to Syria,encountering incomprehensible death tolls firsthand in Damascus. Having been out of communication for so many years, he received the first news of his family, only to find that most had died years earlier. Then, passing through Cairo—the powerful center of the Islamic world that had impressed him so earlier—he found that Egypt's population had been devastated as well. In no small measure disturbed by the cataclysmic world events, he embarked on another Hajj. After a brief respite, however, he saw even the holy city of Mecca struck by the plague. With nowhere else to go, Ibn Battuta headed for home.

As always, Ibn Battuta proved to be a survivor and continued to serve. Upon his return, he placed himself in the service of the sultan of Morocco and would even venture on a military expedition to defend the Muslim communities in Spain.[171] Yet his greatest service would be one that he hardly anticipated. Fascinated by Ibn Battuta's recollections of the world, the sultan would commission a record to be written. Despite the terror and superstition of the plague-ravaged fourteenth century, he gives a relatively objective picture of the political, economic, and religious world of his day that was of great value to the ruler. Even as Ibn Battuta closed out that record with the required flattery and hyperbole for his patron, he gave compact survey of the major powers of the world of his time. Centuries later, it remains an unmatched account of the time.

From the Writings of Ibn Battuta

On his return journey through the Levant, Ibn Battuta finds the devastation of the Black Plague everywhere:

(١) في أوائـل شـهر ربيـع الأوّل عـام تسـعة وأربعيـن بلغنـي الخـبر في حلـب أن الوبـاء وقعَ بغـزة، (٢) وآنّـه انتهـى عـدد المـوتى فيهـا إلى زائـد عـلى الألـف في يوم واحـد، (٣) فسـافرت إلى حمـص فوجَـدت الوبـاء قـد وقعَ بهـا ومـات يـومَ دخـولي إليهـا نحـو ثلاثمائـة إنسـان. (٤) ثـمّ سـافرتُ إلى دمشـق ووَصَلتهـا يـوم الخميـس، (٥) وكان أهلُهـا قـد صامـوا ثلاثـة أيّـام، (٦) فخفّـفَ الله الوبـاء عنهـم، (٧) فانتهـى عـدد المـوتى عندهـم إلى ألفيـن وأربعمائـة في اليـوم.

As Ibn Battuta travels through the Arab countries, he receives news of his family after long separation, reflecting the hardship of travel and the difficulty of communication in his time:

(٨) ثـمّ سـافرنا إلى مدينـة دمشـق الشـام، (٩) وكانـت مـدّة مغيبي عنهـا عشـرين سـنة كاملة، (١٠) وكنـتُ تركـتُ بهـا زوجـةً لي حامـلاً (١١) وتعرفـت، وأنـا بـلاد الهنـد، أنّهـا ولـدت ولـداً ذكـراً (١٢) فحينَ وُصُـولي إلى دمشـق في هـذه الكـرة لم يكـن لي هَمٌّ إلاّ السـؤال عـن ولـدي، (١٣) فدخَلـتُ المسـجد فوُفّـقَ لي إمـامُ المالكيّـة، (١٤) وسـألته عـن الولـد، (١٥) فقـال: "مـات منـذ اثنـيّ عـشرة سـنة"، (١٦) فسـرتُ إليـه لأسـأله عـن والـدي وأهـلي،

---

171 See Lesson 18

Finally returning to his home in Morocco after an absence of twenty-four years, Ibn Battuta finds his return bittersweet:

(١٩) وَصَلـتُ إلى مدينـة تـازى، وبهـا تعرَّفـتُ خـبرَ مـوت والـدتي بالوبـاء، رحمهـا الله تعـالى، (٢٠) ولقـد زاد الله بـلاد المغـرب شرفـاً إلى شرَفهـا وفضـلاً إلى فضلهـا بإمامة مولانـا أمـير المؤمنـين الـذي مـدّ ظـلالَ الأمـن في أقطارهـا.

Ibn Battuta pays respect to his ruler, the sultan of Morocco, and takes care to place this ruler in the (politically) proper context of his world travels. In his extravagance nonetheless emerge Ibn Battuta's most lasting impressions of the world's leaders:

(٢١) فوصلـتُ...إلى حـضرة فـاس، (٢٢) فَمَثُلـتُ بـين يـدي مولانـا الأعظـم الإمـام الأكـرَم أمـير المؤمنـين المتوكّل عـلى ربّ العالمـين أبي عنـان، (٢٣) وصلَ الله علـوَّه وكبتَ عـدوَّه (٢٤) فأنْسَـتْني هيبتُـه هيبة سلطان العـراق، (٢٥) وحسنُه حسنَ ملك الهنـد، (٢٦) وحسنُ أخلاقـه حسـنَ خُلـق ملـك اليمن، (٢٧) وشـجاعتُه شـجاعةَ ملـك الـترك، (٢٨) وحلمُـه حلـمَ ملـك الـروم، (٢٩) وديانتُـه ديانـةَ ملـك تركستان، (٣٠) وعلمُـه علـمَ ملـك الجـاوة.

In the final summation of his many adventures, Ibn Battuta thanks God and his ruler:

(٣١) فوَصَلـتُ إلى حـضرة مولانـا أمـير المؤمنـين، أيّـده الله، فقبّلـتُ يـده الكريمـة، وأقمـتُ في كنـف إحسانه، (٣٢) بعـد طـول الرحلـة، (٣٣) والله تعـالى يشكرُ مـا أولانـيه مـن جزيل إحسـانه، (٣٤) ويمتّـع المسلمين بطول بقائـه. (٣٥) وههنا انتهت الرحلـة المسمّاة تحفـة النُّظـار، في غرائـب الأمصـار وعجائـب الأسـفار. (٣٦) والحمـدُ لله وسـلامٌ عـلى عبـاده الذيـن اصطفـى.

Vocabulary

أوائل (١)	early, the beginning of
ربيع الأوّل (١)	Rabi' al-Awwal, the third month of the Islamic Calendar
حلب (١)	Aleppo, city in northern Syria
الموتَى (٢)	the dead
حمص (٣)	Homs, city in central Syria
خفّفَ (٦)	to abate
مغيب (٩)	absence
ذَكَر (١١)	male
كَرّة (١٢)	time
وُفّقَ لـ (١٣)	be so lucky to find
مالكيّة (١٣)	Maliki, one of the four schools of *fiqh* or religious law in Sunni Islam, the one practiced by Ibn Battuta
سرتُ إلى (١٦)	I moved forward, went on
بقيد الحياة (١٨)	alive
تازى (١٩)	Taza, city in northern Morocco
إمامة (٢٠)	leadership, command
ظِلال (٢٠)	the shade of, the cover of
المتوكّل على الله (٢٢)	having trust in God
وصلَ الله علوّه (٢٣)	expression means: 'May God grant him success and continue his exaltedness.'
كَبَتَ (٢٣)	to suppress, repress
أنْسَتْني (٢٤)	it made me forget
هَيبة (٢٤)	prestige
حِلم (٢٨)	kindness, leniency
دِيانة (٢٩)	faith
الجاوة (٣٠)	Java, in current day Indonesia
كَنَف (٣١)	patronage
أولانيه (٣٣)	he offered me

Comprehension Exercises

A. Answer the following questions in complete Arabic sentences (numbers refer to the lines in which the information can be found):

١.   كم شخصاً مات بالوباء في يوم واحد في غزّة وحمص؟ (١–٣)

_____

_____

_____

٢.   كم سنةً مرت بين زيارة ابن بطوطة إلى دمشق لأول مرة ورجوعه إليها؟ (٩)

_____

_____

_____

٣.   ماذا حدث للابن الذي وَلَدَته زوجة ابن بطوطة في دمشق أثناء سفره؟ (١٥)

_____

_____

_____

٤.   ما الخبر الذي علِمَه ابن بطوطة عن عائلته عند رجوعه إلى المغرب؟ (١٩)

_____

_____

_____

٥.   ما الاسم الكامل لكتاب رحلة ابن بطوطة؟ (٣٥)

_____

_____

_____

B. Find Arabic phrases in the text that approximate the following meanings in English:

1. The early part of the month:_____

2. I had no concern but:_____

3. blotted out, caused me to forget:_____

4. lap of his kindness:_____

5. amazing places:_____

C. Find Arabic synonyms or equivalents in the text for the following words and phrases:

١ . في بداية:_____

٢ . فترة:_____

٣ . بلاد:_____

٤ . قَمَعَ:_____

٥ . جَمَال:_____

D. find Arabic antonyms or opposites for each of the following words in the text and use each in a complete sentence:

١ . أُنْـثـى :_____
_____

٢ . زادَ :_____

٣. حضـور :_____

٤. مُغـادرة :_____

٥. الخـوف والجُبْن :_____

Interpreting the Text

١. قال ابن بطوطة:"خفّفَ الله الوباء في دمشق بعد ثلاثة أيام من الصوم حيث انتهى عدد الموتَى عندهم إلى ألفين وأربعمائة في اليوم." كيف يعكس هذا القول حِدّة الوباء في البلد؟ (٥-٧)

_____

_____

٢. علم ابن بطوطة بخبر وفاة ابنه بعد سنوات طويلة. فما أسباب ذلك وما رأيكم في موقف ابن بطوطة من هذا الحَدَث؟ (١٥)

_____

_____

٣. ماذا حَدَثَ ببلاد المغرب خلال فترة مغيب ابن بطوطة عنها؟ (٢٠)

_____

_____

٤. 'حَمَلَتْ عودة ابن بطوطة إلى بلده في طيّاتِها١٧٢ مزيجًا١٧٣ من المشاعر المُخْتَلَطة'. ناقشوا هذه العِبارة (١٩-٢٠)

_____

_____

_____

٥. ما أبرز السمات المميزة لملوك الدول الذين قابلهم ابن بطوطة في رحلته؟ وما أوجه المقارنة بينهم وبين أبي عنان ملك المغرب؟ (٢١-٣٠)

_____

_____

_____

Grammar, Structure, and Context Clues

In line 24, Ibn Battuta begins a passage: "فأَنْسَتْنِي هيّبتُه هيبة سلطان العراق" and makes frequent use of the verb أنسى. This is a measure-IV (أَفْعَلَ) verb, coming from the familiar root ن-س-ي which you likely recognize as meaning 'to forget.' Like many measure-IV verbs, and similar to measure II (فَعَّلَ), it carries a causative meaning, in this case 'to cause to forget.' Measure-IV verbs, however, are often more polite or imply a less direct action of causation than measure II. Note the following examples:

دَخَلَ (to enter)

دَخَّلَ (to insert)

أَدْخَلَ (to allow in, lead in)

عَلَم (to know)

---

172 carried within itself, reflected
173 mixture

عَلَّمَ (to instruct)

أَعْلَمَ (to inform, apprise)

This conveys in a somewhat poetic sense that Ibn Battuta has been 'caused to forget' the many great leaders he encountered by the surpassing greatness of his own sovereign, rather than implying he has been forced to renounce something. Note also that measure-IV verbs are typically transitive, meaning they do not require a preposition. Further, this one takes two objects (the person caused to forget something, and the thing forgotten). These two factors make determining the subject and objects tricky. In the sentence "فَأَنْسَتْنِي هَيبتُهُ هيبة سلطان العراق" the *damma* on هيبتُهُ marks it as the subject, the suffix ني on the verb makes 'me' the direct object, leaving هيبة سلطان العراق as the other object. Thus, the esteem of the sultan of Morocco is eclipsing that of the sultan of Iraq.

6. In line 10, Ibn Battuta describes his return to Damascus after a long absence with "كنتُ تركتُ بها زوجةً لي حاملاً". The use of a perfect-tense verb following كان is an instance of the compound tense called the 'pluperfect' in English. This tense is usually translated as '…had done…' something. The كان thus refers to the time of Ibn Battuta's departure, at which the other action (تركتُ) had already been completed. Arabic often, inserts the particle قد in between the two verbs to indicate the difference in time frame, but not in this case. Note also that the accusative ending on زوجةً is there because the word is an indefinite object of تركتُ, not because of كان.

7. Note the participle حامِل in line 10, meaning 'pregnant' in this case, is not conjugated for gender, although, by definition, it refers to a female. The word حاملة would refer to something used for carrying or holding, and would thus be the wrong word for 'pregnant,' despite possibly seeming like the logical choice.

8. Finally, note in line 10 Ibn Battuta's construction "زوجةً لي". This is an example of using لِ to break up a possessive structure, and is common-ly used to stress the indefiniteness of the object. Here, Ibn Battuta wants to refer to '*a* wife of mine,' rather than 'my wife,' which would sound much more callous in the situation. As you know, following an indefinite noun immediately by the possessor, either another noun or a pronoun suffix, creates an *idaafa* and makes the first noun inherently definite. To keep the first noun as 'a' or 'an,' لِ is inserted to express possession without creating an *idaafa*. This is slightly different than using واحد من... or أحد..... which mean 'one of...' and would also sound rather callous here. Note the contrast:

صديق الرئيس (the president's friend) / صديق للرئيس (a friend of the president)

Writing Exercises

A. Translate the following sentences into Arabic, using vocabulary from this reading. Hints in parentheses indicate which lines to look at for similar structures:

1. At the beginning of December, I arrived in Damascus (1):

    _____

    _____

    _____

2. God lessened his sickness (6):

    _____

    _____

    _____

3. When I left Morocco, the king was still living (17-18):

_____

_____

_____

4. The beauty of Egypt caused me to forget all other places (24):

_____

_____

_____

5. Ibn Battuta visited many amazing lands (35):

_____

_____

_____

B. Rearrange the words below into coherent sentences:

١. كانت رجوعي عن بلدي عشرين مغيبي سنة عند مدّة

_____

_____

_____

٢. العالم جمال القاهرة جمال كل مدن أنْسَاني مدينة

_____

_____

_____

٣.   أهل فخفّفَ عنهم هذه قد ثلاثة الله الوباء المدينة صاموا أيّام كان

_____

_____

_____

٤.   عائلتي إلى إلاّ لم يكن لي همٌّ السؤال عن بلدي وُصُولي حينَ

_____

_____

_____

٥.   وأنا رحمها في مسافر أنّ ماتتْ الله أمي تعرفت

_____

_____

_____

Discussion Questions

١.   كشفت حكايات ابن بطوطة عن جوانب متعددة في شخصيته، فما أبرزها وما رأيكم فيها؟

٢.   هل كان قرار ابن بطوطة صائباً[174] عندما ترك بلده ورحل ليستكشف العالم؟ لماذا؟

٣.   ناقشوا مراحل تطور الاتصالات ونقل المعلومات على مرّ التاريخ وكيف أثّرت في صياغة[175] عالمنا المعاصر؟

٤.   "في السفر سبع فوائد" مقولة عربية نردّدُها[176] كثيراً في كلامنا، فما فوائد السفر في رأيكم؟

٥.   ما الدروس والعِبَر[177] المستفادة من رحلة ابن بطوطة؟

---

174   appropriate, correct
175   forming
176   say
177   lessons

Research and Presentation

ابحثوا في الإنترنت عن أحد أشهَر الرّحالة والمستكشفين على مَرّ[178] التاريخ واكتبوا مقالا عنه مُبيّنين[179] أوجه التشابه والاختلاف بين رحلته ورحلة ابن بطوطة.

---

178 throughout
179 demonstrating

20
To Mali and Timbuktu

ذكر السفر إلى مالي (Timbuktu, Mali, 1352–53)

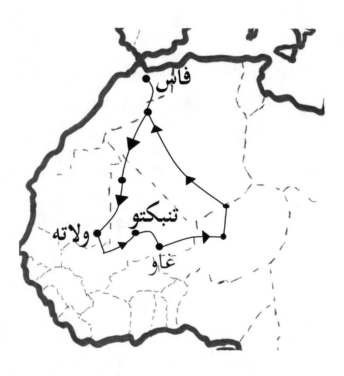

Ibn Battuta's final recorded journey

Chronologically the last of Ibn Battuta's travels, his journey through the Sahara to West Africa, brought some of his most outlandish accounts of life on the frontiers of Islam. After his return to his home in Morocco and the aborted military campaign into Spain, he set off again, this time south on a

1,500 mile journey through the Mali empire. His journey was likely inspired by the reports he had heard in Cairo of the *mansa* (king or sultan) of Mali, Mansa Musa, who had passed through Cairo on his Hajj journey with an impressive caravan of servants and riches. In any case, West Africa was the one last major frontiers of the Islamic world that Ibn Battuta had not visited and his curiosity was natural. Much of what we know today of the Mali Empire comes from Ibn Battuta's account.

The Mali Empire

Islam was introduced into West Africa by the Moroccan kingdom in the eleventh century CE. By 1230, about a century before Ibn Battuta's journey, a powerful kingdom developed centered on the Niger River, in modern-day Mali. By the time of Ibn Battuta's visit, the empire reached its greatest extent. Trade routes from West Africa into North Africa were the heart of Mali's strength. Above all, gold mining was the source of the empire's economic power. In Ibn Battuta's time, almost half the world's gold supply came from Mali. While this resource would later be exploited by colonial powers, the *mansa* of the Mali Empire maintained firm control of the gold trade in Ibn Battuta's time. In fact, it was required that any gold found in Mali be turned over immediately to the *mansa*. Thus, when Mansa Musa I visited Cairo in 1324, his wealth dazzled the citizens.

Like many of the places Ibn Battuta visited, Mali was still in the process of converting from its pre-Islamic past to the standardization of Islamic law and education. The transition was never completed, as old customs continued to mix with Islam, a mixture that Ibn Battuta described in detail. In particular, cannibals feature prominently in his accounts, and the Muslim *mansa's* cooperation with the cannibals comes as something as a shock to Ibn Battuta. Nevertheless, as one whose career was made largely by bringing Islamic law to newly converted lands, the challenge and rewards of serving in Mali must have been quite attractive to him. He praised the diligent efforts of some leaders to impose Islamic teaching on the youth and the *mansa's* efforts to build new mosques and centers of learning, yet was continuously scandalized by the pre-Islamic practices he saw. As in the Maldives, he noted the practice of women going topless in public, yet unlike that ocean paradise, the challenges in Mali seemed overwhelming. In any case, Ibn Battuta did not stay long, returning home in 1354, perhaps not realizing that his travels had finally come to an end.

The long since fabled Timbuktu had just been annexed by Mansa Musa after his return from the Hajj in 1324. Mansa Musa had ordered the construction of a palace and a mosque there, and by the fifteenth century it would become a major center of Islamic teaching and trade. Yet when Ibn Battuta visited, the city was just beginning to grow. For a man who was known to heap lavish praise on the cities he visited, Timbuktu hardly merited mention.

From the Writings of Ibn Battuta

Ibn Battuta meets the sultan of Mali and has cause to laugh:

(١) هـو السـلطان مَنْسَى سـليمان، ومَنْسَى معنـاه السـلطان، وسـليمان اسـمه، (٢) وهـو ملـك بخيـل لايُرجَـى منـه كبـيرُ عطـاء، (٣) تقدّمـتُ فسـلّمتُ عـلى مَنْسَى سـليمان، وأعلمـه القـاضي والخطيـب وابـنُ الفقيـه بحـالي، فأجابهـم بلسـانهم. (٤) ولـما انصَرفـتُ بُعـث إليّ الضيافـة، (٥) وقـال: "قُـم! قـد جـاءك قِـماش السـلطان وهديّتـه،" (٦) فقمـتُ وظننـتُ أنّهـا الخلـع والأمـوال، فـإذا هـي ثلاثـة أقـراص مـن الخبـز وقطعـةُ لحـم بقـريّ مقلـوّ بالغـرتي، وقرعـةٌ فيهـا اللبـنُّ رائـبٌ، (٧) فعندمـا رأيتُهـا ضحكـتُ وطـال تعجّبـي مـن ضعـف عقولهـم، وتعظيمهـم للـشيء الحقـير.

Ibn Battuta hears a story of cannibals in the Niger area:

(٨)أخبرني فربا مغـا أن مَـنْسَى موسى لـما وَصَلَ إلى هـذا الخليـجَ كان معـه قـاض مـن البيضـان يُكنَى بـأبي العبّـاس، ويُعـرف بالـدكّالي، (٩) فأحسـنَ إليـه بأربعـة آلاف مثقـال لنفقتـه، فلـمّا وَصلـوا إلى ميمـة شـكا إلى السـلطان بـأن الأربعـة آلاف مثقـال سُرقـت لـه مـن داره، (١٠) فدخـلَ دارَ القـاضي واشتـدّ عـلى خدّامـه، وهدّدهـم (١١) فقالـت لـه إحـدى جواريـه: "مـا ضـاعَ لـه شيء، وإنّـما دفنهـا بيـده في ذلـك الموضـع،" (١٢) فغضـبَ [السـلطان] عـلى القـاضي، ونفـاه إلى بـلاد الكفّـار الذيـن يأكلـون بنـي آدم، (١٣) فأقـامَ عندهـم أربـع سـنين، ثـمّ ردّه إلى بلـده، (١٤) و إنّـما لم يأكلـه الكفّـار لبياضـه لأنّهـم يقولـون إن أكلَ الأبيـض مـضرّ لأنّـه لم ينضـج، والأسـودُ هـو النضـج بزعمهـم.

A leader of the cannibals visits the sultan of Mali:

(١٥) قَدِمَتْ على السلطان مَنْسَى سليمان جماعةٌ من هؤلاء السودان الذين يأكلون بني آدم، معهم أميرٌ لهم، (١٦) فأكرَمهم السلطان، وأعطاهم في الضيافة خادمة، (١٧) فذبحوها وأكلوها ولطّخوا وُجوههم وأيديهم بدمها وأتوا السلطان شاكرين. (١٨) وأُخبرتُ أن عادتهم متى ما وَفدوا عليه أن يفعلوا ذلك، (١٩) وذُكِرَ لي عنهم أنّهم يقولون إن أطيب ما في لحوم الآدميّات الكفّ والثديُ.

Although Timbuktu was destined to become one of the most legendary cities of Africa, Ibn Battuta's visit there is quite short. He notes few remarkable
features:

(٢٠) ثمّ سافرنا... إلى مدينة تُنْبُكْتو، وبينها وبين النيل[180] أربعة أميال. (٢١) وأكثرُ سكّانها مسّوفة أهلُ اللثام، وحاكمها يسمّى فربا موسى، (٢٢) حضرتُ عنده يوماً، (٢٣) وقد قدّم أحد مسّوفة أميراً على جماعة، (٢٤) فجعل عليه ثوباً وعمامة وسروالاً، كلّها مصبوغةٌ، (٢٥) وأجلسَه على دَرَقة، ورفعَه كبراء قبيلته على رؤوسهم. (٢٦) وبهذه البلدة قبر الشاعر المفلق أبي إسحاق الساحلي الغرناطي (٢٧) وبها قبرُ سراج الدين بن الكُويك أحد كبار التجّار من أهل الإسكندرية. (٢٨) ومن تُنْبُكْتو ركبتُ النيل في مركب صغير منحوت من خشبة واحدة.

---

180   The river which Ibn Battuta assumes to be the Nile is actually the Niger

Vocabulary

مَنْسَى سليمان (١)	Mansa Sulayman, emperor of the Mali Empire, 1341–60
يُرجَى (٢)	to hope for, anticipate
الخطيب (٣)	religious speaker
انصَرفْتُ (٤)	I left, departed
قماش (٥)	textile
الخُلَع (٦) (sing.–خِلعة)	robes granted as a reward
قَرعة (٦)	jar, pitcher
الحقير (٧)	trifling, meager
مَنْسَى موسى (٨)	Mansa Musa, emperor of the Mali Empire, 1312–37
فربا (٨)	farba, a trusted agent appointed by the Mansa to watch over a province
مثقال (٩)	weight used for valuing currency
ميمة (٩)	village in Mali
اشتدّ على (١٠)	to berate, treat harshly
نفاه (١٢)	he exiled him
بني آدم (١٢)	the descendants of Adam (a metaphor for human beings)
مُضرّ (١٤)	harmful
ينضُج (١٤)	well-done, ripe, mature
لطّخ (١٧)	to tarnish, stain, smear
الآدميّات (١٩) (sing.–آدمية)	female human beings
مسّوفة (٢١)	tribe in Timbuktu
فربا موسى (٢١)	Farba Musa, *farba* of Timbuktu
دَرَقة (٢٥)	leather shield
مُفلِق (٢٦)	unique, masterly
أبي إسحاق الساحلي الغرناطي (٢٦)	Abu Ishaq al-Granadi, a poet of Granada
سراج الدين بن الكُويك (٢٧)	Siraj al-Din Ibn al-Kuwayk, a merchant of Alexandria
منحوت (٢٨)	sculpted, made, shaped

Comprehension Exercises

A. Answer the following questions in complete Arabic sentences (numbers refer to the lines in which the information can be found):

١. ماذا بعث السلطان إلى ابن بطوطة كهدية الضيافة عند وصوله إلى مالي؟ (٥-٧)

_____

_____

_____

٢. لماذا لم يأكل الكفار القاضي الأبيض؟ (١٤)

_____

_____

_____

٣. بالنسبة للكفار، ما أطيب الأجزاء[181] في لحوم الآدميّات؟ (١٩)

_____

_____

_____

٤. ماذا جَعَلَ فربا موسى على أمير الجماعة؟ (٢٣-٢٤)

_____

_____

_____

٥. ما أهم معالم مدينة تُمبُكتو؟ (٢٦-٢٧)

---

181 parts

_____

_____

_____

B. Find Arabic phrases in the text that approximate the following meanings in English:

1. one doesn't expect from him:_____

2. their aggrandizement of something base:_____

3. human:_____

4. according to their belief:_____

5. it was their custom whenever:_____

C. Find Arabic synonyms or equivalents in the text for the following words and phrases:

١. منحة : _____

٢. لهجـة : _____

٣. أُرْسِــل:_____

٤. تمجيــد : _____

٥. ألــذّ :_____

D. Find Arabic antonyms or opposites for each of the following words or phrases in the text and use each in a complete sentence:

١. كريـم : ـــ

٢. ثمـين : ـــ

٣. تلطّف مـع : ـــ

٤. مفيـد للصحـة : ـــ

٥. بَكَيْـت : ـــ

Interpreting the Text

١. ماذا توقّعَ ابن بطوطة عندما قالوا له: "جاءك قماش السلطان وهديّته"؟ (٥)

ـــ

ـــ

ـــ

٢. لماذا ضحك ابن بطوطة على هدية السلطان؟ (٧)

ـــ

ـــ

ـــ

٣. لماذا نفى مَـنْسَى موسى القاضيَ إلى بلاد الكفار؟ (٧–١٢)

ـــ

ـــ

٤. ماذا أعطى السلطان مَنْسَى سليمان للكفار عند زيارتهم؟ وكيف تصرّف الكفار بها؟ (١٥-١٩)

٥. كيف غادَرَ ابن بطوطة مدينة تنبكتو؟ (٢٨)

Grammar, Structure, and Context Clues

1. In describing the interrogation of the dishonest official's servants, Ibn Battuta uses the phrase إِنَّا to signal their confession of truth of the situation (line 11). This is a compound of إِنَّ (verily, indeed) and the particle ما. Although ما can have many meanings, including 'no' and 'what,' in this compound, it has the effect of modifying the meaning of إِنَّ from 'verily' to 'but,' or 'merely.' Here, the interrogated servants are refuting the *qadi*'s claim that the sultan's money was stolen from him, "إِنَّا دفنها بيده" (but merely he buried it himself).

2. In the paragraph from lines 8 to 14, we can observe the practice of reverse agreement between numbers and the nouns they describe. The same number is used both in line 9 in "أربعة آلاف مثقال" and in line 13 as "أربع سنين".

Agreement rules for numbers are typically very difficult for non-native students. They often cause confusion and the situation presented here is among the most confusing for learners of Arabic. As a rule of thumb, remember that numbers between 3–10 will have reverse-gender agreement with the basic noun. Thus since ألف, the singular of the noun in the first sentence, is masculine, the number 'four' is feminine. In the other sentence, the singular of سنة is feminine, so the number is masculine. Note that this is not affected by the rule of treating all non-human plurals as feminine singular; the reverse agreement is always with the gender of the basic (singular) form of the noun. While this convention may be somewhat difficult to master, it is a good habit to begin observaing this reverse-gender agreement in numbers 3–10.

For a more complete summary of number-agreement rules:

The numbers 'one' and 'two' (واحد / واحدة، اثنان / اثنتان) agree with the gender of the noun they describe. This also applies to two-digit numbers and higher that end in 'one' or 'two' (11, 12, 21, 22, 31, 32… 101)

The number 'two' is considered a dual word. So, it will be اثنان / اثنتان in the nominative case (في الرفع), and اثنيْن / اثنتيْن in the genitive and accusative case (في الجر والنصب). Both the number 'one' and the number 'two' will agree with the noun in gender. Moreover, the *nuun* (ن) will be dropped when the number is the first part of an *idaafa* structure and the second part is the number 'ten' (عشرة).

Review these examples and complete the missing words:

كتبتُ إحدى عشرةَ رسالةً وقرأت أحدَ عشرَ كتاباً

معي اثنا عشر دولاراً وعندي اثنتا عشرة...............

سافرتُ اثني عشر .... وزُرْتُ اثنتي عشرة ....

As mentioned above, the numbers 3–10 take the opposite gender of the word they describe:

عشر سيدات ، عشرة رجال ، أربعة أبواب ، خمس صديقات ، تسعة طلاب

Numbers 11–12 show the same gender as the noun described (see examples above).

For numbers 13–19, the ten (عشرة) will have the same gender as the basic noun and the ones digit will have reverse agreement:

ثلاث عشرة سنة وسبعة عشر عاماً

This may appear slightly confusing. However this still follows the same rule as for single-digit (3–9) numbers, but now adds the tens digit.

For numbers between 23–99, notice that the base multiples of ten (20–90) are not affected by gender:

سبعون رجلا و سبعون امرأة

The ones digits (3, 4, 5, 6, 7, 8, 9) will take the opposite gender of the noun, as they do in the rules above, while the tens digit (20, 30, 40, 90) do not change:

ثلاثة وعشرون ولداً وثلاث وعشرون بنتاً

3. As we've seen in previous chapters, the particle ف has many uses, and often serves as an important signal marker, especially in long, complex sentences. In previous examples, the particle ف is used to signal the result, or 'then' clause of a two-part statement. It is also used as a connective particle that can be translated as 'and,' 'then,' or 'therefore.' In many cases, it serves as a resumption particle, used to indicate a close connection between words or clauses in a sequence. In these cases, the particle would not be translated in English.

In the first excerpt in this chapter, Ibn Battuta uses the particle in this connective function repeatedly to narrate a story in which one event follows closely upon another. Note how many sentences in the excerpt begin with ف. For example in 3–7:

فأجابهم بلسانهم...فقمتُ ...فإذا هي ثلاثة أقراصٍ ...فعندما رأيتُها...

The alliterative repetition of ف to begin each utterance gives a staccato, poetic quality that might be approximated in a suspenseful English narrative beginning each statement with 'then I…'

Writing Exercises

A. Translate the following sentences into Arabic, using vocabulary from this reading. Hints in parentheses indicate which lines to look at for similar structures:

1. We didn't expect much hospitality from him (2):

_____

_____

_____

2. I laughed at his aggrandizement of this small gift (7):

_____

_____

_____

3. The king loved all humankind (12):

_____

_____

_____

4. This fruit is harmful to your health, because it has not ripened (14):

5. This beautiful statue was carved from one piece of stone (28):

_____

_____

_____

B. Rearrange the words below into coherent sentences:

١. العطاء بخيلاً لا يُرجَى الكثير من منه كانَ الملك

_____

_____

_____

٢. يأكل يظنون مقدّسة لحم البقر لأنّهم الهنود أن البقرة لا

_____

_____

_____

٣. على المسلمين جماعةٌ من المسافرين السلطان قَدمَتْ

_____

_____

_____

٤. لما إلى بيتي سُرقَت بأن بعض نقودي أخبروني وَصَلتُ

---

٥. السلطان و فسلّمتُ هديّة تقدّمتُ على أعطيته

Discussion Questions

١. وصف ابن بطوطة سلطان مالي بالبُخل وتهكّم على[182] هديته. هل تؤيدون ابن بطوطة في موقفه؟ لماذا؟

٢. هل أُصيب ابن بطوطة بصدمة[183] عندما عَلِم بأمر[184] آكلي لحوم البشر[185]؟ كيف تُقيّمون[186] موقف سلطان مالي منهم؟

٣. كانت مدينة تنبكتو عند زيارة ابن بطوطة في بداية تطورها الثقافي والتجاري. ما أدلّة ذلك ؟

٤. ما أكثر الخرافات[187] انتشارا في عصرنا الحديث وما رأيكم فيها؟

٥. ما صور الصراع الثقافي[188] التي يمكننا رَصْدها[189] في هذا الفصل؟

---

182 poke fun at, ridicule
183 shock
184 case
185 cannibals
186 evaluate
187 fables
188 cultural conflict
189 observe

Research and Presentation

ابحثوا في الإنترنت عن أهمية دولة مالي في التاريخ الإسلامي والأفريقي، واكتبوا مقالاً قصيراً عن علاقات مالي مع المغرب ومع الدول الإسلامية الأخرى.

Glossary

Vocabulary terms (words are given in conjugated form where necessary for clarification):

Word	Definition	Lesson
أَبَى	to refuse	1, 5, 14
أَبطَأَ	to be slow, to hesitate	16
أَبلغ	to convey	2
أَتقن	the most perfect	5
اجتَلَينا	we explored	5
أَجزل	to donate and give with generosity	12
أَجفان	scabbards, sheaths	18
أَجمعين	all together	14
احتجب	covered, veiled	12
احتفرَ	to dig	15
احتفل بِـ	to celebrate, be interested in	17
أَحصى	to be counted, be calculated	17
آدميّات	female human beings (collective)	20
أَذرع	cubits, old unit of measurement	7, 13
أَذيال	lower parts, ends, tails	12
إراقة الدماء	killing without a good reason	14
أَرباب	lords, officials	13
ارتحل	to depart	6
إزاء	in the face of	2
إستار	unit of weight	14
استقرَينا	we followed, tracked	5

Word	Definition	Lesson
استقلّ	to declare independence	9
استهلّ	to begin	6
استولى عليه	seized	2
إسداء	giving, granting	14
إسعافُ	complying with, granting	15
اشتدّ على	to berate, treat harshly	20
إطعام	nutrition, feeding	7
أطنب	to exaggerate	17
اعتقاد	firm belief without proof	12
اعتكاف	isolation, retreat	15
أعجميّ	foreigner, non-Arab	11
أعراب	Arabs of the desert, Bedouins	11
أعزّ	to reinforce, strengthen	12
أغار على	to attack, invade, make a raid into	10
إفرانج	Westerners, Europeans	13
أقذار	garbage, junk, trash, filth	13, 16
أقروف	consumer jewelry	12
أقطع	amputee, one-armed person	11
اكترى	to grant or take on lease, hire	11
أكذب	to prove a liar	5
إكرام	performing the duties of a host to guest	9
الأندلس	al-Andalus, the name for Islamic Spain	18
البحر الأعظم	'The Great Sea' — The Indian Ocean	9
البربرة	Barbary, from the African coast	10
التفات	attention	8
الجهة القِبلية	the direction of the Qibla	6
الحَرَم الشريف	the Noble Sanctuary	6
الحرمين الشريفين	the Two Holy Sites	3
الدربين	the two paths	3

Word	Definition	Lesson
الرّوضة الكريمة	a section within the Prophet's Mosque which holds the tomb of the Prophet Muhammad and the first two caliphs.	6
الروم	Rome, Christendom	5
السواحل	the Swahili coast of East Africa	10
ألصق	to stick, affix	17
المسجد الكريم	the Prophet's Mosque in Medina	6
المعمور	civilization, the civilized world	3
الموتَى	the dead	19
الميمنة أو الميسرة	the right-hand side or the left-hand side	8
أُلهِمَ	to be inspired	15
أمامة	leadership, command	19
امتنع	to decline	16
أمر	condition, situation	12
أمنان	unit for measuring weight	15
أمير الركب	Amir (leader) of the caravan	6
أمير المؤمنين	Commander of the Faithful	5
أَنْسَتْني	made me forget	19
إناث	female	1
انتشف	to run dry	6
انتماؤه	his association with	3
انتهت إلى	reached	6
إنزال	lodging or sheltering someone	9
انصَرف	to leave, depart	20
انفرد	to be unique	17
أهل قسطنطينيّة العظمى	people of Greater Constantinople, i.e. Byzantines	12
أوائل	early, the beginning of	19
أوقد	to enkindle, light	13
أولانيه	he offered me	19
أوى/ أوى الى	to be sheltered, moved to	5

Word	Definition	Lesson
أيّد	to support, bless	12
أيا صُوفيا	Aya (Hagia) Sofia Cathedral	13
إيثار	unselfishness	7
إيناس	sociability	1
إيوان	*iwan*, a vaulted alcove	8
بادية	visible, apparent	12
باشر	exposed to	11
بالرغم من	although, in spite of all that	14
بخس	cheap, very low	10
بدَن	body	16
بدرة	sum of money, purse	14
بديعة	terrific, impressive	4
بَرّ	mainland	2
بِرّ	charity, reverent deeds	3
برء	healing, cure	1
برية	wilderness	6
بطش	annihilation, execution	14
بغطاق	conical crown	12
بقيد الحياة	alive, still living	1, 19
بلاد الشام	Greater Syria	6
بني العبّاسي	the Abbasid dynasty	9
بني آدم	the descendants of Adam, humankind (collective)	20
بهجة	joy, delight	5
بين يديه	lit. 'between his hands', an idiom meaning 'before him'	9
تَابَ	to forsake (his ways), repent	11
تبرّك بـ	asking the blessing of	12
تتر	Tatars	8
تَجَبَّر	to behave arrogantly or proudly	9

Word	Definition	Lesson
تَجَلّى	to flaunt, transfigure	2
تُحَفّ به	surrounded by	7
تَحرّى	to seek	12
تَخطئ	to mistake	17
تَخلص	be freed from, cleared of	15
تُربة	land, soil, burial ground	4
تركمان	Turkomen	11
تَصويرُ	making a picture	17
تعظيم	glorification, magnification	4
تعلّق ب	to hang on	17
تَكبُّر	arrogance	9
تنزّه	to keep away, keep far above	16
تواضع	state of humility, modesty	9
تؤخذ	to be taken by	11
توغّل	to go deep into	2
ثغر	a coastal city or town, a fortified border city	2
ثلاثاً	three days of hospitality given to a guest	9
ثمار	fruits	17
جبّة	*jubbah*, a loose outer garment	15
جبل طارق	Gibraltar	18
جِذعِ النخلة	trunk of the palm tree	4
جَزَم	asserted, resolved	1
جزاه الله عن الإسلام خيراً	Islamic expression meaning, 'may God reward him'	4
جزية	the *jizya*, a poll tax paid by non-Muslims living in an Islamic state	15
جعبة	case, frame	13
جلبة	type of boat used in the Red Sea	9
جمادى الأول	Jumada al-Awwal, the fifth month of the Islamic calendar	2

Word	Definition	Lesson
جَمَد	to solidify	11
جنان	paradises	18
جهنّم	Hell	6
جولان	wandering	2
حافل	full of, loaded with	8
حرّة	meritorious	18
حرم	a sacred territory or space	13
حريميّ	characteristic of women	8
حسّ	to realize, feel, perceive by sense	11
حسم	to put an end to	16
حسن	elegance, beauty	9
حسن الجوار	good neighborliness	7
حصّة	group, unit	14
حظّ	chance, fortune	18
حقير	trifling, meager	20
حلَم	kindness, leniency	19
حمّالين	carriers, porters	9
حُمّى	fever	1
حوّات	fisherman	18
حوز	enclosure	18
حيزوم	front of the chest	1
خاتون	khatun, title of a wife of a khan	12
خِباء	tent	1
خَرِب	decayed, destroyed	8
خريدة	virgin girl or pearl	2
خشنة	rough	17
خصومة	lawsuit	16
خطيب	religious speaker	20
خطئ	to make a mistake	17
خفّفَ	to abate (something)	19

Word	Definition	Lesson
خِلع	robes granted as a reward	14, 20
خَيار	the finest	16
دابّة	ride	1
درج رُخام	marble stairs	4
دَرَقة	leather shield	20
دعاء	call, prayer, supplication	16
دواب	animals used for riding	11
ديانة	faith	19
ديس	bulrush	10
ذات قرار ومَعين	fertile and flowing with water, promised land	5
ذاهب	going	2
ذراع	cubit, an old unit of measurement	7, 13
ذكر	male	1, 19
ذو القعدة	Dhu al-Qaʿda, the eleventh month of the Islamic calendar	1
ربوة	hummock, knoll	5
ربيبة	stepdaughter	16
ربيع الأوّل	Rabiʿ al-Awwal, the third month of the Islamic Calendar	19
رجب	Rajab, the seventh month of the Islamic calendar	1
رسوم الشرع	guidelines of *sharia* law	16
رضي الله عنه	May God be pleased with him	7
رطل	unit of weight, approx. a half kilogram	14
رعّادات	catapults	15
رفاهية	luxury	17
رَكْب	caravan	6
رُوعي	my mind	2
رياض	meadows, gardens	18
ريح السَّموم	a severe hot and dry wind	6

Word	Definition	Lesson
زاد، أزواد	food and provisions; supplies	3, 9
زعم	to claim, allege	13
زُقاق	alley, side street, lane	16
زنوج	people of the Zanj (African interior)	10
زوايا	convents	3
سائر	all	16
سار إلى	to move forward, go on	19
سبيل	path	9
ستر	to cover, veil	16
سُرّة	navel	16
ستور	curtains, hangings	7
سَدّ	to be closed up, blocked	13
سراج	lamp, light	13
سقائف	booths, sheds	13
سقى	to give (to someone) to drink	14
سَلَبَ	to loot, sack	11, 15
سلَحْفاة	turtle	11
سموم	a hot wind of the desert, sandstorm	11
سنا	glow	2
سِواهم	others	15
سِوى	except, only	13, 17
شارك	to share	13
شافعيّة	of the Shafi'i school of Sunni Islam	10
شامي	Syrian or Levantine	3
شاؤوا	they wanted	5
شِبر	a measure, the span of a hand	7
شبيه	one like it, one similar, replica	5, 13
شبيهُ عيسى	one who resembles Jesus	13
شدّ	to tighten	1
شَرَطات	incisions	10

Word	Definition	Lesson
شَرَع	to begin, pave	2
شَريف	high-ranking, honored	10
شَقّ	to cleave, split	13
شَمائل	characteristics, manners	9
شَهّر	to publicly expose, denounce	16
شُهِر بـ	renowned as	9
شَوال	Shawwal, the tenth month of the Islamic calendar	6, 16
صالِح	devoted, honest, pious	10
صالَحوا	they made peace with	5
صبر	patience, holding breath	11
صَدّتنا عن	it held us back from, diverted	9
صَدَف	seashell	11
صِدْق	honesty	5
صُفّاح	thin paving stones	13
صنابق	small boats	10
صنف	group, rank	14
صِياح	shouting, yelling	18
ضَجَر	annoyance, unease	7
ضُحى	forenoon, the part of the day before noon	8
ضَريبة	tax	4
يُضيّفون	they host	4
طاغية	tyrant	18
طاف	to circle, surround, patrol	13, 14
طائف	one making the circuit around the Ka'ba	7
طَلَل	remains of something that has decayed or collapsed or been destroyed	8
طيقان	arches	12
ظاعن	transitory	18

Word	Definition	Lesson
ظَرف	elegance, style	7
ظِلال	shade, cover, protection	19
عادة	custom	16
عاق	to prevent, hinder	2
عامّة الناس	the general public	9
عَبْرة	crying, weeping	1
عتيق	ancient, old	8
عجم	Persians or, more generally, non-Arabs	3
عدوة	riverbank, side	13
عَذِرة	excrement	14
عَرَجَ	to ascend, rise	4
عريض	broad, great	9
عزائم	intentions, resolutions	1
عَزَم على	to determine to	5
عشيّاً	in the evening	17
عصَمني الله	God protected/saved me	18
عطاء	gift	12
عطايا	things received as a gift	14
عظم الغَليم	the bones of a small turtle	11
على الضدّ	contrary to, opposite of	10
على حدة	separately, has its own place	8
عُمرة	a minor Hajj, a visit to Mecca conducted any time of the year	7
عَنوةً	forcibly	5
عهد	time, era	6
عِوَض	indemnity, compensation	5
غار	cave	4
غلمان	servant boys, slaves	14
غوّاص	diver	11
فاضل	excellent, kind	4

Word	Definition	Lesson
فائت	utmost, preeminent	9
فائق	supreme, superior, surpassing	7, 9
فأس	axe	5
فتك	violence, cruelty	14
فربا	farba, a trusted agent appointed by the Mansa to watch over a province	20
فَرسَخ	old measure of distance	2
فروة	fur, animal skin	12
فظاظة	crudeness, harshness, roughness, rudeness	9
قُفّة	basket	18
قُرشيّة	affiliated with the Quraysh tribe	8
قرعة	jar, pitcher	20
قِرى	hospitality, receiving as a guest	14
قصد	to head for	9
قضى	to predestine	1
قطّ	never, not at all, in no circumstance	7, 17
قعد	to sit, hold audience	3, 9
قفجق	Kipchak, a Turkic state in Central Asia	3
قلّما	rarely, seldom	15
قمّ	to sweep	13
قماش	textile	20
قنطرة	building with a curved top and straight sides supporting the weight of structures or bridges	13
قوارب	boats	11
كافأ	he responded, compensated	15
كأنّه	it is as if it were	6
كبتَ	to suppress, repress	19
كَرّة	time	19
كُفّار	infidels	2

Word	Definition	Lesson
كلبتين	pliers, pincers	14
كمخا	velvet	15
كنف	patronage	19
كواغد	sheets of paper	17
لا نَبَات بعارضيه	no growth on his cheeks (i.e. no hair, a reference to his youth)	8
لا يتأتى	it is not easy	6
لا يردّهم خائبين	not let them down, not disappoint them	7
لسان	tongue, language	10
لطّخ	to tarnish, stain, smear	20
لطافة	friendliness, courtesy	9
مآثر	finest works	2
مارستان	medieval hospital, usually part of a mosque complex	3
مالكيّة	Maliki, one of the four schools of *fiqh*	19
مأنوس	popular, familiar	2
مبادرة	initiative	16
متأهّب	ready to go	9
متباهية بـ	flaunting, showing off	3
متسعة	vast, wide	12
متصل	linked, connected	2, 7
متناهية في	of the greatest...	3
متوكّل على الله	having trust in God	19
مثابة	refuge, resort	8
مِثْقال	weight used for valuing currency	20
مثوى	dwelling, habitation, home, lodging	8
مُجِدّ السير	diligent traveler	3
مجزّع	dappled, grained , spotted	7
مجعول	had put	13
مُجَلّلة	wrapped, covered up	12

Word	Definition	Lesson
مِخلاة	bag	11
مَجلوّة	shiny, polished, gleaming	8
محاسن	good qualities, advantages	4
مَحَلّة	a city quarter or district	8
مَحَلّة	*mahalla*, a movable Mongol camp	8
مذاق	taste	3
مذخور	is provided, stored	18
مذهب	a school of thought in Islamic law	8
مرآه	its sight, scene	7
مردود	rejected, turned down	10
مَرسى	harbor, seaport	13
مرعز	cashmere	14
مُستدبرين	unwelcoming	6
مستبشرين	optimistic	6
مستحكم	intense, severe	10
المدرسة المستنصرية	the Muntasariya school, built in 1234, one of the first to feature all four schools of Islamic law	8
مُستوفز	confused, excited	8
مسرَجة	saddled	15
مسقط رأس	birthplace	1
مسّوفة	tribe in Timbuktu	20
مسيرة	distance	11
مُشتكين	those with complaints	3
مشقة	difficulty	6
مصعد	elevator, place of ascent	4
مضرّ	harmful	20
معتمداً	intending, targeting	1
مَعرَج	route of ascent	4
مُغَشّى	coated, plated	4

Word	Definition	Lesson
مغيب	absence	19
مفلق	unique, masterly	20
مِقراض	clipper, scissors	11
مقدار	size, extent, expanse	4
مقصورة	private room, compartment	10
مكث	residing, remaining	16
ملازمة	accompanying, guarding	15
مِنّة	merit	6
من جملتهم	among them	15
منحوت	sculpted, made, shaped	20
منسوبة	belonging to, associated with	10
منصّة	podium, dais, stage	5
منفرداً	alone, solitary	1
منفعة	usefulness, benefit, profit	3, 10
منقسم	divided	13
منقطعين	cut-off, i.e. those without support, homeless people	3, 7
منيف	lofty	6
مواهب	aptitudes, talents	10
موكلون	assignees, those charged	14
مؤنة	supply	17
مؤنسة	welcoming, friendly	3
ميد	swaying, shaking	9
مئين	hundredths	10
ناصعة	clear, pure	7
ناظور	observer, watcher	18
نجدّ السيرَ	speed up	1
نَجِس	filth, extreme uncleanliness	13
نحر	to slaughter	10
نزيل	visitor, guest	10

Word	Definition	Lesson
نشز	elevated place	4
نصارى	Christians	4, 18
نصر	victory, conquest	12
نضارة	grace, beauty	3
نضج	to ripen, be well-done, mature	20
المدرسة النظامية	the Nizamiya school, founded by the Seljuks in 1065, one of the leading Islamic schools of its time.	8
نفاه	he exiled him	20
نفقة	a sum of money for expenses	15
نواصي	front of the head, the finest	3
هواء	air	2
هيبة	prestige	19
وارد وصادر	arriving and departing passengers	11
وباء	epidemic, plague	18
نصبا، وَصَبا	pain (in classical usage)	1
وصلَ الله علوّه	May God grant him success and continue his exaltedness	19
وضوء	the wudu'— the Islamic procedure for washing before prayer	8
وُفّقَ لي	be so lucky to find	19
وُكور	nests	1
وليتُ	I administered, governed	16
يباح	to be allowed, authorized	15
يتعدّاه	to exceed, go past (something)	8
يحسن	treat with kindness; give charity	9
يزُكّي	pay zakat (charity) for poor people	11
يكُنى	he is called, known as	10
يومئذ	at this time	1

Grammar and Structure
Points by Lesson

Lesson 1

The verb قضى (to decree)

The absolute object, المفعول المطلق

The verb اعتمد (to intend)

Uses of the particle فَ

The four sacred months

The categoric negative لَا

Lesson 2

Parallelism and rhyme

Use of a fronted predicate in a sentence

The subject of *laysa*, اسم ليس

The verb رأى (to see)

Lesson 3

Components of Arabic names

Use of the particle لِ (belonging to)

Use of the word غير (other than)

The passive voice المبني للمجهول

Forms of blessings on the deceased

Case endings on subject and object

Lesson 4

Forms of blessings for religious figures

The verbal noun of نشز (elevated place)

Names of Quranic prophets

The verb عَرَج (to ascend)

The passive participle معلومة (fixed, specified)

Lesson 5

Direct object suffixes

Separation of verb and object

The verb تَفضُل (to exceed)

Measure I and measure II verbs compared

The compound وإن (even if)

The *tamyiiz*, 'noun of specification,' التمييز with the superlative adjective, التفضيل

The word قرار (place of refuge)

Lesson 6

The *hal* construction (الحال)

Masdar form for hollow verbs

The verb جدّ (to strive, hurry)

Lesson 7

Meanings of the noun طائف

Use of the particle قطّ (ever)

The false *idaafa* construction

Defective nouns

Idioms derived from the verb انقطع (to be cut off)

Lesson 8

Definite *idaafa* constructions

Various uses of the verb ضرب

The word دارس (forgotten, erased)

The compound وأنّ (although)

Lesson 9

The verb شُهِر (to become famous)

The 'five nouns'

The particle ذو (possessor of)

The passive voice المبني للمجهول

Lesson 10

Various uses of the word البربر (barbaric, Berber)

Use of the word الزنج (a region in Africa)

The verb كنّى (to be named)

Lesson 11

Different naming systems for months

Active and passive participles of the verb سار

سائر، مسيرة : (to head to, to move)

The root صدف (to run into)

Lesson 12

Form and uses of the measure-II *masdar*

The *tamyiiz*, 'noun of specification,' construction, التمييز

Recognizing referent pronouns

The false *idaafa* construction

Lesson 13

Uses of the noun أهل (a people)

The 'topic-comment construction,' ...أما (as for)

Uses of the word سوى (equally)

Use of the word الروم (Rome, Christendom, Greece)

The term إفرانج (Franks, Europeans)

Lesson 14

Uses of the accusative case

The expression مع ذلك (in spite of)

The superlative construct with أشدّ (most intense)

Various uses of the verb حلّ

The particle ذو (possessor of)

Lesson 15

The construction قلّما (rarely)

The passive voice المبني للمجهول

Lesson 16

The verb تنزّه (keep away)

Case endings in idaafa constructions

Uses of the particle ما

The phrase ما عدا (except)

Use of the particle مَن (who) in statements

Feminine plural pronouns and verbs

Use of the particle لِ (belonging to)

Lesson 17

The expression لو لا (if not)

The verb احتفل بـ (to celebrate, glory in)

Uses of the particle ما (what, not)

Use of the particle قطّ (ever)

Lesson 18

Uses of the compound بينا (while, however)

The demonstrative pronoun هنالك (the further 'there')

Use of the word الروم (Rome, Christendom, Greece)

Lesson 19

Uses of measure-IV verbs

Use of كان to form the pluperfect (had done)

The participle حامل (pregnant)

Use of the particle لِ (belonging to)

Lesson 20

Gender agreement on numbers

Use of the compound إنّ ما (merely, but)

Uses of the particle فَ

Index of People Mentioned
in the Text

Index of Places

(in Arabic alphabetical order)

Name	Location	Lesson
أزاق	Azaq (today Azov), in Southern Russia	12
أُصْطَنْبُول	Istanbul (at that time, the Western half of Constantinople)	13
أصيلا	Asila, Morocco	18
الإسكندرية	Alexandria, Egypt	2
الأندلس	al-Andalus (Islamic Spain)	18
البحرين	Bahrain	11
البصرة	Basra, Iraq	8
البندقية	Venice	13
الجاوة	Java, Indonesia	19
جبل طارق	Gibraltar	18
الحجاز	Hijaz, Saudi Arabia	1
الخليل	Hebron	4
الخنساء	Hangzhou, a city in China	15
الروم	Rome (usually refers to Christendom in general)	5, 13
الزيتون	Zaytun (now Quanzhou), China	17
السند	the Sindh, region in Pakistan	2
السواحل	the Swahili Coast (Kenya, Tanzania, Mozambique)	10
الشام	the Levant, Greater Syria	3, 6, 19

Name	Location	Lesson
الغَلَطة	Galata, the Eastern half of Constantinople	13
القدس	Jerusalem	4
القِرَم	Crimea	12
القطيف	Qatif, region in Eastern Saudi Arabia	11
الكسوة	Kiswa, Syria, starting point of the Damascus Hajj caravan	6
الماجَر	Machar, today in Dagestan, Russia	12,
المغرب	Morocco	1, 19
النيل	Nile River	3
الوادي الأخيضر	Wadi al-Ahkaydr, a small valley in Northwest Saudi Arabia	6
اليمن	Yemen	9
بجاية	Bejaia, Algeria	1
بغداد	Baghdad, Iraq	8
بلاد الزنوج	the Zanj (an Arab name for the Swahili coast)	10
بيتَ لحم	Bethlehem	4
تازى	Taza, Morocco	19
تبوك	Tabuk, Saudi Arabia	6
تركستان	Turkestan	12
تَعز	Ta'iz, Yemen	9
تُنْبُكْتُو	Timbuktu, Mali	20
تُونُس	Tunis, Tunisia	1
جدّة	Jeddah, Saudi Arabia	7
جُزُر المالديف	the Maldive Islands	16
جنوة	Genoa	13
جهنّم	Valley of Gehenna	4
حلب	Aleppo, Syria	19
حمص	Homs, Syria	19

Name	Location	Lesson
خوارزم	Khwarizm (Oasis in Uzbekistan and Turkmenistan)	12
دجلة	Tigris River	8
دمشق	Damascus	5
دهلي	Delhi	14, 15
ذِيبة المهل	the Maldive Islands	16
رأس دوائر	Ra's Dawa'ir, village in Sudan (now absorbed into Port Sudan)	9
زبيد	Zabid, Red Sea port in Yemen	9
سَبتة	Ceuta, Spain	18
سِجِستان	Sijistan, region in Eastern Iran	11
سُرَادق	Surdak, port in the Crimea region of Ukraine	2, 12
سُهيل	Fuengirola, Spain	18
سواكن	Sawakin, a port in Northeast Sudan	9
صنعاء	Sanaa', Yemen	9
طنجة	Tangier, Morocco	1, 19
عَدَن	Aden, Yemen	9
عيذاب	Aydhab, Red Sea port in Egypt	9
غرناطة	Granada	18
غزّة	Gaza	4
فارس	Persia	11
فاس	Fez, Morocco	19
فرنسة	France	13
قاليقوط	Calicut (now Kozhikode), India	2
قراجيل	the Himalaya Mountains	15
قسطنطينيّة	Constantinople	5, 11
قفجق	Kipchaq, state in Central Asia	3
كُلْوَا	Kilwa (in modern day Tanzania)	10
كولم	Kollam, India	2

Name	Location	Lesson
ما وراء النهر	Oxus, a region in Uzbekistan	12
مالقة	Malaga, Spain	18
مالي	Mali	20
مدينة رسول الله	Medina, Saudi Arabia	6
مربلة	Marbella, Spain	18
مصر	Egypt, also Cairo	3
مَعان	Ma'an, Jordan	6
مقدَشو	Mogadishu, Somalia	10
مَنْبَسى	Mombasa, Kenya	10
ميمة	village in Mali	20
نهر شَنّيل	Genil River, Spain	18
وادي بلْدَحَ	Wadi Baldah, a small valley in North-west Saudi Arabia	6

Index of Places

(in English alphabetical order)

Location	Name	Lesson
Aden, Yemen	عَدَن	9
al-Andalus (Islamic Spain)	الأندلس	18
Aleppo, Syria	حلب	19
Alexandria, Egypt	الإسكندرية	2
Asila, Morocco	أصيلا	18
Aydhab, Red Sea port in Egypt	عيذاب	9
Azaq (today Azov), in Southern Russia	أزاق	12
Baghdad, Iraq	بغداد	8
Bahrain	البحرين	11
Basra, Iraq	البصرة	8
Bejaia, Algeria	بجاية	1
Bethlehem	بيتَ لحم	4
Calicut (now Kozhikode), India	قاليقوط	2
Ceuta, Spain	سَبتة	18
Kollam, India	كولم	2
Constantinople	قسطنطينيّة	5, 11
Crimea	القِرَم	12,
Damascus	دمشق	5
Delhi	دهلي	14, 15
Egypt, also Cairo	مصر	3
Fez, Morocco	فاس	19
France	فرنسة	13

Location	Name	Lesson
Fuengirola, Spain	سُهَيل	18
Galata, the Eastern half of Constantinople	الغَلَطة	13
Gaza	غزّة	4
Genil River, Spain	نهر شَنّيل	18
Genoa	جنوة	13
Gibraltar	جبل طارق	18
Granada,	غرناطة	18
Hangzhou, a city in China	الخنساء	15
Hebron	الخليل	4
Hijaz, Saudi Arabia	الحجاز	1
the Himalaya Mountains	قراجيل	15
Homs, Syria	حمص	19
Istanbul (at that time, the Western half of Constantinople)	أصْطَنبُول	13
Java, Indonesia	الجاوة	19
Jeddah, Saudi Arabia	جدّة	7
Jerusalem	القدس	4
Khwarizm (Oasis in Uzbekistan and Turkmenistan)	خوارزم	12
Kilwa (in modern day Tanzania)	كُلْوَا	10
Kipchaq, state in Central Asia	قفجق	3
Kiswa, Syria, starting point of the Damascus Hajj caravan	الكسوة	6
the Levant, Greater Syria	الشام	3, 6, 19
Ma'an, Jordan	مَعان	6
Machar, today in Dagestan, Russia	الماجَر	12
Malaga, Spain	مالقة	18
the Maldive Islands	جُزُر المالديف	16
the Maldive Islands	ذِيبة المهل	16
Mali	مالي	20

Location	Name	Lesson
Marbella, Spain	مربلة	18
Mayma, village in Mali	ميمة	20
Medina, Saudi Arabia	مدينة رسول الله	6
Mogadishu, Somalia	مقدَشو	17
Mombasa, Kenya	مَنبُسى	10
Morocco	المغرب	1, 19
Nile River	النيل	3
Oxus, a region in Uzbekistan	ما وراء النهر	11
Persia	فارس	11
Qatif, region in Eastern Saudi Arabia	القطيف	11
Ra's Dawa'ir, village in Sudan (now absorbed into Port Sudan)	رأس دوائر	9
Rome (usually refers to Christendom in general)	الروم	5, 13
Sanaa', Yemen	صنعاء	9
Sawakin, a port in Northeast Sudan	سواكن	9
Sijistan, region in Eastern Iran	سِجِستان	11
the Sindh, region in Pakistan	السند	2
the Swahili Coast (Kenya, Tanzania, Mozambique)	السواحل	10
Sudak, port in the Crimea region of Ukraine	سُرَادق	2, 12
Ta'iz, Yemen	تَعز	9
Tabuk, Saudi Arabia	تبوك	6
Tangier, Morocco	طنجة	1, 19
Taza, Morocco	تازى	19
Tigris River	دجلة	8
Timbuktu, Mali	تُنبُكتُو	20
Tunis, Tunisia	تُونُس	1
Turkestan	تركستان	12
Valley of Gehenna	جهنّم	4

Location	Name	Lesson
Venice	البندقية	13
Wadi al-Ahkaydr, a small valley in Northwest Saudi Arabia	الوادي الأخيضر	6
Wadi Baldah, a small valley in Northwest Saudi Arabia	وادي بلْدَح	6
Yemen	اليمن	9
Zabid, Red Sea port in Yemen	زبيد	9
the Zanj (an Arab name for the Swahili coast)	بلاد الزنوج	10
Zaytun (now Quanzhou), China	الزيتون	17

Further Reading

Complete translations of Ibn Battuta's *Rihla*:

Defrémery, Charles, and Beniamino Sanguinetti, trans. and ed. *Voyages d'Ibn Batoutah*. Paris: Société Asiatic, 1853–58. (French and Arabic)

Gibb, H.A.R., trans. and ed. *The Travels of Ibn Battuta*. Vols. I, II, III. London: Hakluyt Society, 1956.

Gibb, H.A.R., and Charles Beckingham, trans. and eds. *The Travels of Ibn Battuta*. Vol. IV. London: Hakluyt Society, 1994.

Books about Ibn Battuta and his travels:

Dunn, Ross E. *The Adventures of Ibn Battuta: a Muslim Traveler in the 14th Century*. Berkeley: University of California Press, 2005.

Harvey, L.P. *Ibn Battuta*. New York: I.B.Tauris, 2007.

Mackintosh-Smith, Tim. *Travels with a Tangerine: A Journey in the Footnotes of Ibn Battutah*. London: Picador, 2002.

Waines, David. *The Odyssey of Ibn Battuta: Uncommon Tales of a Medieval Adventurer*. Chicago: University of Chicago Press, 2010.

Internet Resources:

Ibn Battuta — The Animated Series Interactive Map
http://www.ibnbattuta.tv/travelMap.html.

Internet Medieval Sourcebook. http://www.fordham.edu/halsall/source/1354-ibnbattuta.asp

The Journey of Ibn Battuta: The Man Who Walked Across the World. BBC, 2007. http://www.topdocumentaryfilms.com.

The Travels of Ibn Battuta: A Virtual Tour with the 14th Century Traveler. http://www.ibnbattuta.berkeley.edu